APPLYING LEADERSHIP AND MANAGEMENT IN PLANNING

Theory and practice

Janice Morphet

First published in Great Britain in 2015 by

Policy Press
University of Bristol
1-9 Old Park Hill
Bristol BS2 8BB
UK
t: +44 (0)117 954 5940
pp-info@bristol.ac.uk
www.policypress.co.uk

North America office:
Policy Press
c/o The University of Chicago Press
1427 East 60th Street
Chicago, IL 60637, USA
t: +1 773 702 7700
f: +1 773 702 9756
sales@press.uchicago.edu
www.press.uchicago.edu

© Policy Press 2015

British Library Cataloguing in Publication Data
A catalogue record for this book is available from the British Library.

Library of Congress Cataloging-in-Publication Data
A catalog record for this book has been requested.

ISBN 978 1 44731 684 8 paperback
ISBN 978 1 44731 683 1 hardcover

The right of Janice Morphet to be identified as author of this work has been asserted by her in accordance with the Copyright, Designs and Patents Act 1988.

All rights reserved: no part of this publication may be reproduced, stored in a retrieval system, or transmitted in any form or by any means, electronic, mechanical, photocopying, recording, or otherwise without the prior permission of Policy Press.

The statements and opinions contained within this publication are solely those of the author and not of the University of Bristol or Policy Press. The University of Bristol and Policy Press disclaim responsibility for any injury to persons or property resulting from any material published in this publication.

Policy Press works to counter discrimination on grounds of gender, race, disability, age and sexuality.

Cover design by Andrew Corbett
Front cover: image kindly supplied by Getty
Printed and bound in Great Britain by by CPI Group (UK) Ltd, Croydon, CR0 4YY
Policy Press uses environmentally responsible print partners

For Charlotte, Robin, Sophie and Owain

Contents

List of tables, figures and boxes vi
Abbreviations viii
About the author ix
Preface xi

one Introduction 1
two Sector and scales 21
three Theories, tools and techniques 37
four Strategy and planning 59
five Managing resources in planning people and communications 79
six Managing resources for planning finance and assets 101
seven Managing planning processes 121
eight Managing planning projects, plans and programmes 143
nine Sustainable management and risk 161
ten Personal management in planning 177

References 191
Index 225

List of tables, figures and boxes

Table

7.1   Comparative sub-costs for development management processes   138

Figure

7.1   Process overview for peer challenge   133
7.2   NPIP process method   137

Boxes

1.1   Recommended improvements to PPAs   11
1.2   Key challenges facing leadership and management in planning   19
3.1   McGregor's theory X and theory Y   43
3.2   Likert's four styles of management   43
3.3   Adair's action-centred leadership   44
3.4   What makes a good leader? A view from central government   45
3.5   Which soft power skills do leaders need?   45
3.6   Egan's skills for leadership in planning   48
3.7   National competency framework leadership skills for planners   48
3.8   Peer review systems   49
3.9   Characteristics of managers and leaders   53
3.10   What are the key challenges in management?   56
4.1   Why local authorities should work in partnership with other   63
        organisations
4.2   Principles of strategic management   67
4.3   SWOT analysis matrix template   71
4.4   EU community-led local strategies content   77
5.1   Strategic HR policy   82
5.2   Prohibited grounds for discrimination   83
5.3   The role of recruitment in the organisation   84
5.4   Job description   85
5.5   Job specification   85
5.6   Belbin's team roles   88
7.1   Reasons for providing pre-planning application advice   128
7.2   10 commitments for effective pre-application advice   128
7.3   Definition of development management   135
7.4   Development management key focal points from BPR   136
7.5   Lean thinking principles   139
7.6   Using Lean in a public sector organisation   139

8.1	SMART approaches to project management	145
8.2	The uses of project management approaches in planning activities	147
8.3	Some cost 'rules of thumb'	151
8.4	Definition of TQM	152
8.5	Why is the business case important?	154
8.6	Five Case Model	155
9.2	Identifying hazards in the workplace	175
9.1	United Nations definition of the role of audit	175
10.1	What is the nature of professionalism?	179

Abbreviations

CDA	Comprehensive development area
CEC/EC	Commission of the European Communities/European Commission
CIPD	Chartered Institute of Personnel and Development
CPO	Compulsory purchase order
DCLG	Department for Communities and Local Government
DCO	Development consent order
ESDP	European Spatial Development Perspective
EU	European Union
HBF	Home Builders Federation
IfG	Institute for Government
JR	Judicial review
LDO	Local development order
LGA	Local Government Association
MoJ	Ministry of Justice
NPM	New public management
ODPM	Office of the Deputy Prime Minister
PAS	Planning Advisory Service
PINS	Planning Inspectorate National Service
POS	Planning Officers' Society
RICS	Royal Institution of Chartered Surveyors
RSS	Regional spatial strategy
RTPI	Royal Town Planning Institute
WTO	World Trade Organization

About the author

Janice Morphet has had a career in local and central government and as an academic and consultant. She has degrees in sociology, planning, management, politics and literature. Janice has been a planner for over 45 years and has worked in a range of local authorities including London boroughs, county, district and unitary councils and was secretary of SERPLAN. She was head of a UK planning school and has been a professor of planning for over 30 years. She is now a visiting professor in planning at University College London where she teaches management for built environment professionals. Janice was a member of the ODA planning committee for London 2012 and she has been centrally involved in infrastructure delivery planning since 2007. Her latest research has been on the practices and geographies of devolution. Janice has written extensively on planning, local government and the EU.

Preface

Management has always been an issue that has interested me. I started my professional working life in the public sector. I wanted to know how to do things and how to do them better, to understand how resources work and are allocated, to undertake participation in more effective ways for residents and communities and deliver projects on time and on budget. When I worked on the fringes of economic development as a local authority planner, I realised that the private sector operated differently – not only in its culture, objectives and orientation, but also in its financial and accountancy practices and investment in people who lead and manage their organisations.

Taking advantage of flexitime at work and low-cost education courtesy of the Inner London Education Authority (ILEA), I enrolled on a part-time MA in management at what was then Thames Polytechnic. I travelled to Woolwich for a half day/evening plus a second evening for two years and then completed my dissertation. Frequently, while waiting for the rare bus that took me from the town hall where I worked to Woolwich through the Blackwall tunnel, I wondered if I was wasting my time; there were no other students from the public sector on the course. In group work and coffee breaks, I learned about the private sector, its priorities and practices, similarities and differences with the public sector and this has been invaluable since. My dissertation was on the role of professionals in the public sector, and I used this to help make sense of the obvious incongruities and conflicts between the sector and the role. Since then, I have attended other short management courses and learned that I have to add to my understanding of leadership and management every day. I do not pretend to be a good or excellent leader or manager, but rather one who takes the responsibility seriously in everything that I do.

This book is based on a module that I have taught undergraduates at University College London (UCL) since 2008 as part of an RICS-accredited course focused primarily on planning and development. In this time, I have learned what students have found to be useful and stimulating and where they have gaps in their understanding and knowledge. The students will gain experience through their careers, but this course is focused on providing them with insights and understanding that will enhance their practice from the outset. Many students start the course assuming that they have no relevant experience but then find that their roles in sport, voluntary work or vacation jobs have provided them with opportunities to experience leadership and management at first hand. Some are already experienced leaders of teams, shifts and tasks, and they come to recognise the wider applicability of what they have learned in practice.

I also hope that this book will stimulate some discussion among planners in practice. The book does not give 'recipe' approaches to problem solving, but it does provide methods and examples that may be a useful place to start. Throughout the book, there are discussion boxes that contain some broader questions on leadership and management issues as they relate to planning. These are a starting point to encourage consideration of alternative approaches, even if, after this evaluation, the current approach is accepted as the best available; knowing this provides confidence. The philosophy of this book is one of continuous improvement, not change for the sake of it. Planning is consistently the target of change pressures, particularly from government. This book encourages an understanding of the wider set of actors in the planning process – planning is not only delivered by planners. However, this wider consideration of those involved in the planning system should not distract planners from their own responsibilities to lead and manage as well as they can.

I owe thanks to the students at UCL who have taken this course, for their contribution, participation and feedback. It has been a pleasure to work with them, to see their growing confidence and interest in management issues and to hear that they have later applied some of what they have learned in their own working lives. As ever, I owe thanks to Emily Watt and Laura Vickers at Policy Press for their support and encouragement. I would also like to thank my colleague Ben Clifford with whom I share the management teaching at UCL, for our discussions on how best to undertake this task and the anonymous reviewer of the draft text for their helpful comments, although, of course, the responsibility for the book content is my own. Finally, but not least, thanks go to my family for their support.

Janice Morphet
November 2014

ONE

Introduction

What is the purpose of this book?

Leadership and management are critical to the way in which planning is practised, perceived, resourced and trusted. Yet over the past 50 years, in the UK, planning practice has been criticised by governments, companies and communities for its failure to be 'effective' (Clifford and Tewdwr-Jones, 2013), albeit that these detractors have failed to define the ideal process. These criticisms have been made by both major political parties operating in England (Barker, 2004, 2006; Osborne, 2014). They have primarily been aimed at local government, at the institutional scale that is responsible for the operation of the planning system and at local authority planners, in particular for their inability to manage the planning system in a way that supports the national economic interests. This had led to a continuing process of reforms to the planning system in England since 2004. In Scotland, Northern Ireland and Wales, there have also now been major reforms within the planning system, but the relationship between those engaged in the planning system and politicians has mostly been more positive (Morphet, 2011a, 2011b; Morphet and Clifford, 2014).

However, this is a simplistic view of the way in which the UK planning system operates. Planning professionals are more similar to lawyers than doctors; they advise others who take the decisions. If leadership and management are to be considered, all those with a stake in the planning system have a role to play. In local authorities, this includes councillors, the chief executive, chief officers and the community as well as planners. Part of the planner's role is to evaluate the proposals, policies and projects within the planning framework, identifying 'imagined users' (Ivory, 2013) and ensuring that these conceptualisations are consistent with reality.

In the private sector, the use of the planning system is diffuse. All organisations engage with the planning system and will seek advice from time to time, while some use it as the basis of their business. Some organisations employ planners but the majority use planning consultants who comprised approximately 50% of practising planners in the UK in 2014 (RTPI, 2014). Planning also needs leadership and management in the private sector to be effective. The private sector's relationship with planning has frequently been cast as that of a victim (CBI, 2011; HBF, 2014). In 2011, the British Chambers of Commerce undertook a survey and found three key causes of concern that their members had with the planning system – its cost, complexity and lack of consistency (BCCI, 2011a, 2011b, 2011c). The main cost concerns were not the planning applications fees or contributions to mitigate development, but rather the costs of consultants and the time spent by their own businesses in the planning process. The criticisms of local government were that they provided inconsistent advice within and between local authorities and that there was a negative perception of planning for growth from the businesses surveyed. However, it is also important to note that 71% of the businesses that took part in the survey did not own their business premises and were reliant on others for progressing growth and change in their accommodation. The survey did not report on any positive features of the planning process to the organisations, including adding value, certainty and quality of process (Adams and Watkins, 2014).

So is planning failing to deliver its core purposes? Is it capable of improvement and who would judge this? Would a more focused approach to leadership and management make a positive difference to the way in which planning is conducted, its outcomes and how it is perceived? Planning is now undertaken in a variety of organisations and all three sectors – public, private and third – and the scale of operation will vary from organisation to organisation. Finally, and in common with some other professional groups, the term 'management' is highly charged for planners, both in practice and academia, and the implications of this cultural response will also need to be considered.

This book includes an overview of leadership and management theories, and the tools and techniques that are available and used in planning. Management also operates within a context of both the immediate organisation and the wider political and societal frameworks that create the rules and expectations of its practice. All of these elements consistently interrelate and although they need to be understood individually, collectively they make the biggest demands on managers' time. There is also some consideration of the core components of management, including managing resources, process and project management and sustainability. While these individual elements have to be brought together by those leading the practice of planning in any organisation or locality, it is their integration that is the heart of planning (Stead and Meijers, 2010; Forester, 2013).

When providing advice on planning decisions or choices, planners have to assess the alternative courses of action that are situated in strong cultural or ethical frameworks (Mace, 2013). These also frame the risk assessment and its potential mitigation. However, planners cannot sit on the fence. Once the analysis has been undertaken, planners have to give a reasoned recommendation to their client – whether a councillor, developer or community group. Can the method of analysis and recommendations be improved through leadership and management? This is what we are discussing here.

Without having some view of planning's roles and functions, it is difficult to consider whether management approaches are appropriate and then which tools to apply. In the UK, since 1947, the rights of landowners to determine the use of their land and the form of any development on, above or below it have been removed (Cullingworth and Nadin, 2006). Landowners can now only exercise these rights where they have the necessary planning consents. Even where planning regimes appear to have been made easier for users, in practice, these legal requirements remain. While the planning system determines how land may be used and planners provide advice on how this system is operated, the final decisions on the use of land will be made by politicians. These local politicians are also subject to the strictures of government policy and their own party political agendas, which may provide specific institutional frameworks or encourage particular policy outcomes (Holman, 2013).

Planning embodies specific tensions between national objectives and local decision making (Mace, 2013) that have always existed (Jacobs, 1989). This tension has been multiplied with the introduction of three new planning scales – national, in 2008, sub-regional in 2010 and neighbourhood in 2011 (Smith, 2014). In the UK political system, there is a culture of differentiation rather than cooperation between governance scales. There is no legacy of aligned policies and objectives for places between different tiers of government and this has been detrimental to localities (Lyons, 2007). Differences between spatial objectives at varying scales have been a political 'given' since the creation of local government in its current form in the 1880s (Young, 1988), played out in specific localities including overspill housing estates (Young and Garside, 1982) and new towns (Finch, 2009).

The advice provided by planners to their clients is informed by the assessment of evidence, interpretation of the system and application of judgement to each specific case. This is a source of professional power even if planners do not make the final decisions (Hendler, 1990). Thus planners need to demonstrate how they are operating, the source of their advice and their accountability for the public and private funding that supports their work (Reade, 1987).

Yet there is little discussion on the relationship between the exercise of the planner's professional role and the extent to which this might be capable of engaging with 'management' theories, tools and techniques. This may be an anathema to some who define a professional's role as exercising independent judgement. Others regard management as a tool of neoliberalism and all the attendant issues of corporatism that accompany this (Healey, 1992; Sager, 2009) This book is an attempt to open this debate and to encourage planners and those who lead and manage the planning process to consider if there are theories, methods and tools that might engage with the practice of planning to the benefit of society, its users and the planners who work within it.

Why does planning need leadership?

Leadership is important for all activities and can be exercised at all levels in any organisation. Leadership is required in a number of roles in the planning process. In the private sector, those developing a scheme will show leadership in its conceptualisation and then communicate this to potential funders, landowners and users. This leadership will need to extend to the planning authority and any other regulators that have a role in the process (Wokingham Borough Council, 2014). For all schemes, the individual leader will need to communicate the details of the scheme to local communities, incorporate their views and demonstrate how their views have been addressed in a credible way (Blanchard, 2014). In some cases, the leader will have to promote the development in a competitive environment and demonstrate how it fulfils the needs and requirements of the location (LGA, 2013). In the majority of cases, the developer of a scheme will appoint consultants to promote its scheme and to obtain necessary planning consents (BCCI, 2011a). It will use the consultants to negotiate the scheme and act as a buffer between the regulators and the development leader.

In the public sector, the leaders will be political (Simpson, 2008) and they are supported by planners they appoint, who act as their proxy in negotiation. Some political leaders will have firm views about the type of development they would prefer to see in their areas (Howells, 2012) and others would rather take advice from their directly employed staff or consultants. Politicians may also develop and incorporate citizen and community-based governance within decision making (Foot, 2009). No distinction is made between public and private sector 'clients' in the planning process, although the outcomes that they are seeking may differ. In the public sector, the leaders are responsible for any advice given to politicians and the conduct of the process. The requirements on the operation of planning practice, whether plan making or development management, have to operate within legal frameworks and administrative law. Those taking the leadership role in this planning practice must demonstrate that these standards have to be met, lead a maintained or improved quality of service and lead change. If this leadership role is not exercised by the person designated, it will be exercised by others on an informal basis and focused on other objectives.

Why does planning need management?

Through the regulation of land use, planning manages the access and supply of different facilities, amenities and infrastructure (see, for example, Scottish Government, 2008; Ross with Chang, 2013) and, in part, the quality of this provision through design, maintenance standards and long-term agreements. The operation of planning regulation at the local level means that there is always a tension between national and local policy objectives. Planning allocates resources, undoubtedly creating wealth for individuals, companies and communities. In its identification of needs for housing and other social goods, it affords a positive value to some schemes and a negative value to others – for example those located near proposed waste or recycling facilities, mineral extraction or prisons – where schemes may be regarded as an anti-social use that will have a negative effect on their locality (Clifford, 2006). Planning manages these externalities through the use of mitigation measures including design, control of on-site of activities and environmental operating standards (DCLG, 2006d).

Planning also has an effect on value at the micro scale (Adams and Watkins, 2014). The use of designations such as conservation areas, the delivery of enforcement services and the design of development all have a significant impact on the quality of a place for a community (Carmona, 2010; Adams and Tiesdell, 2012). Comparisons within towns and cities demonstrate that the care and attention paid to different locations within local planning practice can have widely diverging outcomes for citizens, businesses and the community (Morphet, 2007).

The design and layout of development and the provision and location of specific facilities can also have significant impacts on the community. The origins of UK planning in public health have been mostly lost over the past century, but their reunification through local government responsibilities in 2013 has opened the potential for promoting the delivery of health objectives including reducing dependencies such as obesity and gambling, public safety and mental wellbeing (Ross with Chang, 2013).

Finally, the planning system supports the maintenance and delivery of environmental standards and sustainability objectives (Helbron et al, 2011; Owens and Cowell, 2013). In the UK, these environmental policies are pooled within the European Union (EU) (Morphet, 2013), while much of their application is in planning policies and the determination of planning applications against and within this body of environmental regulation and legislation (Cini and Borragán, 2013; Golub, 2013). EU policies are developed over a long period of time and negotiated between all member states. They may be influenced by external agreements such as those on climate change with the UN or in consideration of the wider needs of food security, flooding and water pollution for example. While planning has always had a core responsibility for environmental issues, the legal basis for the EU's territorial role is now more directly underpinned and continues to expand (Barca, 2009; CEC, 2013).

Planning or planners?

Managing planning is different from managing planners and this book discusses both. The planning process engages a wide range of actors and stakeholders, including politicians, communities, the government and other agencies. This needs to be led and managed through a variety of means. Planners have central but not exclusive role in the practice of planning (Farrell, 2014). The management of planning can embrace both the whole process and the contributions of planning professionals within it. With the exception of companies that have development as their core business, all other planning activities within organisations are subservient to wider organisational objectives. Planning is a mechanism, not an outcome.

Within this, planners are organised, trained, resourced and managed to help the delivery these outcomes. As in the delivery of any project or process, those involved can enhance or detract from quality, efficiency and effectiveness. Planners are led and managed and this can be undertaken in a variety of ways and within different cultural parameters. Planners are helping to manage change. This book assumes that managing change includes a commitment to continuous improvement – how can things be done better to improve the outcomes of intervention? This is the question that those leading and managing planners have to answer. Their accountability is to the communities and clients they serve and their ability to make this contribution will depend on the ways in which practice is conducted.

Planners are professionals who are responsible for advising on the management and delivery of places in a variety of roles. This involves managing or contributing to decisions on the use of a major part of any country's capital resources and infrastructure and having a key role in supporting and developing the economy and the economic success of the country. At the same time, planners have responsibilities for undertaking the assessment of the policies, plans and decisions that accompany these investment activities in ways that are sustainable and that support communities and their objectives (Barrett, 2004). The role that planners play in preparing plans for the future and then regulating new investment and protecting environments will mean that they are always likely to be criticised by one group or another. Further, any advice that planners provide has to be legally compliant and transparent. Planning also operates within the code of conduct in public life (Nolan, 1995). This makes it a complex activity and one that is frequently in the firing line.

What needs to be led and managed in planning?

The management of land and development are the sites of the planning leadership and management discussion and these relate to different types of planning activity. Management is one method of demonstrating that the powers and responsibilities of planners are exercised in ways that attempt to make the best use of the resources available, are timely, evidence-based and participative. Management practices enable planners to consider how to undertake their work, to organise it, and to ensure that operational requirements are met. Management tools can also provide ways of supporting decision making in different settings. A general appreciation of management is also useful at every stage in a planner's career. At the start, they will be concerned with self-management and operating within the immediate organisation and at all levels planners will be managed by someone. They will need to consider how they relate to and on occasions manage their own managers. As planners progress, they may take on more responsibilities for management and leadership or become a specialist.

While improvement of the planning system can be effected in many ways, as noted earlier, central government in the UK has become increasingly involved in system interventions that are proposed as improvements to the system. These are set out in the discussion below and are primarily considered to be an English approach. However, many of these changes have been implemented in other nations in the UK through their own devolved powers (Morphet, 2011a; Cave et al, 2013; Morphet and Clifford, 2014).

Plan making and policy

Plan making is the responsibility of the democratic body for the area of the plan. It is undertaken by a core of directly employed staff usually with specialist contributions from consultants. Whoever prepares the plan, it is the responsibility of the accountable body and the democratically elected politicians in the public sector or the client in the private or third sectors.

Preparing a national plan has largely been an anathema to the UK government. While plans for Scotland (Scottish Government, 2014) Wales (Welsh Government, 2004, 2008) and Northern Ireland (DRD, 2014) have been made and updated since 1999, there is no plan for England or the UK. Barca (2009) states that this is one of the most important activities of any government, not least as plans identity the location of future public and private investment (Marshall, 2012). Public plans provide some certainty to the private sector, including how public sector funding on social, environmental and physical infrastructure will be prioritised and located. Plans are also intended to provide some certainty over a longer period than a single electoral cycle, which is normally five years.

All states have multi-level government and the application of subsidiarity means that plan making operates at different spatial scales and has implications for vertical integration (Morphet, 2011a). At sub-national levels and below, plans are framed within the context provided by the national scales, but also represent the territorial concerns of any locality, whether for an administrative or natural area. Sub-national planning approaches in the UK are an outcome of variable geometry, where sub-state plan making is undertaken for Scotland, Ireland and Wales and then strategic plans are used at the scale below this (CEC, 2013; Pemberton and Morphet, 2014). Within England, the sub-state scale introduced in the 1930s was the region. However, since 2010, England now has a similar approach to the rest of the UK with strategic plans for functional economic areas, in practice, made up of groups of local authorities.

At the spatial scale below this, local authorities have been the key institutions for plan making and they make two types of plan. The first is a community strategy that is intended to provide a long-term plan and programme for the future of an area. In England, community strategies had an important role in the local authority when first introduced in 2000 (Lambert, 2006) and then were renewed in 2007 as sustainable community strategies (Morphet, 2011b). These plans are also important as the basis of the local development plan systems that were revised in England and Wales in 2004, Scotland in 2003 and 2015 in Northern Ireland (Morphet, 2011a) and provide the context for local plans.

Local plans are a core component of the local authority's proposals for development, investment and land use regulation. Local authorities have always been slow to prepare plans for their areas (Burgess, 2014). This has been ascribed to a number of reasons, which include the politics of housing site allocation, uncertainties and change in the system and a failure to understand the commitment to implementation and infrastructure delivery included within the revised system (Morphet et al, 2007).

The government has been particularly exercised about this slow progress. This may be in response to two key factors, both linked to housing – the euro and the Organisation for Economic Co-operation and Development (OECD). The links between the UK housing market and its trigger to the UK's membership of the Eurozone have had a significant role in planning policy, particularly in the period 1997-2010. In addition, the OECD has consistently identified the UK housing market as a key component of its economy – whether in growth or recession (Andre, 2012). Although the OECD does not have any executive power over governments, its influence is considerable. The EU also uses these assessments and in the agreements towards the convergence to the EU's 2020 economic programme (CEC, 2010), the UK's housing market and planning system together with its poor performance on infrastructure delivery are three of the four key elements of its agreement (CEC, 2013; HM Treasury, 2013). All of these have led to a significant government focus on plan making as a mechanism through which both housing and infrastructure can be delivered.

In addition to plans prepared for territories, some public bodies make plans. These plans, such as those for utilities or housing are made by hybrid bodies in both the public and in the private sectors. Private utility companies deliver public services and services that were formerly provided by the public sector. Utilities, like many other public sector services, became subject to market forces following World Trade Organization agreements about opening the public sector to competition in 1976 (Woolcock, 2010; Morphet, 2013). Although delivered by the private sector, the pricing processes for utilities are regulated and include the costs of providing infrastructure for new development as well as maintaining the existing infrastructure. Housing associations are rooted in the public sector but operate across all three sectors, with funding being provided from government, local authorities, the private sector and they act as developers in their own right (Malpass, 2000). Transport is also hybrid, with networks owned by the government and a mix of public and private providers (Vigar, 2013). These specialist sectors will make their own plans and will vary in the extent to which they are linked with the public sector adopted plans.

Plans are also made in the private sector by major landowners or developers (Brindley et al, 2013). These can be masterplans for land in their ownership or plans with local authorities (Jones and Evans, 2013). Specialist private sector companies such as retailers have a planning strategy that serves the business strategy (Guy, 2000). This will be focused on locations of stores and distribution. These plans will not be in the public domain and will only emerge in annual reports for shareholders or when specific schemes are promoted either through a planning application or in a local plan-making process.

Plans are also made by communities, neighbourhoods and parishes (Gallent and Robinson, 2012). Parish plans are managed within a democratic framework like local authority local plans, although their methodologies and consultative processes may exclude them from a formal role in the planning process (Owen et al, 2007). The preparation of community plans at a sub-local authority level is a key component of the planning system in Scotland and has been enabled in England through neighbourhood plans (2011 Localism Act). These plans may be prepared by residents, the local authority, community technical aid, specialist consultants or other volunteers. They may be funded by the local authority through parish council precepts on each property or grants awarded from other bodies. Some communities may fundraise to support their plan making.

So what kind of management tools and techniques are important to consider in plan making? A plan is a defined product and making a plan is a project. Project management methods include the systematic assessment of different approaches together with an analysis of the winners and losers from any policy proposals. A process-based approach to plan making can become disjointed and may lead to failure as the final examination.

Development management

A key component of planning is regulation. This is primarily, but not exclusively, undertaken by local authorities, which determine individual planning applications (Cullingworth and Nadin, 2006). There is also an expanding role for central government through national planning applications. These planning applications are submitted and determined according to national policy, relevant EU directives and regulations, local policy and plans and any site-specific issues. Part of the regulatory framework provided by government is the time-frame used to determine planning applications submitted to a local authority, which is eight weeks for a minor application and 13 weeks for a major application. There has been criticism of the time taken to determine planning applications (Burgess, 2014) and successive governments have promoted a range of methods to speed up the process.

All planning application decisions are made in the name of the local authority and until the early 1990s all decisions were made by democratically elected councillors (Thomas, 2013). The government's management intervention initiatives to speed up the planning application process (Allmendinger and Haughton, 2012) have been undertaken in several waves. These have primarily been led by central government reforms of practices in England, but there have also been similar reforms in other parts of the UK, albeit characterised in a less 'top-down' form (HoPS, 2012). The first English reforms were procedural. The government promoted delegation of planning applications decisions to planners within a locally adopted scheme. These schemes of delegation might include exceptions, for example where there had been a number of objectors to the planning application or where a councillor had specifically requested that the application be determined by councillors or the full council. As anticipated by planners, these reforms were expected to give more control in executive decision making. However, these reforms retained the same system of political control, albeit now operated in a different decision-making space. While this created more operational control over decision making, the net effect remained the same or even reduced the space for professional discretion by planners (Gunn and Vigar, 2012).

The second phase of attempting to speed up the planning application process came through incentivising management within local authorities through the means of providing planning delivery grants to those authorities that were performing satisfactorily, with bonuses for those doing particularly well (Addison and Associates with Arup, 2006a, 2006b; Burgess et al, 2010). This incentivisation has also been continued through the new homes bonus (DCLG, 2011), where English local authorities have been able to obtain funding for every new dwelling completed in their area (Sheppard and Smith, 2011). This incentivisation was seen to be weaker than regional planning targets but also to be encouraging local authorities to build in places where housing might not be appropriate (Wilson, 2014), and while it was considered by government to be successful in achieving its objectives, the National Audit Office considered this interpretation to be unreliable (Wilson, 2014, p 23).

The third approach that has been adopted has been punitive, with threats of direct action for English local authorities that have determined the lowest numbers of planning applications in eight weeks. Local authorities were given specific support through the Planning Advisory Service (PAS) and then in 2013, those at the bottom of the league tables with fewer than 30% planning applications being determined within a set period were named and threatened with having their development management powers transferred to the Planning Inspectorate National Service (PINS). In 2014, the regime was changed with an increase in the threshold to 40% and a range of specific conditions and type of development that could be removed from the local authority's control (Branson, 2014; PINS, 2014), potentially making the system more confusing for those applying for planning consent.

The fourth approach that has been used is that of deregulation within the planning application process. The first initiative here has been through the use of planning legislation in England, where deemed consent has been given to more categories of development. This is meant to give more freedom to householders for works on their properties and to owners of certain types of building to change their use in a prior notification process. In practice, these deregulated approaches have caused more uncertainty and in a number of cases local authorities have attempted to reinstate the former regulatory processes. This has made the situation more unclear and has not necessarily improved the performance of local authorities as a result.

A second initiative was initially introduced in 1981 through the creation of deregulated areas or enterprise zones (EZs) (Barnes and Preston, 1985; Cullingworth and Nadin, 2006). These have been implemented in England, Scotland and Wales, with a commitment to introduce a pilot EZ in Northern Ireland (Ward, 2014). Although there has been some evidence that EZs have generated some jobs and economic improvement for their areas, Einiö and Overman (2012) found that this has been at the expense of neighbouring areas so there has been no net additional development as a result of removing planning controls and creating specific financial incentives. Further, Pickvance (1990) has shown that these initiatives become embedded and normative behaviours take over within professional policy communities that serve to undermine the 'special' territorial incentives ascribed through these policies.

A third initiative as been the introduction of local development orders (LDOs) to grant planning consent for an area. LDOs were introduced in England and Wales as part of the 2004 Planning and Compulsory Purchase Act and allow local authorities to extend permitted development rights within a defined area. A survey on their use within English local authorities commissioned by PAS (2014d) found that while LDOs were considered useful they did not necessarily simplify the planning process. Between 2009 and 2014, 47 LDOs have been adopted in England; none has been adopted in Wales, despite considerable support from the Welsh Government (Peter Brett Associates, 2014).

A fourth initiative has transferred the regulatory costs to the applicant and away from the regulating authority. This has been undertaken through planning performance agreements (PPAs) and planning application fees. When the planning system was first introduced in 1947, fees for applicants were low or non-existent, not least as a response to criticisms about the removal of development rights. More recently, planning applications have been accompanied by fees by type of application that have been set by central government. Staff have been employed based on this income and when planning application numbers reduced in the post-2007 recession many planners were made redundant. Some applicants have decided to fund local authority planning officers through PPAs, which were introduced in 2008.

An evaluation of the use of PPAs was undertaken for the Homes and Communities Agency, a government-funded organisation involved in their delivery (McGrath, 2010). This found that PPAs were not being used as frequently as anticipated and that further promotion was needed to improve their take-up. The study identified a number of reasons for this, which are shown in Box 1.1. Further, the study found that any suggestion that the compulsory use of PPAs would be by local authorities and applicants would be problematic, although incentives might be useful.

BOX 1.1: Recommended improvements to PPAs
- Show how PPAs fit within a development management context.
- Take into account the need to tie in with the various other processes that are required in the pre-application period.
- Highlight success stories and present best practice case studies in an attractive way.
- Clarify the status of PPAs, that is, the legality of documents.
- Present a range of models, including short, limited-scale PPAs. There should be more guidance on the different formats of PPAs, including those suitable for smaller projects, and those where pre-application processes are already well advanced.
- Set out best practice approaches to engaging elected members and the community in PPAs and specifically address members' involvement and how issues of predetermination could be avoided or handled.

Source: McGrath (2010)

As Box 1.1 shows, although PPAs have been designed to be helpful to the applicant and the local authority, they are regarded with some suspicion by those who consider that there are problems with their lawfulness. There was also a concern with transparency and the concerns that some applicants may be receiving preferential treatment could be met by through a recommendation that the PPA be shown on the formal planning register of planning applications held by the local authority (McGrath, 2010, p 72).

While the fees for each planning application may be high, they do not cover the full cost of the service and some local authorities such as Westminster have proposed to government that certain categories of planning application should be subject to full cost recovery from the applicant. This may occur in any event when the government eventually passes responsibility for setting planning fees to local authorities, as it has already committed to do (LGA, 2014).

Despite being defined as a 'national' service, PINS has responsibilities in England and Wales; Northern Ireland and Scotland have their own systems. PINS has a major role in determining planning applications through the system of appeal against refusal of planning consent or any associated conditions. Here inspectors make recommendations for a decision to the Secretary of State for Communities and Local Government. Where there are unpopular local development applications, for example for housing or waste facilities, there is a strong temptation within local authorities to refuse the application and if the applicant appeals, to then blame the resultant decision on PINS. The temptation to take this approach is offset by the award of costs against a local authority if the reasons for refusal are poor. This approach also incorporates delay (Ball, 2011), sometimes as a means to bridge election cycles. The system of planning and environmental appeals was reformed in Scotland in 2010, with a focus on improving the customer experience (Scottish Government, 2011).

The second and increasing role of the planning inspectorate in planning regulation is the determination of and award of development consent orders (DCOs) under the national planning system set out in the 2008 Planning Act. Here the policies are set by parliament, and there is an agreed submission process that does not need to argue the case for the development but rather concentrates on its form and effects. These processes are undertaken within a year. The initial approach set up to deal with these applications was through an independent Infrastructure Planning Commission (IPC) that was housed with PINS, which itself was an independent agency. However, in 2012, the two were merged and the planning inspectorate moved to become an in-house part of central government. In these cases, PINS makes recommendations to ministers and parliament. In this system, ministers may be able to override the recommendations, while there is little in this process that promotes infrastructure integration.

In all cases, whether for local authority or national planning applications, there are other mechanisms that can be invoked for decision making. The first is that the Secretary of State for Communities and Local Government can decide to determine any planning application and can overturn or change the recommendation that has been made by the planning inspector. Second, the Secretary of State for Communities and Local Government can also use call in powers to determine the whole application.

All decisions on planning applications and development consent orders can be considered for judicial review (JR) once they are determined. JR is a part of administrative law introduced when the UK joined the EU in 1973. It is a review of the administrative procedures rather than the merits of the case (Morphet, 2013). These reviews may be on the grounds that inspectors did not correctly interpret evidence or the law or did not go through the relevant EU processes. The number of JR requests has increased and are significant in number. In response, the Ministry of Justice has created a specialist planning court to hear these JRs to ensure that the process is efficient and supported by specialists (MoJ, 2013).

What kind of management tools can be used for the practice of development management? Development management may be regarded as a process or a project. Within the regulatory authorities, it is managed as a process, with multiple planning applications or DCOs being managed by the same teams and supported by process management IT systems. However, for the applicant or promoter and their planning advisers, each planning application is a project because they are seeking a specific outcome. While local authorities dealing with major development management projects may see the group of planning applications that will accompany it as a programme or as part of the project that the authority may support, each planning application has to be determined individually and its role within a project does not mean that it has any different status.

Promoting development

One of the core activities in planning is promoting development. In the private sector, planners promote development through planning applications and prompting the use of specific sites through plan making. The promotion of development may be carried out for clients in all sectors and all organisational types (Cullingworth and Nadin, 2006; Morphet, 2011b). Much development is promoted by organisations whose main business in concerned with the use and development of land but many applications will be from organisations that need changes to their premises to suit their own business needs whether for operations or investment. In these cases, planners may be advising at every stage including assessing development potential, managing the planning application process or providing specialist input. Some planning consultants will have a long-term relationship with their clients while others provide advice on an individual and ad hoc basis.

The public sector also promotes development through plans, planning briefs, master planning or specific town centre or regeneration initiatives. In the public sector, the organisation may own the site being promoted for development or may be working in partnership with other bodies. The local authority may have no ownership relationship to any sites in a master plan or planning brief, but will be undertaking this work as part of its wider planning and public functions. These approaches may include design (Adams and Tiesdell, 2013; Carmona and Punter, 2013), regeneration (Deas, 2013) or flooding (White and Howe, 2002). Local authorities will also be promoting planning projects that have been identified in other plans such as those for local enterprise partnerships (Pemberton and Morphet, 2014).

The third sector will also be promoting development and this will also vary according to the organisation's objectives and functions. Buildings constitute the core business for charities such as the National Trust and a high proportion of its assets will be protected in some way, as will the natural landscapes that come under its remit. Planning is a key activity for organisations like this. Other small community organisations may be promoting sports or social facilities, a hospice or other community buildings (Hague and Jenkins, 2013). In the third sector, planning consultants may be used to undertake this work or it can be undertaken in-house.

Promoting development is a project-based activity as there is a defined 'product' at the end of it. This might be an individual building or the re-planning of a major area of a city over a number of years. However, preparing for this development, and considering the order and dependencies of separate projects in the programme or how funding might be managed are all project management approaches.

Implementation

Implementation as a planning activity has been a major concern since the 1947 Town and Country Planning Act (Cullingworth and Nadin, 2006). Initially, this was through comprehensive development areas (CDAs) that were used for post-war remodelling and involved the wholesale purchase, demolition and rebuilding of areas primarily by local authorities. Also post-1945, implementation was engaged in building new and expanded towns and here the main leadership was through central government agencies such as the New Towns Commission (Tallon, 2013). Both approaches included land acquisition through compulsory purchase orders where land could not be acquired by agreement (Cole, 2012).

The implementation role of planning was scaled down in the 1970s. Major redevelopment was criticised for destroying existing urban fabric and being driven by the development industry. Critics of this approach, including Ian Nairn (Nairn, 1956; Darley and McKie, 2013) and John Betjeman (Tewdwr-Jones, 2005; Betjeman and Games, 2009) used the media to demonstrate the negative effects of wholesale demolition of the urban fabric and the failure to recognise the role of existing buildings in the cultural value of places. The second criticism was the failure of policy in real terms as it was not delivering the number of dwellings required and the housing crisis continued as illustrated by Cathy Come Home, the BBC television play about homelessness (Sandford, 1966), and the founding of the charity Shelter.

The community's views about change were not being taken into account – it was too top-down, as demonstrated in the Skeffington report (1969). The encouragement of many skilled and qualified people to move from London and other cities to new towns meant that the remaining areas were left with no jobs or community leadership (Stewart, 1994). As unemployment reached levels of 25% in 1976 in areas of Tower Hamlets, the London boroughs were still prohibited for advertising London as a place to do business.

Since then, the focus on implementation has been more muted. The switch from redevelopment to regeneration to deal with inner-city areas in the 1970s and 1980s (Lawless, 1996) was left in the hands of a new economic development profession and the central implementation role of planning was lost. Planning in local authorities became primarily about preparing plans and development management rather than direct implementation, which was undertaken by others. When the 2004 Planning and Compulsory Purchase Act was introduced following the planning Green Paper (DTLR, 2001), it took some time for the planning community to appreciate that delivery and implementation was now a core role of planning. The introduction of infrastructure delivery planning process as part of the local planning process was established fairly quickly through the support from PAS and a nationally led approach to changing practice (Morphet et al, 2007). However, it has taken planners and the organisations they operate in longer to understand the integration of plan making and delivery and to change their practice cultures accordingly.

Implementation is also central to planning in the private sector and while much of the focus may be on obtaining the planning consent for a development, its delivery will be the objective of the scheme promoter. Even once a planning application has been granted, there may be conditions to be negotiated or changes as the development proceeds (Thomas, 2013). Some aspects of the development may need additional consents and planners will also be involved in discharging any conditions to ensure that the value of the development is unencumbered by any outstanding obligations.

Implementation is a project-based activity and implementation projects might be grouped together in a programme. Implementation is similar to development promotion but includes the delivery phase and in implementation it is the project completion that is the desired outcome, not just a planning consent.

What are the external criticisms of planners?

As already noted earlier in this chapter, government and the private sector have been critical of the way that planning is undertaken within the UK and of the practice of planners within this. These criticisms of planners can be summarised as follows.

Culture and practices: language of separation

Planning culture, including the use of professional argot, is seen to be a key issue in managing planners. Professional cultures can be inward-looking and define who is inside and outside of the group. Within local authorities, planners were once leaders of strategy and delivery but since the early 1990s, the increased legal operating environment and separation of councillors between those who are executive members and those who sit on the planning committee making decisions has served to reinforce this separation. Within local authorities, this also reinforced by councillors who like planning and those who do not, not least because many planning issues are contentious in local politics (Clifford and Tewdwr-Jones, 2013). The nature of planning culture has been investigated as part of a project on spatial plans in practice. Shaw (2006) found that culture change for planners was a critical element of adapting to the new planning system in England that was introduced in 2004.

Skills

Planners have frequently been criticised for lacking the skills to undertake their role effectively, including being part of a wider development team (Egan, 2004), design (Carmona and Punter, 2013), knowledge of the market (Barker, 2006) and effective management of the process (Killian and Pretty, 2008). These criticisms of planners are, however, primarily focused on planning practitioners in the public sector and do not extend to the wider range of networks and agencies included in the delivery of the planning system.

Management of time and process

The way in which planners use their time to manage plans and undertake development management has been criticised by the government and the development industry. Central government supported change in the planning services of local authorities through the use of planning delivery grants. However, a research project undertaken to review the effectiveness of the use of these grants from the perspective of the private sector found, first, that the key problem for local authorities was a lack of resources, and second, that undertaking more pre-application discussion before submission of a planning application leads to a smoother process subsequently (DCLG, 2006a). The study also found that the quality of planning applications was an issue on occasions and that this led to delays in their processing.

Failure to understand planning's role in the economy

The failure of planners to understand their role in contributing to the economy is a frequent one, and is a particular criticism directed at planners by national politicians (Osborne, 2014). This frustration can be attributed to a number of intersecting issues. The first is that through the application of the principle of subsidiarity, it is not possible for nationally elected politicians to exercise control over local decisions nor to provide such tight guidance that fetters local democratic processes. The application of the principle of subsidiarity has led, amongst other things, to the removal of Regional Spatial Strategies (RSS) by the outgoing Labour Government in the Local Democracy, Economic Development and Construction Act 2009 and the abolition of their replacements, Regional Strategies by incoming Coalition Government in 2010. The failure of planners to fully understand their role is shared by civil servants supporting national politicians whose traditional command and control culture provides them with little skill or expertise in a more decentralised state (Thomas and Panchamia, 2014; Cox, 2014). As a consequence, decision making is distributed and can be inward-looking. Attempts to change this through duties to cooperate and the creation of self-selected groupings of local authorities have as yet only been partially successful and cooperative horizontal decision making has yet to establish itself. Unlike vertical integration between central and local government, there are fewer potential benefits and funding in terms of exercising joint working in this way.

The second frustration felt by central government politicians is rooted in a fundamental misunderstanding of the way in which planning operates in the markets. The reports commissioned from Barker (2004, 2006) demonstrate a theoretical approach to the land market, and a misunderstanding that land is a monopolistic good. The government has assumed that more supply of land will reduce the price of housing. Instead, the land market works like that for raw materials and finite goods in that owners will hoard supply and use their ownership to manage the market. Organisations with high land ownership will still use the land to obtain maximum value.

Third, central government politicians have failed to grasp that competition in the use of land has operated most effectively when this competition has been between sectors rather than from competiton within the private sector. The UK had greater numbers of houses being built when the public and private sectors were both building and the problems of the housing market have been exacerbated since the shift to near monopolistic supply in the private sector (Elphicke and House, 2014).

What are the main internal criticisms of planners?

Criticisms of planners within organisations are primarily focused on their roles in local authorities and can be summarised as follows.

Separation through language and legislation

Planners have been criticised by councillors and chief executives within local authorities because they have used legislative processes, including those for plan making, as a means to argue separation and difference. Planners have also used arguments related to legal processes to delay participating in one-stop shops and wider integrated customer initiatives. These differences have been reinforced through the use of a separate language. In addition, those councillors engaged in planning decision making are required to have specific training and to operate in non–political, quasi-judicial ways when making decisions, which separates them from the rest of their colleagues. As a consequence, those councillors can come to see themselves as a specific community and there can be tensions between councillors who are part of the planning decision-making process and those who prefer to remain outside it.

All planning decision making at the local level is contentious within a wider political setting and this again causes a division between those politicians who regard it as a positive contribution to the local authority's work and others who regard it as a political difficulty to be managed (Clifford, 2007).

Silo-based working

One of the key concerns of any institution is managing the different parts of the organisation as a whole to the benefit of all. Many organisations are described as operating in silos and protecting the interests of their own services before prioritising either joint or corporate working approaches. This is recognised as a considerable problem in the public sector and particularly in local government. While there may be leadership towards integrated working from the top, there may also be issues about an unwillingness to integrate within the middle of the organisation, with the role of middle managers being particularly important (Solace, 2014a). Planners have been described as existing in silos and failing to work with other services such as health (Carmichael et al, 2013), or across boundaries (Hamiduddin and Gallent, 2012; Scott et al, 2013) or sectors (Haughton et al, 2010;Whitehead, 2010).They have also been accused of being too inward-looking (Cheshire and Magrini, 2000b; HM Treasury, 2003).

Not sufficiently strategic – only interested in the small stuff

The role of planners as key actors in developing and delivering strategic direction in local authorities (Friend and Jessop, 1969; Friend and Hickling, 1987; Solesbury, 1974) has long passed and now few chief planning officers sit on the management boards of local authorities. In a report on planning for economic growth, local authority chief executives considered that planning was regarded as a negative feature of attracting growth and it was an area that attracted least interest in investment by the chief executive (Solace, 2014b). In the survey that accompanied this report, planning was not included as one of the key services for support and development over the coming five years (Solace, 2014b, p 4) and planning-led growth schemes were the least important of all cited (Solace, 2014b, p 11). Finally, the local authority chief executives were advised to 'perform the lead role in shaping local places, being proactive and taking advantage of the unique understanding of local economies' (Solace, 2014b, p 15) but nowhere in this report are planners identified as contributing to this approach. Rather they are regarded as an area of damage limitation against negative perceptions from potential investors. The challenges facing leaders and managers in planning are set out in Box 1.2.

BOX 1.2: Key challenges facing leadership and management in planning

- Not being able to sit on the fence and being required to make a recommendation
- Being identified with regulatory restrictions rather than problem solving
- Operating in a political environment
- Managing complexity
- Managing in a changing economic context
- Managing within a public service orientation
- Managing within an ethical framework

TWO

Sectors and scales

Introduction

Planners are employed almost equally in the private and the public sectors (RTPI, 2014). Most of the research and literature that specifically deals with planning and management issues is directed at the public sector and at its policy, planning and regulatory roles. In the private sector, advice for practitioners is available from the websites of professional bodies (the Royal Institution of Chartered Surveyors, Royal Town Planning Institute and Chartered Institute of Personnel and Development). It is also important to consider the management issues of professionals in specialist consulting and corporate organisations.

Planners are also active in the third 'not for profit' sector in community and charitable organisations (Wates and Knevitt, 2013). While the numbers of planners employed in the third sector is small, many planners also volunteer for planning aid activities. In the third sector, planners may also be involved in lobbying government or working within community technical aid or in development trusts directly with groups or individuals seeking to respond or participate on local issues (Warburton, 2013). These may range from a planning application, a local or neighbourhood plan or a national infrastructure project. This chapter discusses the ways in which planning is managed and delivered within organisations in each sector and at different scales of organisation.

Leading and managing in the public sector

Planning responsibilities in the public sector are held by a range of different bodies and organisations. These include central government and its agencies, local authorities including neighbourhood and parish councils, and national parks. Each of these organisations is accountable to democratically elected politicians and this is what distinguishes all public sector bodies from those in the private and voluntary sectors. Planners are also employed in utilities, including those providing energy and water, which are hybrid organisations whose operations are split between the public and private sector. Here the market is managed by the public sector through regulatory offices that report to government ministers and parliament, while the supply companies are in the private sector and operate within this publicly regulated and accountable framework. Planners are also employed in housing associations, which are also hybrid bodies and span all three sectors.

There are key issues to consider in the role of leadership and management in the public sector as employees 'remain the most negative about their senior managers', with low levels of trust and confidence in their senior leaders (CIPD/Halogen, 2014). These findings create a continuing challenge for public sector leaders.

Accountability

The planning responsibilities of each type of public sector body are an important consideration in their leadership and management. The democratically elected politicians who hold the executive power in a public sector organisation are also subject to scrutiny by peers who do not hold this power. Utilities in the UK come under the scrutiny of parliamentary select committees, which have the power to interview witnesses and issue reports, although these reports are not binding on the executive politicians making decisions and have a varying degree of influence (Hindmoor et al, 2009; Benton and Russell, 2013). Parliament also has powers of scrutiny in England for planning, transport and energy, as well as for local government together with an overview of local government. In Scotland, Wales and Northern Ireland, scrutiny functions are undertaken by the relevant parliament or assembly. In local authorities, national parks and parishes, it is councillors who have powers of scrutiny, but again, the executive is not required to implement any recommendations they may make in their subsequent reports (Ashworth and Snape, 2004). Planning, as a local service, has been subject to scrutiny since its introduction (Allmendinger et al, 2003). It is not one of the most popular areas for scrutiny and is more likely to be scrutinised in relation to its role in delivering wider local authority objectives such as public health (CfPS, 2008) or town centre regeneration (Hammond, 2012).

All public bodies operate within the code of conduct in public life, which applies to executive politicians and paid employees including planners (Nolan, 1995). This means that any individual cannot be involved in consideration of an issue or take a decision on a matter that involves any personal interest such as family member or business associate. It also includes the conduct of meetings and site visits, which should be taken in a formal way and not on a private basis. Finally, any politician or official should not accept any hospitality from an organisation that has a decision under consideration. At other times, any hospitality offered, whether accepted or not, should be entered into an organisational register.

Legal framework

Each sector is set within a different legal framework. The public sector is set primarily within the administrative law where it is possible to challenge a decision by questioning the procedures used (McEldowney, 2003; Hartley, 2007). Public bodies are subject to all other sets of law that apply to organisations including those for employment and health and safety. Second, public bodies are known as 'creatures of statute', that is, they are set up through specific legislation set by parliament and although there is operational and organisational scope within this legislation, it sets the terms and responsibilities of these bodies (Wollmann and Thurmaier, 2012).

The government also has to implement the principle of subsidiarity in governance and decision making (CEC, 2007, 2013; Morphet, 2013) to ensure that decisions are taken at the lowest possible level (Toth, 1992; Craig, 2012). This has started to force the introduction of new scales such as neighbourhoods and devolve more functions to local authorities in England and governments in Wales, Scotland and Northern Ireland. There is also greater devolution of strategic functions to sub-national functional economic areas such as local enterprise partnerships (LEPs) in England and strategic development plan areas in Scotland and Wales (Morphet, 2013; Pemberton and Morphet, 2013). In local government, the application of the subsidiarity principle has led to the introduction of a general power of competence for local authorities (2011 Localism Act).

Third, all public bodies are managed directly or indirectly through democratic representatives. In central and local government, these are directly elected politicians, whereas in other areas such as health, strategic development plan boards in Scotland or LEPs in England, they are appointed from within directly elected politicians. However, the leadership of these bodies is under frequent change and it is likely over time that public bodies with indirect democratic accountability will move to a more directly accountable model such as has occurred for the police (Sampson, 2012).

The distinctive feature of managing in the public sector is the diffused form of governance. This differs from the private sector. The legislation for charities and voluntary organisations is moving closer to that for the public sector. Some organisations have multiple organisational structures – so local authorities may also have development companies and charities may have trading companies.

Central government

The structure of government departments is established by the government of the day and may be changed at any time. Since the devolution process commenced, UK central government has responsibility for planning, transport, local government and allied matters in England; elsewhere, they are the responsibility of the relevant parliament or assembly. All policies within the UK operate within the framework set by EU policy and legislation where it has been pooled with other member states (Morphet, 2013). Much of the work of all parliaments and assemblies is the delivery of these pooled policies and legislation within their own territories.

In England, change is managed though processes known as the 'machinery of government' (Peters, 2012). However, as White and Dunleavy (2010) demonstrate, changes to reshape government departments at speed, frequently without any preparation and at time to suit political rather than management challenges, can create problems. Unlike in other organisations, these changes are frequently announced as part of a reshuffle of ministerial responsibilities and have to be put into effect immediately. This may cause a productivity dip and loss of morale for staff, and, as a management of change approach, is unlike that in any other sector. Government decisions are subject to administrative law and can be challenged, including those in planning.

In central government, ministers are selected by the prime minister and they work with civil servants not appointed by them, although there is pressure for this to change (Cabinet Office, 2012; Riddell, 2013). The majority of civil servants are generalists and are defined as being administrators rather than managers. Professional specialists such as planners have always formed a small part of the civil service and this remains the position, with very few professionally qualified planners employed, although there are a number of departments that have some responsibility for planning issues (Farrell, 2014). Within each government department, ministers are not responsible for internal organisational management and it is the responsibility of the civil servants to advise on and to deliver projects. However, delivery is defined as legislation or the successful allocation of responsibility for action to be taken by another body. Few central government departments have responsibility for the direct delivery of decisions. If there is a delivery or policy failure in central government, the minster responsible will resign or be sacked.

A particular issue in this approach to managing government business is the silo nature of government departments and the lack of coordination between them. This was a major concern of the Blair government of 1997-2007, with a number of coordinating initiatives being implemented, particularly in the first period (Morphet, 2008). This was reinforced through joint contracts between government departments and local authorities, but the separation has remained in practice. In Scotland, all government departments have been merged into the Scottish Executive and it is argued that this might be a more effective way to promote an integrated approach to policy and delivery.

One of the key issues to consider within the civil service is the relationship between ministers and civil servants on leadership issues. Notwithstanding the subservient connotations of their job title, Chapman and O'Toole (2010) discuss the joint leadership role that civil 'servants' have enjoyed with ministers throughout their existence and that is embedded within the culture of government. Since 1997, civil servants have become increasingly concerned about the erosion of this role (Butler, 2004; Hallsworth and Rutter, 2011). However, as Smith (2011) argues, steering reform from the centre is not likely to be successful as it is built on a Whitehall model. A local government model has also been used. Former local government chief executives have been appointed to senior positions in the civil service in England and Scotland – roles that were previously closed to external applicants. External applicants have also been appointed to departmental boards to manage finance and other specialist corporate functions.

The culture of management is not strong in central government and among civil servants. While there are discussions about new public management and public management cultures (Hood, 2000; Bouckaert et al, 2010), there is little detailed consideration of the antipathy to the practice of management within the civil service (Hallsworth and Rutter, 2011). Rather there is a focus on the general ethos and then the management roles and responsibilities of specialists such as accountants, lawyers and personnel professionals (McCrae and Randall, 2013; Kerslake, 2014). This failure to embrace the requirements of a management role in comparison with other public, private and voluntary organisations comes from the top (Paun and Harris, 2013) where a policy advisory role to the ministerial team takes precedence over managing the organisation.

Central government has not typically had a role in the direct delivery of planning outcomes, but has rather sought to manage at arm's length. Using planning legislation, ministers have always retained the power to determine some strategic planning application decisions and this facility has been used regularly. However, while the Planning Inspectorate National Service (PINS) has had responsibility for determining planning appeals, it has not had responsibility for promoting development. Nevertheless, there have been moves towards a more proactive stance. First, central government has begun to identify national infrastructure plans and policy that have been approved by parliament and may then be managed within PINS. Local authorities may play a part in considering planning applications in their area, but they do not have final responsibility for planning decisions. Second, although the government does not promote specific schemes within this regime, the process does not allow any questioning of the need for development. This provides a more certain form of planning process, albeit that democratic accountability is central rather than local. In this, PINS identifies its role as being a (government) planning authority rather than a regulator (Southgate, 2013).

Local government

In local government, governance is in the hands of the executive, which is made up of a directly elected mayor or small groups of councillors from the majority party. The remainder of the elected councillors serve in back-bench and regulatory roles (Morphet, 2008). The split in responsibility for planning within local government is reflected in this governance model. Executive councillors are responsible for promoting schemes and policies, while other members are responsible for regulation including determining planning applications (Statutory Instrument 2853, 2000).

All councillors together will agree the council's strategic plans, including the budget and the local plan. The pattern of roles and responsibilities within this governance structure will vary within each local authority and the portfolio roles held by executive councillors will have different names and clusters of accountabilities. The distribution of power between councillors and then between councillors and paid officers is set out in the council's constitution and then in the standing orders and/or schemes of delegation (Stoker et al, 2007). The constitution is expected to be reviewed every five years, while the standing orders and delegations schemes are adopted annually at the first council meeting of the new municipal year, which is usually held in May. In a local authority, the chief executive is appointed directly by councillors and is responsible to them. If there is a service failure or problem, the chief executive is expected to leave the authority.

The main drivers that inform management in local government are derived from political priorities, which in turn reflect commitments in manifestos and party ideologies. The modernisation of local government since 2000 has resulted in some slippage between the respective roles of the political leader and the chief executive (O'Reilly and Reed, 2010), reducing or replacing the practical role of the chief executive in the organisation. There is a strong commitment to public service, although methods of delivery may vary and include multiple providers from all sectors (Lowndes and McCaughie, 2013). Priorities will also be informed by community preferences. However, local authorities are also agencies of last resort for people who may be homeless or have specific needs. Further, unlike the private and the third sector, local authorities provide services to all and cannot select their customers. This brings service and budgetary pressures, particularly at times of specific crisis or changes in demographic trends. For example, a higher than anticipated proportion of children in the population places pressure on local authorities to build new schools or extensions to existing school buildings.

The funding of the public sector is primarily derived from taxation. Other contributions are from bonds raised in the market or loans made by the European Union or European Investment Bank for specific activities such as transport infrastructure and more recently housing. This system and approach applies in all parts of the UK. In local government, the mix between funding sources varies in relation to the size of local authorities. A key contributor to this is property and local authorities are estimated to own two thirds of the public estate by value in England (LGA, 2014). In 2008, more than 25% of smaller local authorities generated more than 50% of their income from sources other than taxation, which includes fees and charges for services, parking and use of accommodation (Audit Commission, 2008). Some local authorities have also returned to providing services to other local authorities and organisations following the removal of a ban imposed in 1990 that prohibited such activity.

Larger local authorities provide social care services that use a higher proportion of taxation funding although some of this is generated locally through council taxes. Each local authority will also receive a portion of centralised business rates. In the past, local authorities received numerous incentive payments for specific activities or services but these have now been centralised. In the Localism Act 2011, local authorities were empowered to establish private sector companies and although these powers have been available before, they are now less circumscribed (LGA, 2013). Some local authorities have begun to take advantage of these powers and have established companies for house building and maintenance, for joint development with the private and third sector and to provide energy through wind farms. Increasingly, the local government sector is also considering the use of its asset base to generate investment funding through bonds to support local development, although local authorities may develop anywhere.

Management culture in local government is more developed than in central government but is not as strong as the private sector. In some local authority services, management tools and techniques such as business process re-engineering are used to reduce process costs. Some local authorities have used a balanced score cards approach (Kaplan and Norton, 1996) to support priority setting methods and strategy selection. Many local authorities have in-house management and leadership training, although they are more likely to have group development sessions on specific issues such as quality and customer service. Few staff in local government will have any management qualifications or systematic management education and this may have implications for the introduction of management tools and techniques. However, local authorities are experienced at change management as this is a constant in their organisations. Change may be managed in a contained and limited way rather than considering the implications for the organisation as a whole.

While local authorities are frequently described as being very similar, in practice there is a variance between their internal organisation, leadership, performance and innovation (Andrews and Van Der Walle, 2013). Much of the focus on local government since 2000 has been investigating how management and leadership make contributions to changing each of these four dimensions. Much of this effort has been through central government improvement programmes and the work of the Audit Commission and has been a central feature of the new public management (Bouckaert and Van Dooren, 2009). However, after 2007, the focus of change and improvement shifted within the sector, although the improvement agenda has been overtaken by the cuts and economic efficiencies required after the financial crisis in 2007.

Hybrid public sector bodies

Until 1980, the majority of public services were owned and delivered by the public sector. However, in 1976, there was an agreement to open public sector services to competition to the private and voluntary sectors as part of the General Agreement on Tariffs and Trade (a multilateral agreement regulating international trade). This was subsequently implemented and extended by the World Trade Organization (WTO) and regulated by the European Commission in the EU (Morphet, 2013). This has resulted in a split in the roles of the client or commissioner of services that is non-transferable and remains in the public sector and the contracted provider of these services that may be in any sector. The contracting process is managed within EU legislation that is compliant with WTO agreements and the contract periods may vary between five and 20 years, depending on the type of services or goods being supplied or the level of risk. The introduction of competition has been accompanied by political and management expectations of increased efficiency and improvement that are appropriate to each sector.

Other organisations including universities and housing associations are mixed governance bodies. Universities receive some student and research funding from taxation, but also from individuals and the private sector, and all will also have a charitable arm. The focus on management in universities is on the quality assurance processes of their core activities, that is, the delivery of degrees and diplomas. The second main focus of is on the management of financial and human resources, as these are the organisation's main costs. Universities are major property developers and own more property that major retailers (AUDE, 2013). Housing associations are also hybrid bodies, acting as social landlords but also as commercial developers (Malpass, 2000). Other public bodies such as utilities are primarily funded through fees and charges including their capital investment programmes, although in some cases, like railways, the service has been taken back into public ownership through a specially formed company.

Health services are also now located within this hybrid category where funding is provided from general taxation but services are provided on a commissioned and competitive basis. In the NHS, Bloom and colleagues (2010) consider whether the introduction of competition has improved the quality of management, while Ackroyd and colleagues (2007) considered the effects of reforms that accompanied competition on the management of professionals within the public sector. In both cases, the prevailing culture and proximity to private sector activities was influential on the extent of change.

In these hybrid sectors, there is a stronger focus on management and those working in these sectors are more likely to have formal management education than in the public sector. As the corporate systems in hybrid sectors are closer to those used in the private sector, there is a greater interest in improving management quality, not least as this has a direct relationship with the finances of the organisation and its ability to attract more funding. Planners are not generally employed in these hybrid organisations in a corporate role. When these organisations wish to manage or extend their premises or develop their land, they are likely to behave like the private sector and use consultants, although the National Health Service (NHS) has had a central property team that was managed in-house. Since 2013, when competiton was introduced into the NHS, this service has remained but operates as a company and is in competiton with others to attract business.

Managing professionals in the public sector

Within the public sector, the role of the professional may be different from that in the other sectors. In the public sector, the client can be the organisation but also may be the community, the political leadership of the organisation itself or an individual. There may also be an expectation that professionals working in the public sector will have a different ethical position from those in the private sector and be motivated by a commitment to public service (Anderson and Pederson, 2012). Professionals within the public sector may also be defined as 'internal' professionals whose careers are constructed within the internal institutional sphere, rather than between sectors and organisations as in the case of professional planners (Kletz et al, 2014). While public sector planners operate as professionals, the extent to which they focus on a particular sector as opposed to the planning element itself will depend on the individual and the culture of the organisation they work in.

Silos or layers?

Organisational structures in public bodies can be in silos, as in the case of local authorities and government departments, or layered, as in the case of health services, where accountability is managed in tiers. In some service areas, problems that are not communicated across boundaries cause difficulty such as criminal records across police boundaries and working with children between agencies (Williams, 2012). In planning, the duty to cooperate, first introduced in Scotland in 2003 (Local Government in Scotland Act 2003) and in England and Wales by the 2004 Planning and Compulsory Purchase Act and reinforced though the 2011 Localism Act, has proved to be the most challenging management and political issue. In this case, local authorities are expected to work together to consider issues that cross administrative boundaries, such as infrastructure provision, housing markets and catchment areas. While many local authorities work with some of their immediate neighbours, establishing wider working relationships has proved challenging and in many cases has led to a failure to have a local plan adopted. In some cities, combined authorities have been set up to support strategic integration, although planning has not been included in the first tranche of activities earmarked for integration (AGMA, 2011; Local democracy economic development and construction Act 2008).

A further issue in the public sector is managing across different professionals or teams that can operate as silos within organisations. While there can be interactions between teams, collaborative working is voluntary and informal (Kahn and Mentzer, 1996). Working within multidisciplinary teams can be difficult. This may be due to each discipline having a different culture, aspirations and interpretations of the outcomes. Some professionals may not have a high regard for another profession and this can create difficulty from the outset, particularly when individuals appear to operate within professional stereotypes. Baunsgaard and Clegg (2013) discuss whether these relationships are based on walls or boxes, where the decision making and rationality between professional groups may be similar but where each group operates as a policy or knowledge community, privileging information between its own members rather than between project- or initiative-based teams.

Discussion Box: **Managing in the public sector**
- Who is responsible? Politicians or officials/officers?
- Who holds public sector to account?
- Is the public sector effective?
- How does the public sector deal with change?

Managing in the private sector

Business structure and accountability

Managing in the private sector is focused on the profits of the organisation, and its ability to survive, maintain and increase its market share. In the private sector, ownership takes three key forms. Large organisations are more frequently set up as companies and owned by their shareholders who hold shares to generate income to fund pensions or wealth for other companies or individuals. The shareholder pattern of ownership extends to smaller companies, but here the shares are more likely to be owned by family and other businesses. In some cases, such as business start-ups, shares may be owned by entrepreneurial investors. Where business angels provide funding for start-up companies, this may be in return for shares or a longer-term return from the business (Harrison et al, 2010). Companies are registered and their liabilities are limited by guarantee. They must report to their shareholders at an annual meeting and obtain their agreement on key decisions.

Some businesses are established as partnerships, where ownership and risk are shared between the partners. This has been a typical arrangement for professional organisations such as lawyers and distinguished by the terms LLP (Limited Liability Partnership). Another form of joint ownership is a mutual or cooperative where the company is owned by the employees. In the UK, the most well-known company with this business framework is the John Lewis Partnership. Here, employees share in the profits of the business and there is a workers' council that has an important role in business decisions. Although the organisation has a traditional management structure, its actions and performance are not subject to shareholder considerations (Cathcart, 2013). In 2011, the UK government promoted the creation of partnerships and mutuals being set up particularly to transfer public sector activities into the third and private sectors (Birchall, 2011). The last common business form is that of a sole trader, an individual who may be registered to undertake work.

In all forms of management in the private sector, apart from the sole trader, there will be a separation between the board of the company and the internal management. The board will comprise both individuals, who are employed by the company, and those who are external to it, as non-executive directors. The directors have a responsibility to the shareholders or owners to take decisions that will support the company's maintenance and growth strategies. Some of the directors may be family members or in the case of a family-owned business the family may comprise the entire board.

External non-executive directors are expected to represent the interests of investors as well as the company, to provide direction to managers and to hold them to account. However, there has been a wider debate on the effectiveness of non-executive directors and their degree of influence and engagement within companies (Zattoni and Cuomo, 2010). This may be related to the amount of information that is shared or the number of non-executive roles held by individuals, crowding out their specific sense of accountability (Boxall et al, 2013). Non-executives have also been used in the public sector in government departments and in the NHS, and the issues pertaining to the operation of these bodies are similar to those found in the private sector (Wright et al, 2012; Endacott et al, 2013).

In the private sector, public life standards also apply, particularly in financial and professional services. Within a company, there may be a 'Chinese walls' approach separating teams advising clients on the same deal or working for different parts of the same business. In professional services, companies providing audit services are banned from engaging in other types of risk work for the same organisation. Some organisations ban partners, spouses or family members from working in the same company, which may also apply in the other sectors

Funding

Private sector organisations are funded in a variety of ways. Initially, companies may be funded from the investment of capital by their founders or their families in return for a share of the ownership. As companies grow, they may invite others to invest, including suppliers or customers. As companies increase in size, they may issue shares or spilt their own holdings. When companies wish to raise more funds for investment, they can make a rights issue. This increases the number of shareholders and potentially dilutes the dividend paid to existing shareholders, who then receive preferential terms for the receipt of newer shares to encourage them to agree and to attempt to preserve their interests.

Companies may also grow and develop through mergers and acquisitions. Companies merge with others producing similar goods and services and expect operational efficiencies through combining. Companies merge with or acquire businesses that are synergistic to their own and serve to develop their product range and innovation. Where companies are listed in the FTSE 100 index, there will be considerable pressure to grow each year in order to support stock market and investor confidence. In most cases, this growth may only be sustained through mergers and acquisitions, or, in the case of the retail sector, additional floor space. As Auerbach (2008) has identified, there are a number of issues to consider on the benefits and issues of mergers and acquisitions. While there may be internal business-led reasons to merge with or acquire another company, there may be other factors as work, including the objectives of managers who may gain through these processes. Despite due diligence being undertaken before mergers and acquisitions go ahead, there is also experience of failure (Cooper and Finkelstein, 2012). Mergers and acquisitions are common in planning consultancies, both between companies within the sector or from companies in other sectors seeking to develop or extend planning capability.

New start-up businesses may seek funding from banks or other institutional investors. Businesses that are largely state-owned can move into the private sector by using government funding or guarantees. Companies also form from other companies. This is a common pattern during a recession where larger companies can no longer sustain their workforce. The employees may opt for redundancy packages to found new companies or consultancies. This is a frequent form of new firm formation in planning. The newly formed company may have strong relationships with clients or make have specialist functions that continue to have a market through the recession. Also any individuals being made redundant from their roles or retiring may set themselves up as small consultants or work within a consultancy network.

Once a company is established, it generates income from a variety of sources. The first is through its sales of goods or services and this is the main source of funding for the majority of companies. In some cases, the company may have a patent that will generate licence revenue and this is typical of IT companies. Some companies generate their business on a franchise model. This is another form of licence but the parent company provides all the operating systems and advertising (Nijmeijer et al, 2014). Another way of generating revenue is through a company's fixed assets, particularly property, and a company may also raise funds for growth through loans against assets. Some retailers use property purchase as a means of blocking rivals and then use these sites for other purposes such as housing.

The main business drivers in the private sector are to maintain and grow the company, to generate enough sales to create a surplus that can be used to pay a dividend to shareholders and also to create funds for further investment in the company. For some businesses, sales are seasonal and the advent of 'black Friday' in late November represents the first weekend of profit for the year. In tourism and leisure businesses, sales may be primarily made in the summer and much of business development concerned with filling or using capacity during less busy times.

The role of planning in private sector organisations

Planning has a role in the life of all companies. Planning also affects business at all scales and where companies hold little property, such as those in the creative sector, this creates problems in securing funding. All companies use consultancies to undertake their planning work, even where they have their own in-house teams, and the scale and cost of this consultancy is a concern for all companies (BCCI, 2011a). Large retailers have in-house teams of planners concerned with policy and business strategy for store types, locations and so on. However, they are likely to engage planning consultants to obtain planning consents for new or existing stores.

Planning consultancies vary between large companies to sole traders. Businesses may be entirely focused on obtaining planning consent or supportive policies, but planning may also be part of businesses with wider interests including engineering, environmental consultants or land and property surveyors. The largest planning consultancies in the UK each have over 100 planners whilst the top 16 employ over 40 planners each, although these may be distributed around the country in local offices (Sell, 2013). This is a larger number than most local authority planning departments.

> Discussion Box: **Managing in the private sector**
> ▪ What is the balance of interest between shareholders and managers?
> ▪ How can non-executive board managers be effective?
> ▪ Would the private sector be more effective if there was less government regulation?
> ▪ What role does planning have in all organisations?
> ▪ Are planning consultancies different from other companies?
> ▪ What management challenges do planning organisations have?

Managing in the third sector

Structures

Many organisations operate in the 'not for profit' or third sector. The third sector comprises both national organisations, including charities, professional bodies and think tanks, and local and community groups. Third sector organisations may be similar to those in the private sector in the way that they operate but their governance will be closer to that in the public sector, particularly when they are registered as charities with the Charity Commission. The main motivation for third sector organisations is to serve a specific group or a need that is perceived as not being met by the public or private sectors or not in ways that those affected can afford. Some are devised to create a self-help model (Hibbert et al, 2002, 2005) and others are established through donations and then run through income generated from facilities such as hospices. Some charities are founded in gratitude for services received, particularly medical help, or in memory of an individual who has died. Many organisations in the private sector work for charities and voluntary organisations on a *pro bono* basis. Private sector companies frequently have schemes that enable their employees to be volunteers to support projects or to provide leadership for a fixed period on secondment. This is intended to aid the recipient organisation and to serve as a professional or personal development tool for secondees, which in turn supports the sponsoring organisation.

Funding

The most difficult issue for third sector organisations is obtaining funding. Many voluntary organisations are funded on a short-term basis, perhaps for one to three years, and much of the time of the organisational leadership will be spent on fundraising to maintain the organisation (Boltanski and Chiapello, 2007). This funding might be to meet a specific need, to undertake a project such as developing a community building or a neighbourhood plan, or to create a community activity. For some charities, the funding is more likely to be provided by donors or sponsors. Some charities have long-term investments and use their income to support projects, while others may rely on single donations to fund a particular project. They have multiple legal personalities including as a charity and a company in order to undertake their work.

In the UK, charity registration brings benefits, including tax relief and gift aid. Voluntary organisations may be structured as cooperatives or mutual. Other are grant-giving bodies for research in the areas specified in their charitable objectives. Third sector organisations require accommodation for their work and activities. Some charities are established as single units, whereas others are individual organisations working within a federated structure, working within a national organisational umbrella. Some charities are set up specifically to provide planning support to trusts and community organisations. These may be development trusts or community technical aid organisations or organisations with centrally funded activities, such as the government-funded Planning Aid.

Accountabilities

Accountabilities in third sector organisations are similar to those in the public sector. There is a board of registered trustees with legal obligations towards the trust or charity that are met through providing guidance, leadership and oversight (Charity Commission, 2014). Most charities have trustees who have direct experience in the work of the charity. As charities grow in size, trustees will have experience in finance, legal or personnel matters. The trustees have a responsibility to the funders and also to the clients who use the services (Hind, 2011). They may also have responsibilities to the wider community or members.

Challenges

One of the key management challenges for charities is the role of the founder, who may remain dominant and make it difficult for the organisation to grow. If a charity is registered, it will be constituted as a trust and be managed by trustees who will primarily be volunteers, although they may be paid in some larger organisations. There may also be a question mark over the legitimacy of these trustee boards if they are not elected (Taylor and Warburton, 2003).

Management in the third sector will have the same range of issues as in both the private and public sectors, although there is a further dimension that, in this sector, much of the work is undertaken by volunteers. There are skills required in managing volunteers and in those organisations that deal with vulnerable adults and children, including youth work, sports clubs, play and work with older people, all volunteers will need to undergo a Criminal Records Bureau check.

Since 2000, there has been enhanced interest by governments to include the third sector as part of main stream public service delivery (Brandsen and Pestoff, 2006; Ishkanian and Szreter, 2012). This creates hybrid organisations and generates tensions between the objectives and culture of the original organisation and its relationships with the powerful clients who seek its services. Like the private sector, the third sector may become dependent on the client relationship, building its organisation to offer the contracted services. Moreover, when the government is the client, the power relationship may drive the charity into activities where it has less interest or competence. Billis (2010a) argues that these issues can be addressed by building an explicitly hybrid organisation so that these pressures can be incorporated without destabilising the whole. Brandsen and Pestoff (2006) argue that this change may be engendering a crisis in the third sector where individual organisations may find their roles blurred as they take on the characteristics of the public sector.

The use of co-production to describe the third sector's increasing role in public service delivery, albeit as a contractor, may be blurring the distinctiveness of the sector (Osborne and McLaughlin, 2004). Carmel and Harlock (2008) suggest that this is a process of harnessing and systematising the role of the third sector into the state governance apparatus as an alternative means of delivering public services, providing a challenge to both the public and the private sectors. The third sector also has an important role in delivering places (Thake, 2001; McGregor et al, 2003; Molyneux, 2007), which has also been incorporated by central government (HM Treasury and Cabinet Office, 2007), although the diffuse nature of localities and their approaches to issues may focus this strategy on empowering organisations rather than on specific service delivery.

Discussion Box: **Managing in the third sector**

- How is managing change in the third sector different form other sectors?
- What issues arise from having a founder leader?
- What are the issues in working with volunteers?
- What are the key challenges of short-term funding and perpetual fundraising?
- What effect does the economic climate have on charities?
- Are there any specific issues arising from the legal framework of the organisation?
- Does government's third sector policy make third sector organisations more like businesses rather than charities?

Conclusions

While there is a common core of planning practice, related to legislation and processes, as this chapter has shown, the ways in which this practice is undertaken will vary between different sectors and scales. These variations will be related to the particular focus of the organisation and its primary interests in the planning process. There are also differences between those organisations promoting schemes that have planning as a key component and those responsible for regulating planning applications. There will also be differences between the objectives and aspirations of different clients and the importance of planning in relation to them.

Regardless of their specific role in the process, planners also have an understanding of the wider context whether this is the proposed development in its wider locational context or its role in delivering strategic policy objectives.

Where planners are involved in devising policies, in all sectors, they are aware of the relationship between these and those of other partners and stakeholders and how they will interact. Finally while being employed in one sector, planners are always aware of the role and priorities of other sectors. One of the key challenges in leadership and management in planning is how these different objectives, scales and sectors can work together to create successful places.

THREE

Theories, tools and techniques

Introduction

Leading and managing planning and planners is critical to the delivery of sustainable places and the effective use of land. Planners provide leadership by advising their clients or their organisation. They manage the resources available to them, particularly people and finance. Planners do not make final planning decisions unless they are in political or other executive roles, although they do take many management decisions that influence the way that the planning is delivered.

In the private sector, planning decisions are made by the client acting on behalf of the owners or shareholders of the organisation and these decisions will be framed within due diligence and audit frameworks. The resources required to advise on any decision can be provided from within the organisation, from an external consultant or through a combination of the two. In the public sector, decisions are made by politicians and although they may delegate the determination of smaller planning applications to the planners employed in their organisation, politicians retain responsibility. In the third sector, decisions will be made by trustees or board members, who are legally responsible for the organisation.

When considering the leadership and management of planning, understanding this advisory role is paramount. However, planners have considerable informal power and influence over the way that the planning system is interpreted and applied through the work that they do (Eversley, 1973; Gunder, 2014). This has to be transparent, and the selection of evidence, its application and interpretation are open to scrutiny and challenge. Planning decision making is influenced by public consultation and participation, which are core features of the planning process and also reflect the relative power relationships between consultees and those making the decisions (Rydin, 1999; Campbell and Marshall, 2000; Conrad et al, 2011).

Leading and managing professionals

In the 1980s, there was a concern that professionals were losing their independence when operating within a corporate environment whether in the private or public sector and in the latter where there has been a greater focus on performance management and closer examination of practices (Haughton, 1997; Carmona and Sieh, 2004; Wong, 2013). This might be viewed as a version of 'Taylorism' (Lawrence, 2010), where the process approach overtakes the professional's discretion in undertaking any specific case (Neyroud, 2011). It is important to note that:

> As professionals belong to occupational systems but also increasingly work inside organizations, new linkages between occupational and organizational domains are required, but they are difficult to develop. Occupational principles and professional standards are usually considered to be at odds with managerial and organizational control principles. (Noordegraaf, 2011, p 1349)

In any organisation, as Noordegraaf and Schinkel (2011) state, there are tensions between managers and professionals and each may attempt to appropriate each others' roles. The ways in which professionals think and respond to issues may also differ from managers (Schon, 1982). There has also been a debate about a new collaborative role for professionals (Clifford and Tewdwr-Jones, 2013), particularly where there is a stronger role for clients and consumers. In health, this newly emergent role is defined as the 'expert patient' where an individual with a particular condition and their family can become more expert than most doctors. In developing the notion of 'new professionalism', the Cabinet Office (2008) identified professionals as those in the best position to introduce innovation and change in their roles with clients, customers, consumers and citizens within their organizations, although within the UK civil service there is a focus on professional skills rather on the employment of professionals (Riddell, 2013).

Leadership styles and repertoire

Definitions of leadership can focus on its wider application or its more specific uses in practice as these two definitions demonstrate:

- Leadership is 'about the ability to influence people by personal attributes and behaviours' (CIPD, 2014, p 1)
- 'Leadership is two types – charismatic that carries hearts and minds or transactional that is task focussed' (Macmillan and Tampoe, 2000, p 197)

There has always been a debate about whether leaders are born or made, that is, whether there are genetic or experiential factors that are more likely to influence the development of leadership traits and abilities. Mole (2004) argues that leadership cannot be taught, but that it is possible to teach leadership competences and observable practices. Whatever skills an individual possesses, their life chances have a strong influence on leadership opportunities – whether through formal or informal activities. In the UK, there has been continued concern about the quality of leadership and management (BIS, 2012). Social class at birth has been a determinant of life changes despite numerous attempts to promote more equality, as Macmillan and Vignoles (2012) have shown. Recruitment into state institutions, particularly in central government and the professions such as medicine, has frequently been dominated by social class and although there have been initiatives to improve opportunities, recruitment patterns have frequently 'flat-lined' after some initial change (Kerslake, 2014).

Most managers will be given training in leadership. In the professions, individuals are promoted on the basis of experience gained during their careers rather than specific leadership training or qualifications. Nevertheless, specific training to support the transition from a specialist to a generalist and from being a problem solver to an agenda setter may be required (Watkins, 2012). Those without a professional qualification may undertake a management qualification as an alternative. Individuals may manage their careers to ensure wide-ranging experience or they may be more opportunistic. There may also be gender traits at play, with more men choosing a career path that aims at a specific role and women being more opportunistic and less linear in their career development, although among younger people and in different sectors these patterns may be converging (Lewis and Fagenson, 1995; Billing, 2013).

Leadership development can be supported through coaching and mentoring. Coaching develops individual skills, for example in sport, and can focus on specific issues including performance improvement, managing change or working with people. Coaching is specifically tailored to the individual's needs and practitioners have become more effective in identifying appropriate programmes (Passmore and Fillery-Travis, 2011; Peltier, 2011; Segers and Inceoglu, 2012). In contrast, mentoring provides support from those with more experience. This may be a colleague or manager or may be someone external to the organisation. Mentoring is a means of developing the potential of individuals earlier in their careers while coaching may be provided in mid- to later career. Organisational culture to support coaching and mentoring is important to its success (Zachary, 2011; Klasen and Clutterbuck, 2012). Mentoring will usually last longer than coaching and can remain following job or role changes for either the mentor or the mentee.

Leadership roles and models

Leadership is central to all types of organisation and all sectors. Leaders attempt to build the social capital of their organisations (Putnam, 2000), developing a sense of allegiance and organisational norms that will be the basis for internal judgements of individuals. Leadership also occurs in malevolent situations or in the 'dark side' of the organisation where opaque organisational allegiances and their associated behaviours can be a significant component in its culture (Linstead et al, 2014). Local leadership may reinforce internal or 'local' values or welcome people from outside who can inject new ideas (Gouldner, 1957).

Professional and technical competence

Individual leadership competence can be important where there is a strong technical or professional component in the organisation. Those who lead technical teams of planners are expected to have a least some knowledge of planning and how it is operated. However, in all careers, there is a point where the responsibilities of the leader are wider then their own experience. The ability to make the transition from managing tasks to more strategic issues is critical to the success of a leader (Hirsh, 2004).

Provider of stability and calm

Organisations look to a leader to provide stability and calm when it is facing difficulties or a crisis. It is important for a leader to create confidence but also to provide ideas and inspiration about the future (Mulgan, 2010). The personality or experience of the leader may need to be culturally aligned to the organisation to be accepted. Some organisations only recruit from within and view external appointees as people to be managed or worked around.

Leading change

Leading change is a significant activity. In planning, this might be to implement new legislation or a new IT system or when priorities are reset by new managers or politicians or through changes in the market. Leading change is an important part of resource management. Change also occurs every day in small ways and these changes need to be kept under review in case they bring unintended consequences (Margetts et al, 2010).

The likely success of change implementation within an organisation will depend on a number of factors (Cameron and Green, 2012). First, is the organisation's culture supportive of change or is it a culture where change is not welcomed or seen as a threat? Second, the leaders of change have to 'walk the talk' – that is, they need to demonstrate that they are committed to the change underway. Further, they need to implement the changes that are required rather than assuming that it is the rest of the organisation that needs to change.

While smaller changes may be instituted on a regular basis, there are also times when a step change is required. This needs a different and more considered approach. Change leadership is accompanied by project management, which identifies key objectives, resources available for changes, milestones and potential problems. Those leading change are likely to be the senior responsible owners of any project, ensuring that change is led within the team and organisation.

In planning in England, the changes in the local planning system in 2004 and in the strategic planning system in 2014 have both been moments when fundamental change leadership has been required. In 2004, the changes to the local planning system were not recognised as a step change by practice (Morphet et al, 2007; PINS, 2007). The introduction of the term 'spatial' into local planning in England in 2004 was meant to signal the changes and this was accompanied by additional guidance (ODPM, 2004d, 2004e; DCLG, 2008). Despite support and incentives to planners, there was not an adequate context for the leadership of change to support implementation (Morphet, 2011b).

Crisis leadership

Leadership in a crisis can be critical and will be more successful if preparations have been made for crises, including risk, resilience or emergency planning. Leadership in a crisis depends on being able to provide both direction and reassurance. The extent to which a crisis can be managed successfully will be based on the perception of how it could have been avoided. In this case, the blame culture (Hood, 2013) and formal procedures will be an essential component of the organisation's response. If the crisis has been unexpected and could not have been anticipated, such as first-time flooding, much of the leadership will be focused on short-term measures to stabilise the situation and then an investigation on the causes of the crisis to see whether anticipation might have been possible. This will then be included within risk management processes and procedures.

Leadership scales

Leading teams

The role of team leader may be one of the first formal leadership roles given to an individual as their career develops (Hirsh, 2004). Teams can be the smallest units of leadership disaggregation in the organisation but they can also have a highly specialist and significant role in the whole. Team leadership requires many of the same skills as leading an organisation (Adair, 1987, 2010) and will include identifying tasks, allocating resources to achieve the task and setting the standards for its performance. Also managing a team management may be the first opportunity for a leader to gain experience of relating to the wider organisation within a framework of responsibility. As Schein (1978) identifies, the experience of a professional may be one of their career anchors as they develop and demonstrating some technical and functional competence may be a requirement before attaining a leadership role.

The formal requirements of the team will be set by the organisational objectives and team leaders will be managed and led in the same way as they lead their own teams. Many team leaders spend time managing upwards, that is in their relationship with their immediate manager, and less time in managing the work of their team.

Team leadership requires a range of skills that include interpersonal relationships within, between and outside the team. The ability to motivate and to manage will also be important and it is at team level that the interrelationships between leadership and management become apparent. It is also at this level that leadership can be most difficult if it is focused on change and improvement (Storey, 2004a). Most organisations might expect team leaders to maintain the status quo with incremental improvements than provide internal challenge.

Leading departments

The leadership of departments may provide a significant challenge as it may be the first occasion on which any individual has to manage activities or professions that are outside their experience. It may also be the point where individual motivations to take on a leadership role may become more apparent. Sturges (2004) identifies these motivations as career orientations characterising individuals as influencers, experts, self-realisers and climbers.

Whereas team leadership may rely on some experiential authority to support its role, this is a significantly different situation when the department comprises those skills, disciplines and activities outside the experience of the departmental head. This may be accompanied by resentment or separation from these specialist activities, not least when the departmental manager is attempting to make changes or improvements. This may result in the departmental leader concentrating on those areas with which they are familiar. It may also result in the reverse, a concentration on those areas where these is less experience and leaving familiar areas to a softer leadership approach based on influence rather than direction (Nye, 2004).

In practice, the effective leadership of departments requires internal leadership of all teams and activities and external presentation of these activities in some integrated way. Organisations group activities either because they identify some synergies between them or because they assume some functional relationships. Those who lead departments require both an understanding of specialist activities and other professions and some broader leadership skills.

Leading organisations

Leadership is most commonly considered in relation to organisations. Here leadership can be defined as charismatic (Storey, 2004b) or heroic and distanced from the organisation. Another form of leadership is transformational, where a leader can move an organisation to develop new approaches to its own activities and be a change management leader. In the public sector, leadership may also operate within a broader partnership or governance context (Broussine, 2012).

Organisational leadership skills are similar to those exercised within teams and departments. At the organisation level there may be more emphasis on external rather than internal leadership, although both will be exercised. Leadership of organisations may need to be more openly strategic and long term, although there will be difficulties for the organisation if there is a gap between external promise and internal performance and delivery. Leaders of organisations have to work within the framework of their board, shareholders, trustees or democratically elected politicians, who will also be exercising leadership roles. Where these work together, the leadership can be dynamic and effective but conflict, difference or distrust between organisational leaders and those to whom they are accountable may be destructive and damaging and ultimately will lead to some change or schism.

How can leaders be effective?

Leadership theory considers the ways that leaders can be effective in three key ways. We examine each in turn.

Personality, traits and styles

In early management literature, there was an interest in identifying leadership styles, particularly with a view to understanding which would be more effective in the workplace. McGregor's theory X and theory Y (1960) was one of the first to be considered and was based on two types of leader and their traits as shown in Box 3.1.

> **BOX 3.1:** McGregor's theory X and theory Y
> - X is authoritarian and works on principle that people have to be coerced to work.
> - Y is democratic and assumes that people will do their best to contribute.
>
> Source: McGregor (1960)

This was followed by the work of Likert (1961), who developed four management styles, as shown in Box 3.2. Likert and McGregor shared the view that organisations needed to be supportive of their employees and that leaders should recognise this rather than being authoritarian or controlling (Pugh and Hickson, 2007).

> **BOX 3.2:** Likert's four styles of management
> - **Exploitative:** uses threats, hierarchical
> - **Benevolent authoritarian:** rewards, but in prescribed power framework
> - **Consultative:** communication up and down but boss makes the decisions
> - **Participative:** high level of involvement
>
> Source: Likert (1961)

Later research on leadership and management focused on the needs of the employees. Maslow's hierarchy of needs (1954) is frequently represented as a pyramid that has basic human needs at the bottom for shelter, food and safety and then progresses though love and belonging, self-esteem and self-actualisation. When this latter has been achieved, Maslow identified that people were more creative and problem solving. Maslow's work was developed by Herzberg (1966), who researched the two-factor hygiene theory of job satisfaction. He argued that specific attitudes were required to help people to engage more with their work.

Organisational and contingent leadership

From this personality and trait-based approach to leadership, theories developed to consider whether different types of leadership and management would be more effective if tailored towards the tasks being undertaken. Fiedler (1967) developed the style of contingent leadership, which was based on the relationship between the task, leader and group where the leader needs to be trusted and liked by group, lead the task and interact with the organisation.

Adair (2003) developed the task focus to action-centred leadership (ACL) through three circles of need. These overlap and focus on achieving the task, managing the team and managing individuals. Adair (2010) regards ACL as primarily strategic but also operating in implementation. In ACL, the manager's job is to lead in all three areas as shown in Box 3.3.

BOX 3.3: Adair's action-centred leadership
- **Planning:** seeking information, defining tasks, setting aims
- **Initiating:** briefing, task allocation, setting standards
- **Controlling:** maintaining standards, ensuring progress, ongoing decision-making
- **Supporting:** individuals' contributions, encouraging, team spirit, reconciling, morale
- **Informing:** clarifying tasks and plans, updating, receiving feedback and interpreting
- **Evaluating:** feasibility of ideas, performance, enabling self-assessment

Source: Adair (2010)

Another approach, proposed by Handy (1993), suggests that a 'best fit' between the leader's characteristics and the organisation are critical for success. Here, the leader's values need to fit with the organisation, while the leader should also have technical competence and be able to demonstrate their combined contribution to any group's work. The relationship between members of the team is also important. Handy argues that team members have their own expectations of the role of the leader and their contribution of knowledge, skills and experience. He argues that there needs to be alignment between the team and the task, otherwise the leader may not be respected or have influence. Handy also suggests that past experiences of the group may be central in this relationship, not least where teams have worked in a particular way and may only accept a leader who works in a similar way.

Distributed leadership

There is a growing view that leadership in organisations needs to be collective rather than exercised by individuals. Spillane and colleagues (2004) describe this as distributed leadership, with different constellations of leaders working together on different tasks. Spillane (2012) sets this approach against the 'heroic leader' approach (Brown, 2014). Bennett and colleagues state that:

> Distributed leadership is not something 'done' by an individual 'to' others, or a set of individual actions through which people contribute to a group or organization … [it] is a group activity that works through and within relationships, rather than individual action. (Bennett et al, 2003 cited in Bolden, 2011, pp 251-2)

Distributed leadership can be viewed as normative with its main focus on performance improvement and organisational effectiveness rather than an ethical or philosophical approach to power sharing or more democratic decision making (Kempster et al, 2013; Jones, 2014). Further, Oborne and colleagues (2013) suggest that distributed leadership is a means of gaining acquiescence to change.

Distributed leadership may also be characterised as collaborative leadership, a term frequently used within planning (Healey, 1997). However, Bolden (2011) argues that it represents a different set of characteristics and while distributed leadership may be normative, collaborative or shared leadership may be ethical or political, seeking a different set of normative outcomes.

BOX 3.4: What makes a good leader? A view from central government

1 Know your own style and be authentic
2 Be prepared to lead, offer continuity and admit if you are wrong
3 Win and retain respect of others – for you and your role
4 Relationships are more important than tasks
5 Set a vision
6 Communicate vision constantly
7 Lead delivery
8 Manage your energy
9 Build the right team
10 Trust your instinct
11 Learn lessons from mistakes and move on

Source: Fraser (2014)

BOX 3.5: Which soft power skills do leaders need?

'Among the soft power skills are emotional intelligence (emotional self-control and the ability to use emotional cues to attract others); vision (an attractive picture of the future that balances ideals, objectives, and capabilities); and communication (the ability to use words and symbols to persuade both an inner circle and a broader audience). With regard to skill in the use of hard power resources, two hard power skills are particularly important; organizational capacity and the Machiavellian political skills of bullying, buying and bargaining in the formation of winning coalitions'

Source: Nye (2014, p 121)

Levels of leadership

Leadership is required at all levels of the organisation. At the level of team or department this might be considered primarily as part of a management role with a switch in focus appearing at the level of the organisation. However, as discussed below, leadership is exercised at all levels, including the smallest teams. The extent to which leadership is exercised at different organisational levels may depend on the function of the group or at different times, including those of change or crisis, but there is an underlying need for leadership in daily management. The way in which leadership is exercised and the challenges involved is now considered at the three most common levels – the team, the department and the organisation.

Strategic leadership

Strategic leaders provide vision and aspiration for the organisation. They give direction and purpose through demonstrating why one strategic pathway is more important than another. They also articulate and represent the organisation's values, demonstrating their alignment to them and their embodiment of them (Adair, 2010). Strategic leaders need to communicate the direction and strategy throughout the organisation and to external stakeholders (Bovaird, 2012). In the public sector, this strategic leadership operates within a political context.

Operational leadership

Operational leaders need specific skill sets demonstrating their technical expertise and experience. Leadership styles will be blended depending on the situation and the task. This may mean listening to those who have detailed experience of a process and likely problems. Failure to do so may result in an alternative *de facto* leader being designated by the team. While paying lip service to the *de jure* leader, the team will follow the *de facto* leader. Competition or lack of respect between these leaders may cause problems and the quality of outputs may suffer.

All operational leaders are likely to have their behaviours observed at close quarters and be responsible for more immediate actions than a strategic leader. This means that the personal behaviours of operational leaders need to be openly aligned with the leadership messages that they are projecting.

Task leadership

Task leaders use their experience in accomplishing set objectives using past experience and training. Task leaders need the confidence of the organisation in achieving their defined outcomes on time and on budget and need experience in team management and team building (Adair, 1987).

Working with volunteers

Leadership of volunteers can be through an organisation or informally through the group. Volunteers may be recruited to undertake a particular project, such as carrying out a survey or preparing a community plan, or a physical task, such as landscape improvement. Volunteers are recruited within an equal opportunities framework, and must operate within a safe environment, but otherwise do not have the same employment conditions as other staff members. As such, they may experience different forms of leadership. Volunteers are unlikely to be responsive to management and leadership styles found in organisational settings and institutions (Farmer and Fedor, 2001). Boezeman and Ellemers (2014) argue that leadership of volunteers has to be undertaken in ways that communicate the influence of the project and its positive outcomes in order to contribute to the volunteer's experience and esteem.

Discussion Box: **Leadership skills**
- Do all leaders need the same skills and experience?
- What leadership skills are required in a crisis?
- Do all organisations need the same type of leader?

Leadership in planning

Leadership skills for planning

Leadership in planning operates at different scales and within different sectors, and the interrelationships between sector and scale may be significant. In the private sector, leadership may constitute large teams of consultants working with a range of clients. Within the organisation, work has to be completed on time and budget and the client should be satisfied with the outcome. In the private sector, there may the need for a 'heroic' leader who can represent the organisation externally and be associated specifically with the company. In smaller private sector organisations, leadership may converge with management. Here, leadership may be more distributed, especially if individual team members have a higher degree of autonomy in identifying priorities and delivering work.

In the third sector, there is also a strong need for strategic management that relates to the organisation's core purpose and its direction for the future, even if the organisation is a small one. Hudson (2011) also points out that it is important for third sector organisations to identify their vision and strategy so that they can align with others in partnerships. Third sector organisations may now be hybrids (Billis, 2010b), delivering contracts for government or major developers, particularly for consultation. Does this mean that there is a blurring of the lines between the different strategies for the organisation or does it become so dependent on the contracted work that rather than supporting its founding objectives? Harris (2010) discusses the potential effects of these contradictory environments, noting a trend for third sector organisations to be more varied rather than broadly similar to each other as before. In planning, this hybridity can create uncertainty for potential donors and volunteers.

In the public sector, leadership is exercised in a context of formal procedural relationships. This has been reinforced in England through the separation of the executive and judicial roles of councillors in local authorities since 2000. Planning leadership within the public sector and particularly local authorities has to work with the wider leadership initiatives within local government.

Enticott (2006) identified leadership within planning in local government as being of critical importance. He states that the relationship between planning leadership and development management activities is less easy to identify than in strategic planning or place making and in his research, he found that the managerial characteristics between the higher and lower performing development management authorities were the same. This suggests that other issues within individual local authorities may have a stronger influence on performance than the leadership of the planning service.

Leadership skills for planning is also a concern of government. A report on skills (Egan, 2004) was followed by the establishment of an Academy for Sustainable Communities. This focused on specific skills identified by Egan as being important for leaders (set out in Box 3.6). The ASC undertook its own study of skill requirements (ASC, 2007) following this although it focused more on geographical distribution than a skills diagnostic.

BOX 3.6: Egan's skills for leadership in planning
- Focus on place shaping
- Boundary spanning
- Networked
- Partnership working
- Relational
- Fluid
- Collaborative

Source: Egan (2004)

The academy was integrated within the HCA in 2008 and there is little evidence that the leadership work it undertook has had any noticeable effect. Since then, government initiatives in England on developing planning leadership have been channelled through the Planning Advisory Service (PAS), funded by central government and with governance shared between central and local government. Here the focus on leadership development has been through local authority councillors. Leadership skills for planners have been identified in the national competency framework (PAS, 2013a), which is administered through a self-assessment questionnaire. The leadership attributes it identifies are in Box 3.7.

BOX 3.7: National competency framework leadership skills for planners
- Take ownership appropriate to the task
- Be inclusive
- Inspire and be open to inspiration
- Influence the behaviours of others – and be open to influence
- Work cooperatively

Source: PAS (2013a)

The national competency framework includes leadership as a component skill for change management. The competency framework is useful, but does not set the context nor give guidance on the self-assessment process or what action may be taken subsequently to improve leadership skills. As yet, it has had little impact in practice, although it could prove more effective in the future.

The other initiatives led by PAS to improve the leadership skills of planning officers include peer review. Here the assumption is that recommendations based on comparison and evaluation in a peer-led environment will be respected and adopted. Peer review has gradually replaced central government inspection regimes in the public sector since 2007. The peer review process outlined in Box 3.8 works in a similar way to government scrutiny functions and uses an investigative/inquisitorial process to examine a service against normative benchmarks or a framework. Like scrutiny, its recommendations are not binding. While members of the peer review team share their views and judgments, the group will make a collective report that is transparent. Peer review provides a sympathetic and experienced understanding of a planning service and this is regarded as a prerequisite for making any critical or improvement judgments.

BOX 3.8: Peer review systems

Peer review is the process whereby an organisation invites a small team or an individual to review the operational standards and working practices of one of their teams or services. It is sometimes known as a sector-led process and reduces the external inspection culture, focusing rather on those who can make judgements and recommendations based on their own experience.

The process of peer review includes the development of a framework by the sector and then a submission from the organisation and department about the way it is performing against this framework. In adopting the framework, there needs to be stakeholder engagement and professional agreement.

Once the report has been prepared, a small external team made up of those with experience appropriate to the scale and type of organisation visit for a short period of one to three days. In this time, they will observe, hold discussion sessions and agree between them the judgements and recommendations that they are making as a peer group.

This judgement is delivered verbally to the organisation, and submitted in draft and then in final form. Throughout these stages, the organisation has the opportunity to comment on the report.

The organisation's responses to the report are made at its own discretion and there is no obligation to act on any of the recommendations.

Peer review has been used in planning because it is a complex activity and each local authority will have its own cultural and territorial dynamics that inform its leadership and practices. Planning has been identified as an inward and self-referring activity that has been resistant to change. Peer review in planning demonstrates leadership by the sector. Despite its use, there is no evidence that the peer review process has specifically changed performance or leadership in any situation, although engaging in peer review suggests an openness to change.

In Scotland, the responsibility for promoting improvement has been shared between the Improvement Service and the Heads of Planning in Scotland (HOPS, 2012), which have focused on skills development associated with the planning performance framework. This is a softer approach that has been supported by specific events and training programmes that are led by local government and funded by the Scottish government. The Scottish approach is more collegial and joint than that in England. Some have commented that this is because there are fewer local authorities in Scotland, which means that it is possible to have more face-to-face discussions. However, the differences may also relate to differences in economic pressures and criticisms of the English housing markets and infrastructure planning process from the EU (CEC, 2014) and the Organisation for Economic Co-operation and Development (OECD, 2011).

Leadership in and of places

The leadership of places is now identified as a significant element in their wider economic success (Krugman, 2001; Charbit, 2011) and the alignment between functions of place, their governance and administrative boundaries makes places more economically successful. Leadership and advocacy of place has always been a core local government activity, whether in seeking new jobs or defending existing ones, arguing for resources, investment and the needs of communities (Solace, 2013).

The role of the local authority, particularly relating to its territory and place, took a specific turn in England through the Lyons review on place shaping (2008). This emphasised local place leadership as a critical element for all local government activity and embodied a new approach to widening the governance of place to include leadership through partnership and by communities (Madden, 2010), conflating the roles of community and place. The review had few explicit recommendations for planning, although there were links with the spatial planning approach introduced in 2004 (Morphet, 2007; Morphet et al, 2007). These were identified by the Local Government Association (LGA, 2008), although planning was identified primarily as a delivery mechanism rather than contributing to strategic or shaping activity.

Another study in England by Gibney and Murie (2008) reviewed the leadership of place using a multiple-theory approach with a particular focus on the role of boundary spanners – people who are outcome-focused and can persuade a range of individuals and organisations to work together (Williams, 2012). This study contrasted traditional and post-modern leadership of place. It described traditional leadership approaches as being focused on function/organisation and operating in an hierarchical way with linear relationships. The authors found that in the traditional model of place leadership, personal networks are important and that the focus is on specific problems and tasks within departments, and is based on professional skills, rather than on a more strategic view. Finally, the study argued that the traditional view of place was centralist in its overriding culture and output-focused. Post-modern, cross-boundary, collaborative/relational approaches were identified as more holistic and leading to better results. This decentred approach was outcome-focused. Moreover, in contrast to traditional approaches, this type of place leadership was more fluid and focused on place shaping and working within partnerships. The core competencies of leadership of place were identified as direction, vision, mission, strategies and values, all of which are aligned to the specific place.

Collaborative working may also be difficult. Using an example of joint working across city and county economic boards in Ireland, Rigg and O'Mahony (2013) found that there are conditions that make collaboration more difficult, including where there are differing cultures between organisations, more pessimistic expectations of the likely success and institutional instability. Further, while there is considerable public policy support for collaborative working, this remains a tenet of public policy implementation rather than necessarily being evaluated as more effective than other ways of working (Sullivan et al, 2012).

Private sector organisations may be major landowners with many sites or their activities may be concentrated in specific locations. Private sector organisations may also be major developers when they relocate or change their business, and their contribution to major regeneration, redevelopment or other initiatives such as those for town centres may be significant (Guy, 2000; Harrison, 2013).

Leadership from the community?

There is a growing view that leadership should come from outside the organisation and be more participative in style. Morris and Leung (2010) argues that such approaches to localised decision making are more typical to those countries with growing economies and that the difference between participative and centralised approaches to governance may have economic consequences. Another issue to consider is the role of those who work in the public sector and live within the community it serves. These employees can have a major influence on the way in which the local authority is perceived and trusted and many employees will regard the local authority as a lifelong employer rather than move around between authorities in the course of their career. This may create a norm of reciprocity between the organisation and the employee where the organisation is supporting the community and the employee supports the organisation in return (Gouldner, 1960; Ni et al, 2014). There may also be an organisational memory which can be strong and be based in the social memory of the organisation that can provide a strong sense of identity and worth to the employees (Rowlinson et al, 2010). These relationships can be important in developing credible community leadership.

There has been a strong focus on community leadership in Scotland through single outcome agreements organised through community planning approaches. These agreements are developed by the community and then set out in quasi-contractual form binding their delivery through the primary public sector agencies in the area. In this approach, community planning offers a more integrated approach across a range of public service issues including health and education, and is less narrowly defined than might be the case with community planning approaches in England. The development of neighbourhood planning in England is narrower and focused primarily on the role of development in contributing local services rather than coordinating the roles of the agencies that manage their delivery (Gallent et al, 2008; Gallent and Robinson, 2012).

Discussion Box: **What are the main issues for leadership in planning?**

▪ Is leadership in planning important and can it make any difference?

▪ Is it necessary for a planning leader to be a professional planner?

▪ Does leadership in the private sector require different skills from those required in the public and third sectors?

▪ Are there any particular issues in leading volunteers in planning?

Leadership and management

Management has been defined as 'the art getting things done through people' (Follett, 2003) and 'organising individuals to achieve desired objectives' (Likert, 1961). Planning is about the management of scarce resources – land and buildings – and their use. It is also about the management of planners to deliver planning and the processes that support these wider decisions on public, private and community investment. In many situations, these issues combine into a single system, and both need to be managed together.

There are differences between leadership and management as set out by Storey (2004a) and shown in Box 3.9. However, as noted earlier, despite these differences on many occasions and in some roles individuals may have to combine leadership and management roles using them appropriately in different situations.

Management approaches vary according to the type of activities being managed. The first approach is *process* management where the challenge is to maintain delivery at the required rates within the resources provided. This may mean considering specific action to cover for loss of resources, coping with seasonal demand and dealing with the management of product resources provided though supply chains. Many service organisations are process-driven, with the same tasks undertaken each day. Management interventions are related to improving the processes, resource use and outcomes. In local authority planning organisations, development management is a process management activity where there is a

BOX 3.9: Characteristics of managers and leaders

Managers	Leaders
Are transactional	Are transformative
Seek to operate and maintain current systems	Seek to challenge and change systems
	Crate new visions and new meanings
Accept given objectives and meanings	Empower
Control and monitor	Seek to inspire and transcend
Trade on exchange relationships	Have a long-term focus
Have a short-term focus	Focus on the strategic big picture
Focus on detail and procedure	

Source: Storey (2004a, p 7)

regular supply of planning applications to be determined within a time constraint, with fixed resources and specific processes and outcomes quality to be considered.

The second approach is *project* management, of one-off or episodic activities. This type of management is typical in private sector planning organisations where work tends to be project-driven, and in all sectors where plans are prepared. Projects may be undertaken to implement a specific building or facility, or to implement a new policy or legislation such as that for collecting developer contributions. In some cases, once projects are completed, they pass into process management – keeping the system operational or managing a building facility. Other projects, such as converting properties for sale, may be single activities; once the activity is completed, a new project is undertaken.

The third type is *innovation* management, undertaken where activities are less formal and traditional forms of management may be anathema to invention and new ways of working. Providing the right environment for invention may require softer management techniques, as innovative and entrepreneurial people tend to be more self-managing than others.

Outside of these approaches, 'management gurus' and business leaders may attempt to share general principles derived from their own experiences (Huczynski, 2012). There are gurus for different times and types of business. These 'How I did it' stories may be useful in demonstrating that management is as much an art as science (Goleman et al, 2002) and also that not all management decisions end in success. Overcoming and learning from failure is a positive attribute for those starting new businesses (Edmondson, 2011; Shepherd et al, 2011). Some management thinkers such as Peter Drucker and Charles Handy have something to say to most generations of managers. There appear to be no management gurus in planning.

More recently, there has been a shift to management by concept. This may be described as post-charismatic or post-transformational management (Storey, 2004b), where the manager is more attuned to the needs of the individuals and the leader builds a team around them. In this literature, seemingly simple ideas provide key business and management insights that can make managers more successful. These include the 'tipping point' (Gladwell, 2006), 'nudge' (Sunstein and Thaler, 2008), 'emotional intelligence' (Goleman, 2006), 'freakonomics' (Levitt and Dubner, 2010), 'cognitive surplus' (Shirky, 2010) and 'black swan' (Taleb, 2010). These authors offer a more fragmented approach to management in an age of social media where attention spans may be short.

Most concept books rest on sound behavioural science that has been popularised for general readers and their intention is to stimulate thinking about management practices. The concepts are based on the principle of continuous improvement, where current approaches and repertoire are subjected to constant scrutiny. Best (2006) also argues that such concepts are short-term fads and part of the process of innovation.

Discussion Box: **Leadership and management**
- Is there any difference between leadership and management?
- Can someone be a leader and a manager?
- Do management tasks vary between different sectors?
- What role do new management ideas play? Are they helpful or not?

Key components of management

Meeting the organisation's objectives

The role of management is to implement the organisation's objectives. All organisations have explicit objectives, although there may also be unwritten cultural expressions of organisational priorities. Some organisations, including those in the public sector, may be unclear about their objectives if they provide a range of services. In the voluntary sector, where organisations are charities or trusts, the objectives of the organisation are more likely to be set out in the information required by the Charity Commission when establishing the charity. In the private sector, all organisations identify their objectives for their shareholders, clients and suppliers. These may be set out in reports in the public domain and described in more detail within the company as objectives are achieved.

Achievement of the task

Management is the means through which organisational tasks, however strategic or minor, are achieved using the resources available. All individuals exercise some control over resources in any job. It is also important to note that management is usually described as a process of managing down in an organisational hierarchy, but most people also manage their own managers. In terms of trust and confidence, degrees of individual freedoms and promotion, upward management is a significant component of the daily management activity (Schilit and Locke, 1982).

An important aspect of management is maintaining relationships with external clients and contractors. This is undertaken at all levels in an organisation. Failure to manage these relationships effectively can generate risks and potentially result in failure, loss or poorer performance levels. Failure to manage a client may also lead to additional work, changed priorities and disputes. In planning, external contractors are frequently used to provide specialist input into planning application assessments or plan making. The failure of a supplier to undertake the appropriate work or deliver a project on time may be problematic. At the same time, managing suppliers also requires some skill in constructing a brief so that it is fulfilled appropriately.

Consultants also have to be managed (Sturdy and Wright, 2011). The use of consultants has benefits, as they provide specialist knowledge and offer external credibility. At the same time, they may not understand some of the mechanics and culture of the organisation they are working in and may provide a routine response to a management brief rather than one tailored to the specific situation. Nesheim and colleagues (2014) argue that better results can be achieved when consultants are not managed as external to the organisation but as part of the internal structure, particularly where they are adding capacity.

Maintaining performance

A core management objective is maintaining and improving team performance. This can be undertaken in a variety of ways, including through continuous improvement initiatives, focus groups, customer feedback and investment in new technology. Managers tend to be more effective when they work with staff, especially when they are new to an organisation or must tackle difficult issues such as underperformance. Staff often have the best understanding of their team's problems, and may have suggestions about how best to solve them, and as such they are pivotal to the manager's approach.

Communication

All management requires communication, both inside and outside the organisation. Inside the organisation, formal communication is within local cultures relating to the operation of the organisation. Much internal communication is informal and most organisations have multiple internal networks that are established through friendships or experience of working together and create positive organisational capital. Some organisations foster these internal networks through sports and social activities, volunteering and work-related 'away days'. Internal communication may relate to new initiatives or feedback on current activities or objectives. Sometimes internal organisational communication is negative and serves to undermine the organisation or to defeat its objectives. These communication networks may seek to influence decisions or to have some control over individuals and are generally present in every organisation. Sometimes they are known as the dark side (Linstead et al, 2014).

Communication outside the organisation is important. This may be with customers, shareholders, clients, users or the wider community. Such communication is part of reputation management and is necessary just to retain the status quo. Much external communication is undertaken through social media. Many organisations across all sectors provide business services through their websites. There has been a use of channel strategies so that reaching communities, stakeholders, customers or suppliers will be managed in different ways, including websites and social media. It is becoming more and more common for organisations offering services to the public to engage with their clients online, as this is a cheaper way to run their business. In retailing, the introduction of 'click and collect', whereby customers order goods online and collect them from the shop at a later stage, integrates two processes. This mode of shopping has also been found to engender additional sales during collect visits and so enhance business.

> **BOX 3.10: What are the key challenges in management?**
> * Achieving tasks consistently
> * Optimising organisational culture
> * Relating to the external environment
> * Managing internal conflict
> * Implementing change
> * Motivating individuals
> * Managing upwards

> Discussion Box: **Managing in planning**
> ■ Are there any particular issues to consider in managing planning teams?
> ■ How can planning managers motivate their teams?
> ■ How can a planning manager introduce change?
> ■ How could planning management fail?

Conclusions

Wherever planning is undertaken, it has to be led and managed within the organisation. This is always challenging as shown in Box 3.10. At some levels, this leadership and management will be implemented by planning professionals managing projects and processes but in most organisations planning will be led and managed by those who do not have a professional planning background. Bridging this point may be critical to the organisational success for planning outcomes.

As this chapter has shown, planners operating at all levels have some leadership and management responsibilities in the exercise of their role. The development of individual leadership and management skills and experience is gained by most planners 'on the job' and without specific training, but all leadership and management practice can be enhanced by a wider consideration of the issues related to these roles. Achieving successful outcomes can be enhanced by being aware of different theories and methods of approach. There is no single leadership and management style that will always be appropriate. However, this chapter has shown that some alignment between leadership and management styles and the tasks in hand are more effective for practice.

FOUR

Strategy and planning

Introduction

While much management activity is concerned with the day to day,

> management has no choice but to anticipate the future, to attempt to mould it and to balance short-range and long-term goals. It is not given to mortals to do either of these things well. But lacking divine guidance, business management must make sure that these difficult responsibilities are not overlooked or neglected, but taken care of as humanly possible. (Drucker, 2011, p 8)

Strategic management is concerned with the long-term direction of any organisation, its objectives and associated business plans to achieve these ends. Strategic management will primarily be concerned with positive action for the organisation such as growth and development. At its core, strategic management makes decisions that will affect the organisation in the future. These actions may also be defensive such as preventing other organisations from taking market share by purchasing land or through other actions such as mergers and acquisitions.

Planning is a key element of strategic planning. If an organisation is planning growth, it may need more accommodation for production or delivery of services. Developers may take options to purchase land. Some organisations have large land holdings that have been in their ownership for hundreds of years and they will take a long-term view of their own development programme as patient investors.

What is strategic management?

Strategic management comprises of a number of components. First, there is a review of long-term objectives set in the context of the purpose of the organisation. This review may confirm the objectives or result in their amendment, following which the objectives will be implemented. Some organisations translate this objective-setting process into a mission statement that is then used to set organisational priorities (French et al, 2001; Fang et al, 2013). These may vary in their effectiveness (Braun, 2012) as organisations seek to maintain the status quo. Finance and budgets are then aligned to the objectives and this is where difficulties arise, as groups within organisations can resist the reallocation of resources (Frow et al, 2005).

Organisational leaders adopt a strategic stance when they take proactive, reactive and defensive actions in response to the external environment (Andrews et al, 2012). While strategic managers can set the future direction, most organisations are focused on delivering immediate objectives. Daily tasks always seem more important that long-term changes and unless there are clear communications and internal engagement, there is likely to be resistance to change. Organisations that are founded on change, such as those in the high-tech industry, may also face change management challenges as they grow (Flamholtz and Randle, 2012).

What is strategy?

Strategy has its origins in political philosophy, including the work of Machiavelli (1513) and Clausewitz (1832). Both were focused on the ways in which rulers could retain power and remain key references for strategic management (Jay, 1970; Powell, 2011). These thinkers alert the leader to the need to plan for the future and implement this strategy. Machiavelli and Clausewitz also encourage consideration of the use of resources and operational programmes. Both demonstrate that command and control management is likely to be unsuccessful (Mulgan, 2010; Margetts et al, 2010). Kornberger (2013) also stresses that Clausewitz saw that strategy could only be developed though a combination of theory and practice, and that theory has no place alone.

The leading strategic management thinkers are Ansoff and Drucker. Ansoff (1969) was interested in the role of business strategy as a tool of problem solving and, within this, incorporates multiple initiatives that are not necessarily linked. As a result, Ansoff's approach creates a strategic action programme, but does not necessarily create a strategy. Ansoff's problem-solving approach may not be any better than muddling through (Lindblom, 1959). Drucker (1977, p 421) took a different view:

> Strategic decisions – whatever their magnitude, complexity or importance – should never be taken through problem solving. Indeed in these specifically managerial decisions, the important and difficult job is never to find the right answer, it is to find the right question.

It is this tension between problem solving or 'fire fighting' and thinking about the organisation in the long term that lies at the heart of strategic leadership, management and planning. Should strategic planning be focused on solving problems such as housing or economic growth, or should it take a wider view of the area and its longer term future (Barca, 2009; CEC, 2013)? Mulgan (2010) argues that the aim of public sector management is to set the ends and devolve the means. In considering its future approach to public sector reform, the World Bank has opted for a problem-solving approach over a more strategic one for the period to 2020 (Pollitt, 2013), relying on performance management and outcomes. This creates another means of 'muddling through' (Pritchett, 2013) and suffers from the same criticisms that there may be no overall direction. However, these actions may have normative consistency if not coherence. While the strategy is not overt, it may be implicit.

At different periods in planning history in the UK, the problem-solving approach has prevailed over long-term strategy. In the period 1945-65, the main focus was on problem solving of post-war reconstruction within a wider context of the national economy. In the period 1965-85, a more strategic approach was applied that used technical methods to construct alternative futures in strategic plans (McLoughlin, 1969; Lee, 1973). These strategic plans progressed at a variable rate and were sometimes products of administrative and political convenience rather than strategic direction (Solesbury, 1974). They were also methodologies located within the culture and temporal context (Goetz and Meyer-Sayling, 2009).

Strategic plans were also formulated at two scales. Those at the regional scale were led by central government, with civil servants chairing regional planning boards and organising internal consistency within government (Rodgers, 1965). These boards were supported by economic planning councils that offered advice, but the government was clear that it would not necessarily adopt any of their proposals (Morgan and Alden, 1974; McCallum, 1979). The tension between spatial and economic strategic regional plans continued (Glasson and Marshall, 2007) until both were abolished in 2010 and replaced by a economy-led approach (CEC, 2013).

The second scale of strategic planning was the structure plan, introduced in 1968 and accompanied by a manual (MHLG, 1970). Structure plans were prepared by upper-tier authorities and designed to deliver the regional strategic plans. They included cross-boundary working and promoted economic, social and environmental wellbeing. In the period when Margaret Thatcher was prime minister, government intervention in policy making became more assertive and this was also the case in planning (Thornley, 1991). Since 1985, there has been a predominant focus on central government intervention in planning and planning practice has increasingly operated within the contract set for it. Central government took leadership of a new regional planning system in 1991. Local authorities were engaged in preparing regional plans but were primarily focused on preparing local plans in conformity with the regional policies.

This had the effect of reducing the role of structure plans, which became less strategic and more focused on determining delivery of allocated housing and employment land targets (Cullingworth and Nadin, 2006). While structure plans had a focus on coordination and delivery, they were less detailed and specific than the plans prepared under the previous system and were eventually abolished in 2004. In 2010, they were replaced by strategic economic plans, prepared by local enterprise partnerships (LEPs), which are strategic and incorporate delivery programmes. This suggests a return to a more encompassing approach, reminiscent of the period 1965-2004 but this time more closely associated with programmed delivery (Pemberton and Morphet, 2014).

Strategy in central government

While strategic leadership is seen as a theoretical concept, there is also evidence that it is being used in an operational way within organisations. In the UK, there is a more pragmatic than strategic approach to policy and delivery (Depledge and Dodds, 2014). This has continued to be identified as a problem. Before Tony Blair came to government in 1997, he was concerned that the well-oiled machine he would find would not support the new government's agenda. Instead, he found that the notion of a 'machine' had little substance (Blair, 2010) and created the Prime Minister's Strategy Unit (PSU) to meet this strategic gap.

The PSU operated from 1999 to 2010 and its objective was to provide coordination and direction to the strategies set out by the government in its cyclical spending reviews, which occurred every three to four years (James, 2004). It was set up in parallel with the Prime Minister's Delivery Unit and published over 130 papers. Mulgan, who was the director of the PSU from 2002 to 2004, favoured Drucker's strategy model and argued that strategy should be undertaken at the centre of the organisation, 'setting the overall direction and priorities, with a strategy function to do this at a high level and to address cross-cutting issues' (Mulgan, 2010, p 119). Mulgan also associates this strategic function with the allocation of resources and the ability to track and manage implementation performance. He identifies three ways in which the centre can achieve this – by command, by coordination and by influence – and that these three styles of management should be used appropriately within different situations. Hood (2000) argues that the culture within which these strategic approaches are undertaken is also critical to their success

After Mulgan's term as director, the PSU prepared its *Strategy survival guide* (PSU, 2004). This follows the Ansoff approach of strategy as problem solving. It was also a centralising approach to delivery (Smith, 2011) and served to undermine more decentralised, devolved and localist rhetoric. Another criticism is made by Sainsbury (2013), who argues that, in comparison with other sectors and despite claims of excellence, there is no evidence to demonstrate that central government policy making is anything other than 'amateur' (p 263) and ad hoc, despite the reforms discussed here. He also criticises the role of quasi-independent experts or tsars (Levitt and Solesbury, 2012) who are brought in to provide an alterative view from that prevailing, providing minsters and civil servants with some 'wriggle room'. However, this is not a new approach, as Smith and Young (1996) demonstrate.

The strategic choice approach in local government

In local government, the consideration of strategy and strategic choices was more common in the pre-Thatcher era. Making strategy and then acting on it was central to a local authority's activities. Friend and Jessop (1969) set out an operational research approach to strategic planning, and the choices involved within it, in the context of Coventry City Council. They demonstrated that making strategy was an issue that had to be operated within a live rather than a theoretical context. Importantly, they identified that the main route within the local authority to determining this strategy and implementing it was through the planning process.

This work was continued by Friend and Hickling (1987), who defined strategic choice as a way of operating rather than as a level of operation. While they understood the need for major decisions, Friend and Hickling also emphasised the linkages between decisions and the consequences (intended or otherwise) they can have on each other (Margetts et al, 2010). Further, they stressed that strategic leadership should include the expectation and management of uncertainty.

Friend and Hickling approached this through techniques of strategic problem identification, comparison and choice based on the methods used by Friend and Jessop. This approach was based on live examples and offered a way to continue to make strategy, but by the 1980s, the culture and climate of local government had moved to a more short-term approach, when the pressure was on inward looking efficiencies and reforms. The loss of this local government strategic approach was precipitated by changes in the public sector, characterised by the introduction of competition in 1976 and its associated neoliberal philosophies (Stewart and Walsh, 1992; Hood, 2000). Efforts to contain, control and harness this competiton ethos have not resulted in a new strategic approach in the public sector, but rather one that has been dominated by the conceptual leadership of best value, performance management (Carmona and Sieh, 2007) and localism.

Strategic leadership in partnerships

The role of partnerships in strategic leadership within communities comprising all three sectors has become more important since 1997 and is now a key policy. Such partnerships straddle the whole community. In Scotland, they have been enabled through community planning partnerships and, in England, through local strategic partnerships formed in local authorities from 2000 (Morphet, 2008). These partnerships were imposed on local authorities and other partners for a range of reasons set out by Blair (1998) and shown in Box 4.1. For the majority of local councillors, leadership was now split between the local authority and the community (DTLR, 1998). Further, there has been a strong push for directly elected mayors to promote local leadership, although this has not proved a popular move in practice (Greasley and Stoker, 2008). In return for these reforms in governance, local authorities were offered more powers (Armstrong, 1997; Blair, 1998).

BOX 4.1: Why local authorities should work in partnership with other organisations
- Localities lack a clear sense of direction
- There is a lack of coherence and cohesion in delivering local services
- The quality of local services is variable

Source: Blair (1998, p 2)

The Organisation for Economic Co-operation and Development (OECD, 2001) sets out some lessons on partnership approaches and experience from a range of countries. It argues that communities benefit from partnership governance, as they provide an opportunity for the voice of communities in strategic decision making. It also argues that public services and local authorities benefit through better targeting of their initiatives and services and that this results in higher satisfaction from the population. It also identified the growing role of the third sector in these arrangements, not only to participate but also to deliver some of the solutions.

Partnership approaches to strategic leadership have a number of tensions. First, those organisations pressed by central government into forming partnerships will have differing policies, resulting in inconsistency and a subsequent lack of credibility and maturity (OECD, 2001). Second, the imposition of a partnership and its associated shared governance may be resented by those forced to give up some of their power (Wilkinson and Craig, 2002). Third, those who are being asked to take a role in partnerships governance may be unwilling to do so or may not give it much attention (Morphet, 2008).

A further issue is whether the partnership has symbolic or real power – can it make any decisions and does it have any control over budgets or staff? Does the partnership commit all partners to action or are some partners engaged in advising on the decisions of the local authority (Davies, 2004)? There may also be competiton between partners rather than collaboration (Lowndes and Skelcher, 1998). While the partnerships exist, the real decisions may continue to be taken elsewhere or in the same ways as the past. Having more partnership working does not necessarily create more public involvement (Lowndes and Sullivan, 2004). Finally, there is an underlying concern about the democratic legitimacy of partnerships and their decision making (Geddes, 2006), particularly on priorities or funding. Partnerships are not accountable in the same way as democratically elected politicians and this remains a core objection to this governance form.

Can partnerships provide strategic leadership? This question has been an open one and, while some partnerships might have exercised some strong strategic leadership in some areas, there is no clear evidence either way. Partnerships have also been subject to policy shifts. Local strategic partnerships in England had been developing and maturing in many local authority areas and their role had been reinforced in the Local Democracy, Economic Development and Construction Act 2009. However, a change in government in 2010 meant that they were reduced in status and subject to the policy insecurity risk identified by the OECD (2001). However, the LEPs introduced in 2010 in England have been confirmed as a continuing policy by all main political parties and this may support their developing role in strategic leadership until 2020 (Healey and Newby, 2014). In Scotland, partnership structures have been subject to fewer changes, and if anything their role has developed and increased in importance. New partnerships have been introduced at a more strategic level and have been fitted into existing structures and legislation, unlike the approach in England, which has been outwardly more informal although changes to the role of former civil servants and more coercive pressures to work in particular ways have operated behind the scenes (Heseltine, 2012).

What is the opposite of strategic management?

Undertaking strategic management rather than problem solving may seem like a luxury in many organisations faced by daily management issues. Organisations may adopt processes of 'muddling through' (Lindblom 1959), resulting in disjointed incrementalism, making a series of daily or short-term decisions without necessarily considering their wider consequences or long-term effects. Decisions taken in one part of the organisation may influence those taken elsewhere, but this is not considered at the point in decision making. Also multiple small decisions may contribute to larger decisions in the long term and these may not be a good outcome for the organisation.

A middle way of proceeding is to consider the application of fuzzy logic or approximate thinking (Kruse et al, 1994), which can be used to consider a range of options. De Roo and Porter (2007) and Haughton and colleagues (2010) have used the term 'fuzzy' in planning to suggest a lack of strategic direction and a form of political muddling through. Another variant of this is the use of complexity theory (Waldrop, 1992), which considers the boundary between order and chaos. Muir and Parker (2014) locate complexity in public services between the poles of bureaucratisation and competition, and argue that neither has solved the issues that arise in the state. They argue instead for a territorial and localised approach to integrated delivery that appears to duplicate the role of local government (John, 2014). In effect, not having a strategy is a strategy – the short and medium term is favoured over the long term, and this is how the organisation will respond.

The strategic business planning process

The strategic planning process can vary between organisations and for different purposes. However, there are some core components of a business plan that have a dynamic and iterative character. As information and assessments are fed into the business planning process, they inform decision making. For planners, the business planning process has many similar characteristics to plan making, including developing a vision, use of evidence, alternatives, strategy, implementation, monitoring and review. These are considered in more detail below.

Stage 1: objectives

The first part of a business plan is to develop a statement of the strategic vision and objectives. These may be evaluated and renewed as part of the business planning cycle and will relate to the current business. In business planning, it is possible either to undertake an incrementalist approach or to introduce more fundamental changes. While the objectives or vision may start broadly, these are then developed into defined outcomes. This will be critical for later evaluation of alternative methods for achieving these ends. The objectives may not be new, but linked to what has been prioritised in the past. Etzioni (2014) argues that the future should be viewed as 'a fixer-upper rather than as a new construction' (p 617), that is, the future needs to be considered within some construct of the present.

Private sector organisational objectives may be focused on maintaining profits and achieving further growth. This is similar in the third sector, although the profit is distributed to the aims of the organisation rather than to shareholders. In the public sector, different objectives are likely to be identified including promoting equity and economic growth, reducing welfare dependency and delivering last resort services in times of environmental, economic or personal disaster. Each public sector organisation will have its own objectives that are related to its territory and population within its economic context and its institutional and political cultures.

One of the key functions of defining the vision and objectives of an organisation is to create a comparative advantage over other similar organisations (Lehrer, 2001; Krugman, 2011; Porter 2011). This has applications in all three sectors. In the private sector, this may be a cost or product advantage that gives one organisation an edge over others and makes it more attractive to existing and potential clients. This may be created by a variety of means, including institutional factors such as taxation or the legal operating framework (demonstrated by the operating practices of some multinational companies), or by knowledge or management. In the third sector, advantage may lie within or between different causes. Third sector organisations may be compared for their effectiveness and efficiency, with those spending less on administration or helping more people being favoured by some donors (Billis and Glennerster, 1998). Third sector organisations have also been used to promote comparative advantage in their delivery of public welfare policy outcomes through government-encouraged, cross-sectoral partnerships. However, success may depend on the sectors cooperating within these partnerships (Andrews and Entwistle, 2010). In the public sector, the comparative advantage of the place or territory of a local authority area may have an important role in the way that authority can manage its own organisation and deliver services. Also the ability to attract national investment in infrastructure is strongly contested (Storper, 2011) and is a key local objective to support economic growth and further investment (Asheim et al, 2011).

In the public sector, Osborne and Gaebler (1992) have argued that government should be able to use the strategic principles of the private sector and apply them in ways that would make the public sector more effective. These principles have formed the institutional framework for local government reform within which local objectives may be established and delivered, as shown in Box 4.2.

BOX 4.2: Principles of strategic management

1. Steering rather than rowing
2. Empowering rather than serving
3. Injecting competition into service delivery
4. Transforming rule-driven organisations
5. Funding outcomes, not inputs
6. Meeting the needs of the customer, not the bureaucracy
7. Earning, not spending
8. Prevention rather than cure
9. From hierarchy to participation and teamwork
10. Leveraging change through the market

Source: Osborne and Gaebler (1992)

Stage 2: assessing the future

Part of the purpose of the business plan is to consider the future and how it is likely to affect the organisation. This part of business case development is to attempt to predict the future and the role that the organisation may play within it. The processes used to consider the future may depend on the type, sector and size of organisation and have different degrees of formality. Larger companies may need to demonstrate that these processes have been undertaken as part of their maintenance of shareholder confidence. The key methods of considering the future are as follows and may be undertaken in-house or by external specialist consultants.

Horizon scanning

Horizon scanning is a technique for 'detecting early signs of change through a systematic examination of potential threats and opportunities, with emphasis on new technology. It has been used where there is a need to consider a new issue that has emerged' (Amanatidou et al, 2012) and environmental issues such as threats to biodiversity (Sutherland and Woodroof, 2009). This method determines what is constant, what is likely to change, and what constantly changes. It explores novel and unexpected issues as well as persistent problems and trends, including matters at the margins of current thinking that challenge past assumptions' (OECD, 2014).

Horizon scanning may combine methods that include desk research, small group discussion and specialist expertise. There is a growing use of web-based horizon scanning methods (Palomino et al, 2012) that allow a variety of inputs and provide a means to scope and relate issues when these may be new or have multiple information sources.

Scenario building

Scenario building uses a technique of translating ideas about alternative futures into models that can be communicated to the organisation. Scenario building does not use extrapolation based on past events to project to the future, but uses a range of alternate 'what ifs'. As De Jouvenel (2000) states, scenario building 'aims not to predict but rather to help shape the future' (p 37). These scenarios can be varied and may offer three or five alternatives across a spectrum. It is also a technique used by military and political organisations. However, as Terk (2013) states, scenario building may include specific bias depending on the point of view from which the scenarios are built and it remains a methodological problem to find ways of moderating the scenarios to identify any bias. Scenarios are also used in stress testing the resilience of any organisation's ability to cope with expected or unexpected change.

Scenario building is a useful challenge technique where organisations and individuals assume that the status quo will be maintained. However, scenarios may be dismissed if they are too distant from the current position, as participants may find them unreal. The role of scenario building has been considered in planning (Ratcliffe, 2000) and in strategic property planning and transport (Shiftan et al, 2003) where comparisons can be made between expected and desired scenarios and address any issues that arise as a consequence of this gap.

Taste and fashion

Some organisations, particularly those concerned with retail and consumer goods, may employ experts in taste prediction to make short- and medium-term projections based on the wide range of alternative new products and likely habits in different groups of the population (Fishbein and Ajzen, 2011). This includes the use of new media by different demographic groups or in different locations, predicts sales methods and influences the organisation's activities. These approaches also have a role in the public sector in determining new forms of service delivery.

Tastes and fashion can both influence and be influenced by societal trends. Changing delivery methods, for example through the use of supermarket convenience stores, parcel lockers in stations and stores, and home delivery, can have a wider influence on the core business, and reduce the use of larger out-of-town stores. These changes may reflect changing lifestyles but also influence long-standing habits. In public services, the role of camera phones and the use of social media may change the nature of reporting faults or crime incidents and this needs to be recognised through the provision of new service channels.

Forecasting and modelling

In some organisations, statistical modelling and forecasting are used to predict the future, particularly where long-term investment is required in infrastructure such as roads, rail, energy provision and flooding. Forecasting techniques are based on using statistical data to predict the future from the present and may be used in conjunction with scenario building by taking alternative options as the basis of forecasts. Forecasting may also include modelling. This attempts to replicate an existing pattern of activities and then, through the use of a constructed model, consider what might happen in the future through the use of different data or criteria. Some forecasts and models may use specific techniques to focus on population change or consumption such as time series analysis (Box et al, 2013) or the use of technology (Porter et al, 2011).

Forecasting and modelling have been criticised in a number of ways. First, models may only include what is easiest to count and some issues may not be susceptible to data collection and analysis. Second, there are implications arising from who chooses what is measured and how this selection might skew the results. Third, there are concerns that models are normative and will only operate within the parameters that are set for them. Further, the ways in which models are interpreted may be significant, not least when more weight might be applied to them than the statistical validity of the data might support. Lastly, while appearing technical and independent, models may include a range of judgements and values that are exclusionary. They may also provide a technical support for political judgements and give them a quasi-independent status that may not be justified in practice.

Models and forecasting are used in strategic planning and were a leading method in the 1960s and 1970s when they were incorporated into a systems view of planning (McLoughlin, 1969; Lee, 1973). This took a more technical approach to strategic planning and was frequently criticised as being a centralist and normative 'predict and provide model' that was counter to community involvement and decision making.

Innovation

A key approach to examining the future is to consider the role of innovation within the organisation and in wider society. Innovation may be required to ensure that organisations can maintain their market lead or role. It may also be part of encouraging employees to contribute to change from their own experiences. One way of introducing innovation into the organisation may be through creating different work patterns or cultures or through inserting some disorganisation into the prevailing system (Clegg and Birch, 1998). These are positive disruptions that may be inserted through creating new work, project teams or cross-organisation groups for problem solving, or directly engaging users in service and product design.

Some private sector organisations do not invest directly in innovation but purchase smaller start-up companies for testing new products or processes. This process of mergers and acquisitions may also prevent smaller companies from becoming rivals in the longer term. This technique is most frequently observed in high-tech companies and is also used in other sectors such as pharmaceuticals and food. In most cases, organisations do not purchase innovation from other organisations but copy it in ways that suit their own services or products. Some organisations use their own younger employees – sometimes described as 'space cadets' – to advise on the potential for future developments.

Unknown futures: known unknowns and unknown unknowns

Finally, in most organisations there is some attempt to identify what the American politician and businessman Donald Rumsfeld (2011) described as known unknowns and unknown unknowns. Known unknowns means preparedness for change, generally from what has happened in the past or what has been developed through scenarios or other methods to identify the range of activities being undertaken. However, Rumsfeld also recognised the need to be prepared for unknown unknowns – those changes that cannot be anticipated and occur outside expectations. These may range from terrorist attacks to people responding to new regulations in unexpected ways.

Discussion Box: **Planning and futures**
- How does planning use methods of thinking about the future?
- Is one particular method of thinking about the future better than another in planning?
- How can communities be involved in vision for their area?
- Is it more difficult to discuss a strategic or a local vision?

Stage 3: SWOT analysis

Organsations have explicit and implicit objectives that need to be explored and examined in the business planning process, as both will have an impact on business plan delivery and its outcomes. A key component in assessing the strategic objectives of an organisation is through the use of SWOT analysis (Helms and Nixon, 2010; CIPD, 2013d), a structured planning method that considers the future vision and objectives of an organisation as well as assessing its strengths and weakness and the opportunities and threats that it may face. Strengths and weakness are internal to the organisation and the process of identifying them is stronger if undertaken with a range of people from different departments or sites. The issues identified have no specific boundaries.

The second set of considerations – opportunities and threats – relates to the external and operating environment of the organisation. Again, these are best considered by a wide range of people involved with the organisation and may include any issue that is a potential threat or opportunity. These four elements are generally shown on a simple matrix, as shown in Box 4.3. There follows a discussion of their respective weightings, dependencies and counteracting effects, and the SWOT analysis is then used to build the framework for the strategic plan and may be used to assess preferred strategies.

BOX 4.3: SWOT analysis matrix template

Strengths (internal)	Weaknesses (internal)
Opportunities (external)	Threats (external)

There are criticisms of the use of the SWOT analysis method. As Perdicoulis (2011) notes, this approach encourages people to make lists rather than to see the organisation as whole. However, such concerns can be addressed through secondary examination and discussion of the SWOT analysis. Further, SWOT analyses may be undertaken on different issues or may specifically target organisational integration strengths and weaknesses.

Stage 4: status quo projection

The next stage in preparing the business plan is status quo projection, that is, asking what would happen if nothing else is changed in the organisation. This stage is important, as it may provide an indication of whether the current organisational strategy will remain fit for purpose in the future. This consideration may be internal, including an assessment of capacity to manage current pressures or of whether the existing market or activity patterns will remain constant in the future (Vespermann and Wald, 2011). Externally, the status quo needs to be tested against any potential changes in priorities, demography, demand, taste and operating environment. This is an important feature because changes in the external operational climate may require a response from the organisation. This is particularly the case in organisations that deal in natural resources such as water (Qaiser et al, 2013). The status quo projection considers the current workforce and market and whether these will remain the same. It is quite likely that even if no specific changes are envisaged, some change will need to be included in the business plan to maintain the status quo.

Stage 5: assessment of strategic alternatives

The next stage in business planning is to assess alternative strategies for delivering the vision and objectives and evaluating them. Such strategies may be distinctly different or be variants of the same approach. Both the generation of strategies and methods of evaluation are individually and mutually important in this process. As Steiner (2010) has demonstrated, assessment is influenced by a range of factors including the cognitive and cultural frameworks of those taking part in the process as well as technical evidence and analysis that might be subject to the same soft influences. The process of assessing alternatives is important in all sectors.

The assessment of strategic alternatives is particularly used in strategic environmental assessment (Therivel, 2012. The method includes establishing a baseline, linking the proposals to other strategic actions, identifying the alternatives, predicting their impacts, and evaluating and mitigating them. In the EU, these are formal processes that are required by legislation (CEC, 2001) and applied in UK plan making (Smith and Sheate, 2001)

Stage 6: gap analysis

The next stage is to undertake an analysis of the gap between the status quo and the alternative strategies. This identifies where the biggest gaps are and where each strategy will provide a good fit with the current organisational situation (Morden, 2012). Gap analysis has a second role in identifying where to take action to implement the business plan. This might identify skills gaps, new activities or locations or additional investment. By the end of the gap analysis, there should be some understanding of the relative merits of alternative strategies in relation to the existing position.

Stage 7: options appraisal

The next step is to appraise the options available. This is undertaken through examining the strongest strategies that best fit the organisation and its objectives and meet as many issues as possible identified in the SWOT analysis. At this point, the financial assessment of the alternatives may be more detailed and forms part of the selection of a preferred strategy. Financial appraisal frequently uses modelling methods to apply monetary values to alterative outcomes and then to compare the differences between them. Options appraisal may include other methods, such as discounted cash flow and the use of geo-spatial data to examine optimum alternative locations, for example, sites for infrastructure (Blainey and Preston, 2013). Financial appraisal models are subject to the same kinds of criticism as other forecasting and modelling approaches – that is, they are prone to reinforce normative values and only produce outcomes related to the quality of the information included and the model used.

A method of strategic options appraisal that combines both quantitative and qualitative judgements is the balanced scorecard method (Kaplan and Norton, 1996). This is used as part of the assessment of alternatives and analyses a mix of financial and non-financial information. It focuses on the most relevant information from all that available. Finally, it is a method that seeks to turn the whole organisations towards the defined objectives and strategy, and seeks to achieve this through communication and goal-setting programmes, and by aligning the strategy to reward systems inside the organisation. The balanced scorecard method has been used by the heads of planning in Scotland to approach the implementation of Scotland's planning performance framework (HOPS, 2012).

In planning, options appraisal will also be used to examine alternative delivery programmes or asset portfolios for property (Isaac et al, 2010) and environmental impact assessment methods (Smith and Sheate, 2001). It has also been used for local plan making (Eastleigh Borough Council, 2013), where an options appraisal is a central component of selecting the approach that is to form the plan.

Stage 8: strategic choice

Once these evaluative processes have been undertaken, a strategic option is selected. The remaining part of the business plan process is concerned with turning this into an operational model. This may involve more detailed business plans within departments or activities. Where there are projects required to support implementation, these may also be included.

The criticism of strategic choice methods is that they may not fully account for the political processes that may carry a stronger weight than any other factors. Methodologies for undertaking strategic choice processes may be captured by organisational interests and become institutionalised (Friend and Hickling, 1987; Beckert, 1999). Strategic choice methods may also be criticised for being normative and having a limited scope in the way in which they are applied.

Stage 9: implementation plan and programme

The implementation plan and its accompanying programme are developed in ways that may assign responsibilities within the organisation and monitor outcomes. They include resource allocation. Even where there is no change to the allocation of resources, this represents confirmation of the business strategy. This implementation plan is set within a time frame so that any dependencies between identified activities can be included. IT or business systems and staff skills may also require investment to meet new activities. Implementation includes the management of change and this may meet resistance (Doherty et al, 2014).

Stage 10: monitoring

Once the business plan has been implemented, the next stage is to monitor and manage its progress. As business plans develop, there may be unforeseen changes required that influence the development and delivery of the plan. These may include the economic climate or changes in the market. There may also be changes in regulation and requirements that may affect the outcomes. Monitoring may be a routinised activity that may become an end in itself rather than be used to steer and possibly modify actions to achieve business plan objectives.

As Eckerson (2010) points out, monitoring of the implementation of the business plan is not an activity to be left to the end of a programming cycle or undertaken annually but rather needs a range of monitoring tools and techniques that measure the outcomes within the organisation's activities and across different and appropriate time periods. This may provide the opportunity to take action if the proposed plans or programmes are not having the expected outcomes or are too difficult to implement.

Stage 11: review

In public sector organisations that are run by directly elected politicians, these business planning processes might align with electoral cycles. Elsewhere business cycles might dictate the period of time that a plan lasts before it is reviewed and renewed. In the EU, this period is seven years, although the European Commission operates a double process so that as the current business plan is being implemented the business plan for the subsequent period is being developed (Morphet, 2013).

Stage 12: renewal

At the end of the review process, the business plan cycle begins again with renewal. Although the business planning processes discussed here have been described as sequential, in practice organisations may have several strategic plans operating within different time frames. Moreover, different organisations within partnerships may also have different strategic plan renewal dates. In some partnerships, there is a focus on aligning programmes and budget cycles to support easier strategic planning and joint working (DCLG, 2013a; HM Government and LGA, 2014) and there will be choices to be made about which strategic approaches to take (Marlow, 2013).

What is the role of strategic planning within the planning process?

Strategic planning considers the future needs of society to ensure that they can be provided in ways that are environmentally and economically sustainable. The strategic plan includes an organisation's vision (Improvement Service, 2009a, 2010a, 2010b) and objectives, as well as alternative options, similar to those identified in the business planning process. Strategic plans are likely to focus on a few key issues (Albrechts, 2004) and provide a framework for plans at smaller spatial scales. They will include major investment proposals for infrastructure, long-term population movements and the future for the economy, including managing growth or decline. One of the key challenges in strategic planning is implementing the plan through the organisations that contribute towards its formulation and delivery.

Strategic plans involving places are led by organisations in the public sector (Kunzmann, 2000), although their leadership may take different forms over time. Until the 1990s, strategic planning in Europe was undertaken directly through public bodies, with consultation with other sectors. However, since 1992, strategic planning governance has begun to adopt a distributed leadership model (Ray et al, 2004). In this case, there is still leadership from the public sector but rather than prepare the plan, its role is to set the framework for decision making and encourage cross-sectoral working to achieve the ends as agreed (CEC, 2013).

Strategic plans are prepared for the largest level of jurisdiction. The most strategic plan for the UK is the European Spatial Development Perspective (ESDP) (CEC, 1999), which was prepared by an informal council of EU ministers (Duhr et al, 2010). This plan has an advisory role within the UK and strategic plans have referred to the wider context that it provides. Since the Lisbon Treaty (2007) and the inclusion of a territorial dimension into the principles of cohesion, there is now an opportunity to prepare a more formal plan for the whole of the EU. Work on this is likely to be considered in the next EU budgetary period 2021-27.

Within the EU, the UK is the only member state without a national plan (Barca, 2009). However, there is a national infrastructure plan (HMT, 2013) as well as national policies for issues such as national parks. In Scotland, Wales and Northern Ireland, plans have been undertaken at a 'national' scale, that is, for their whole jurisdiction. There is no such plan for England. In 2011, the Royal Town Planning Institute established a project to create a 'map for England', an effort to identify those national policies that have already been agreed at this scale in an attempt to stimulate discussion and to identify what policies already exist (Wong et al, 2012).

In England, strategic planning was undertaken at the regional scale between 1934 and 2010, albeit not by any directly elected body. Instead, a range of institutions including economic planning councils, central government and latterly regional assemblies (partnership-based organisations) took responsibility for the plans. At the operational level, strategic plans were implemented through structure planning procedures at county level and on an administrative area basis between 1970 and 2004 (Glasson and Marshall, 2007; Wray, 2014). This system was abolished in 2004, leaving regional spatial strategies as the only strategic plans, with a proposal to replace these with regional strategies in 2010. However, the regional spatial strategies were themselves abolished before any reform could take place, and were replaced by plans made at the sub-regional scale based largely on functional economic areas and undertaken within a format regulated by the EU (CEC, 2013; Pemberton and Morphet, 2014).

In London, strategic planning has always operated under a different system from that for the rest of the country. In the London Government Act 1963, the Greater London Council was given responsibility for strategic planning and this was undertaken initially through the Greater London Development Plan (GLC, 1976). When the GLC was abolished in 1986, joint approaches to strategic planning were managed by the London Planning Advisory Committee (LPAC), which was set up as part of the abolition legislation in 1985 and was itself abolished in 1999. LPAC's role was to prepare guidance on strategic issues for the London boroughs but it did not have statutory function in direct strategy or development. During this period no plan for London was developed.

This changed with the Greater London Act in 1998, which established a directly elected mayor for London with executive responsibility for the London Plan and since then strategic planning has been one of the capital's most active policy areas. Each mayoral term has been accompanied with at least a partial if not a full review of the plan. The mayor's London Plan provides the strategic context for the London boroughs local plans, although the two scales of plan spring from different planning traditions. One of the differences is that the London Plan does not engage with issues such as infrastructure planning and implementation, which are incorporated into borough plans as a result of the 2004 Planning and Compulsory Purchase Act. Furthermore, the mayor has responsibility not only for making the plan but also for ensuring its delivery through executive responsibility for transport, redevelopment, housing and public health.

Strategic planning in Scotland was undertaken by strategic regional authorities between 1975 and 1996 as part of a two-tier local government system. In 1996, the strategic regional authorities were replaced by unitary local authorities for the whole of Scotland with responsibility for both local and strategic planning. Following the introduction of devolution in 1999, strategic planning became the responsibility of the Scottish Executive (Morphet, 2011a), which embarked on a series of national planning frameworks (2004, 2009, 2014) that have become increasingly focused on infrastructure investment and economic delivery. In 2006, four strategic development planning (SDP) areas were created for the cities and peripheries of Edinburgh, Glasgow, Dundee and Aberdeen. These SDP areas have operated within a new two-tier system for planning, where local plans operate as part of the SDP in a dual role but operate singly within other parts of Scotland. The SDP approach includes the development of plans and programmes and in 2014, Glasgow negotiated a city deal with the UK government, which extends the SDP process by creating a specific contract with the UK government for spatial and economic initiatives. City deals were introduced by the UK Government in 2013.

Strategic planning in Wales was undertaken by upper-tier authorities between 1974 and 1996 when the local authorities moved to a unitary system. Following devolution, the Welsh Executive prepared the Wales Spatial Plan (2004, updated in 2008), which identified areas for strategic planning together with a process lead by assembly members (Morphet, 2011a). Although these strategic planning groups met once or twice, they never took hold at a strategic planning scale and most focus has been at the local level. In 2013, Wales identified three city region areas – Cardiff, Swansea and North Wales – and the government announced that these would be developed in the same way as the SDP areas in Scotland.

In 2013, methods for strategic planning were set out by the European Union in Regulation 1303/2013, article 33, as shown in Box 4.4.

BOX 4.4: EU community-led local strategies: content

A community-led local development strategy shall contain at least the following elements:

(a) the definition of the area and population covered by the strategy;

(b) an analysis of the development needs and potential of the area, including an analysis of strengths, weaknesses, opportunities and threats;

(c) a description of the strategy and its objectives, a description of the integrated and innovative features of the strategy and a hierarchy of objectives, including measurable targets for outputs or results. In relation to results, targets may be expressed in quantitative or qualitative terms. The strategy shall be consistent with the relevant programmes of all the EU Funds concerned that are involved;

(d) a description of the community involvement process in the development of the strategy;

(e) an action plan demonstrating how objectives are translated into actions;

(f) a description of the management and monitoring arrangements of the strategy, demonstrating the capacity of the local action group to implement the strategy and a description of specific arrangements for evaluation;

(g) the financial plan for the strategy, including the planned allocation from each of the ESI [European Structural and Investment] Funds concerned.

Source: CEC (2013)

Discussion Box: **Strategic planning methods and processes**
- Can strategic planning processes use business planning methods?
- Which elements of the business case method might be most useful for developing a strategic plan?
- Is finance important when developing a strategic plan?
- Could a strategic business case benefit from more community involvement?

Conclusions

Making strategy and strategic planning are essential components of all organisational processes and, as discussed above, are required even to maintain the status quo. This chapter has discussed the alignment between strategic planning roles and process in organisations and that undertaken as part of the planning process. The practices of strategic planning in the past were aligned to forecasts and models but the convergence between the practices of businesses and large organisations and that of planning has been less discussed. However, planning practice is now returning to focus on the strategic planning scale and this alignment between organisational strategy and strategic planning methods may be an essential feature in cross sectoral and partnership working.

FIVE

Managing resources in planning: people and communications

Introduction

People are a key resource and cost in any organisation, particularly those in the professional services sector. In delivering planning, staff are the main cost, whether in a public service or consultancy. Planners may make up the majority of employees in an organisation such as a planning consultancy or they may be part of a larger organisation, such as a local authority. Although the majority of planners in the private sector may be employed in organisations primarily focused on planning, some are part of larger management consultancies or retailers (RTPI, 2014). Some planning consultancies employ more planners than local authorities (Sell, 2013).

The structure of the organisation and the way that planners are managed within it will have a key effect on employees' contribution to the organisation as a whole, and in particular on its efficiency in serving its community or clients. Since then, both the number of chartered town planners and the proportion of planners employed in the private sector has grown. While planning in the private sector has experienced major growth, local authorities have experienced financial pressures. This has led to planning services being scrutinised in an attempt to identify cost-cutting and income-generation activities. At the same time, there have been reductions in specialist staff such as heritage officers (IHBC, 2013). There has also been an increase in the volume of delegated planning applications, which cost 90% less than applications put to councillors for decision (PAS, 2008). Planners and support staff have increasingly been employed on short term contracts to increase resource flexibility. Contract staff are more expensive to employ in the short term but save organisations money in long-term costs such as pension contributions.

The development and training of planning staff is also an important consideration of their management within the organisation. There are two responsible bodies here. The first is the employing organisation, which has responsibility for in-house staff training and development as part of its own risk management strategy and due diligence remit. The second is the planners themselves, who need to be alert to changes within the legislative and operational systems in which they work. They also need to commit to continuous professional development in order to maintain membership of the Royal Town Planning Institute and other professional bodies. The usual procedure here is for the planner to prepare a personal development plan (PDP) and keep a log book on the ways in which the plan is implemented.

People in the organisation

People are a key organisational asset and those employed within an organisation are frequently referred to as its human capital (Baron and Armstrong, 2007) as distinct from financial capital or investment funding. Human capital includes all the skills and contributions that employees make as part of their employment. In any organisation, people contribute to the innovation, production and delivery of goods and services. Their costs are attributed to different activities within the organisation. In the private sector, the ways in which human resources are used may be an important issue for shareholders or clients. Consumers may be influenced by factors such as how much a company pays its staff or where it sources its goods (Sharma et al, 2011). Some brands promote their goods as being ethically sourced (Singh et al, 2012) and this is a key pointer to the employment conditions involved in the production of those goods (Memery et al, 2012).

In service businesses, people are the greatest cost, while in extractive industries employee costs are lower in relation to the value of raw materials or infrastructure. Service industries include government, retailing, professional services, banking, education and other public services. Some organisations such as transport providers employ large numbers of staff, but the staff costs may be lower than the capital investment in the infrastructure used to provide the service. Where people are the main agents of delivery, they are both a key asset and the main source of risk of service failure.

In any organisation where planning is undertaken, the proportion of costs attributed to planning, and particularly to planners, will vary. Where planning is the main function, such as in a consultancy firm, salaries will be a greater proportion of running costs, other overheads such as accommodation, energy and services will all be associated with staff numbers. Staff here may comprise of professional planners, support staff and allied professionals. In other organisations in the private and public sector, where planning may be one of many functions then some of the costs attributable to staff will be distributed across a greater base and may be lower per capita. However, in all sectors, the cost of employing staff to undertake planning functions is now attributed to income. Increasingly in local authorities, different initiatives have been developed to generate more income to contribute to staff costs including charges for pre-application advice, raising income from major applicants to support specific posts and outsourcing some of the planning functions.

Employment law

Since 1986, UK employment law has been aligned with that of the EU through the Single European Act (Morphet, 2013). Since then, employment rights – including the freedom to seek work anywhere within the EU, equal opportunities, unfair dismissal procedures, holiday and sickness entitlement, and transfer of employee regulations following mergers and acquisitions – all operate within this EU legal framework. This framework is negotiated and implemented by all the EU member states.

The creation the Single European Market in 1986 also made it easier for EU citizens to gain employment in other member states. Before this, European citizens had the freedom to move within the EU but it was harder to find employment because of differences in employee contribution schemes, such national insurance, and the lack of equivalency systems for measuring educational and professional qualifications. Now free movement is only restricted when a country first joins the EU and is significantly economically disadvantaged compared with existing member states. In this case, a member state may delay the introduction of total freedom of movement and restrict access to contributor benefit schemes. Here any member state can delay the introduction of free movement for a period time and can restrict access to contributor benefit schemes. Where there are restrictions, job applicants are assessed against a points system based on their skills and the labour market.

Citizens from Commonwealth countries were free to move to the UK before it joined the EU in 1972. Since then, however, Commonwealth economic migrants may only work in the UK if they satisfy the requirements of a points-based application system or gain employer sponsorship. Employees from other countries such as the United States also need work permits and visas.

Free movement of labour has been a key issue in planning, particularly during periods of planner shortage. However, few planners from the EU have been able to fill the UK skills gap, as the planning systems, regulatory institutions, professional training schemes and work cultures are so different among member states. UK employers must rely on planners from Commonwealth countries such as Canada, South Africa, Australia and New Zealand where the planning systems are comparable.

The human resources function

In most organisations, there is a human resource (HR) function. 'Human Resource management refers to all those activities associated with the management of work and people in organisations' (Boxall and Purcell, 2011, p 1) or 'the management of work and people towards desired ends' (Boxall et al, 2008, p 1). People, like materials, are a resource, funding intellectual property or assets, and while employers may be expected to treat employees with due respect, inevitably the main responsibility of any organisation is to produce goods or services that are sold directly to consumers or funded through taxation. Those responsible for human resources have a number of key roles, as shown in Box 5.1:

BOX 5.1: Strategic HR policy
- Recruitment
- Performance management
- Skills and culture
- Managing change
- Training and development
- Diversity and equality

Strategic HR

The scale of strategic HR may vary depending on the size of the organisation. The main role of strategic HR is to ensure that human resources in the organisation are fit for purpose and that the organisation can respond to change. The links between organisational and HR strategies are fundamental (Mabey et al, 1998). Primarily, they are concerned with ensuring that people within the organisation are able to support and deliver its objectives.

There is also a strategic consideration of cost-effectiveness, including the use of salary packages to attract and retain employees. Most organisations prefer to retain staff, as turnover brings recruitment costs. Some organisations find it difficult to make staff redundant This was once the case in the public sector in particular, although this has changed in recent years. In some organisations, job vacancies may be filled internally by existing employees who have developed their roles through training or gained sufficient experience to be promoted. Other organisations rely on external recruitment. Some people may stay in the same role for many years. It is important to see employees as an organisation's key ambassadors. In many public organisations, such as local authorities, a high proportion of employees live locally and the people who work in the organisation can transmit both positive and negative messages about its quality to the wider community, friends and family.

Strategic HR policy is also concerned with recruitment and employee development, including training. Staff may be recruited through social media, newspapers or recruitment consultants or agencies, and terms and conditions of employment are legally binding. In some key posts, organisations regard recruitment as the means of attaining strategic advantage, not least if individuals have a good management record. Organisations might also operate 'golden handcuff' policies to retain staff so that they do not move to other organisations. It is common for outgoing senior civil servants or managing directors of leading companies to be prohibited from working for a rival company for a fixed period of time. Other retention policies may include bonuses, company cars or other incentives such as subsidised housing. Some organisations identify the core competencies and skills they wish to retain and these are purchased externally from consultants or employees on fixed-term contracts.

At times when the market is buoyant, planners can be in short supply. Specific retention policies may be used in the public and private sectors such as higher salaries, bonuses or promotion being offered to retain planners and higher starting salaries for planning graduates. Where planning schools have employer-related projects, these may be used to recruit graduate planners. When the market for planners is much less buoyant, in times of recession, experienced planners may be made redundant as work reduces and then fill what would formerly have been graduate roles. When the market is in recession, graduate planners that have managed to gain some experience through vacation working or internships are more likely to be successful in the job market.

Strategic HR is also aligned to organisational culture. Some organisations may be paternalistic or operate closed systems where staff can expect employment for life. These organisations have strong internal cultures and may have an upper age limit for initial recruitment. One example is the UK civil service (Pyper and Burnham, 2011), where mainstream entry is restricted after the age of 27 and all promotion is internal. Some public bodies in areas of high unemployment see themselves primarily as providers of employment, and many local authorities have had a strong tradition of providing apprenticeships and professional training for local school-leavers.

Discussion Box: **Strategic HR**

- Is it important for an organization to have strategic HR policies?
- How important are people within an organifation delivering planning?
- How can strategic HR help to deal with planner shortages?

Diversity and equality

The role of diversity and equality in employment practice has increased since the 1970s when the first Equality Acts in the UK was introduced in 1970. All employment practices, including pay, recruitment and redundancy procedures, and accessibility, are subject to legislation, and employers may not discriminate on the grounds set out in Box 5.2.

BOX 5.2: Prohibited grounds for discrimination

- Age
- Being or becoming a transsexual person
- Being married or in a civil partnership
- Being pregnant or having a child
- Disability
- Race including colour, nationality, ethnic or national origin
- Religion, belief or lack of religion/belief
- Sex
- Sexual orientation

Source: Equality Act 2010

Diversity within organisations needs to be positively managed (Roberge and van Dick, 2010), while organisations with a diverse workforce are also seen to have benefits (Ellis and Keys, 2013). An organisation found by an employment tribunal to have discriminated against an employee or volunteer on any of these grounds may be liable to pay damages to the claimant.

Recruitment

Much of the management of people within organisations rests on their recruitment and the subsequent talent management policies of the organisation. Recruitment is a core activity for all organisations and it matters for a variety of reasons, as shown in Box 5.3.

BOX 5.3: The role of recruitment in the organisation
- Can add value to the organisation
- Can find talent that may be rare and give the organisation a competitive edge
- Sets the organisation apart from others through its selection processes
- Can support and strengthen rest of organisation

Source: Orlitzky (2007)

Recruitment may be undertaken inside or outside the organisation and through a variety of means. However, one of the primary purposes of the recruitment process is to promote awareness of the organisation. Attracting potential applicants to a website to read about a company and its job opportunities can have positive organisational outcomes even when the reader is not a potential applicant. The way in which any job is advertised is also part of the organisation's brand.

Once a post has been identified, a job description (Box 5.4) and person specification are prepared (Box 5.5). These are part of the recruitment process and the subsequent employment contract. The job might be a replacement for an existing member of staff or a new post, where job design may be a significant issue (CIPD, 2013a). The job description and specification may be designed from the perspective of the skills required or other specific characteristics, or it may be more motivational, particularly in the case of a leadership or management role. The recruiting organisation will expect candidates to illustrate their suitability for the job in terms of skills, knowledge and experience, whether gained though employment, volunteering or internships. While it is important for candidates to set out an organisational career history, it is also important to identify specific skills that the candidate can offer.

The choice between internal and external recruitment may depend on the nature of the job and the culture of the organisation in question. Organisations may favour either internal or external appointments or may use varying methods at different levels within the organisation. Some organisations favour one method, while others use both types of recruitment according to the seniority of the appointment. Internal recruitment, particularly at junior levels, can provide promotion opportunities for existing staff and help retain experienced employees. The choice of recruitment method may also depend on the job market and the

BOX 5.4: Job description
- Explains the job to the candidate
- Includes a list of likely specific tasks to be undertaken by the postholder
- Includes a list of generic tasks
- Identifies accountabilities of the post holder for staff, resources, outcomes within the organisation
- Identifies line manager and position in the organisation
- Forms part of contract of employment

BOX 5.5: Job specification
Criteria for selection, including:
- specific skills or professional membership
- educational attainment
- interpersonal skills
- specific experience
- specific competencies such as:
  - communication skills
  - people management skills
  - team skills
  - customer service skills
  - results orientation
  - problem solving skills

Source: CIPD (2013c) and the author

number of potential applicants for any specific post. Some organisations prefer to recruit their most senior managers externally, in order to maintain competiveness and to inject new ideas. In family-run businesses, management positions are often filled by family members who rise through the organisation's ranks, although there may be instances where there are no obvious family candidates (Kellermanns, 2012). Those family firms that survive for long periods tend to be specialist providers where both skills and clients are handed down through generations (Gomez-Mejia et al, 2011).

When recruiting externally, organisations may advertise jobs through newspapers or websites. Some organisations use employment agencies and these enable the employer to use employees in a flexible way and on demand, obviating the need for open recruitment. It may also be quicker to recruit through an agency. When appointing senior executives, organisations may use recruitment consultants to identify potential candidates on their behalf – not just those actively seeking employment, but also those who might be persuaded to consider a new job.

Within planning, recruitment of planners is undertaken through a number of means including web sites, social media and networking. In some cases, particularly in the private sector, staff may be approached directly particularly at senior levels or where they have a known specialism. In some cases, teams may follow directors and move between consultancies. Recruitment may also feature as part of new firm formation where former colleagues who worked together in previous roles join new consultancies. Planning is a highly networked profession, and these networks are generated through common initial planning education and subsequent professional activities and these networks have a role in recruitment.

Selection

Organisations will use a combination of methods (Zibarras and Woods, 2010) that may include an application form or a curriculum vitae. Selection methods can include one or more rounds of interviews, group discussion, written tests, a technical appraisal, a meeting with peers or a meeting with councillors if it's a local authority job. External references, either formal, informal or both, are usually followed up to establish a candidate's suitability for a job. The combination of methods used will depend on the post, with more interview rounds and other types of selection processes used for posts that are more senior within the organisation.

Selection for a post will involve assessing applications against the job description and person specification. This may be a relatively simple task where there are few applicants or where the post is a senior one requiring very specific experience and career progression. The selection process must be non-discriminatory and will be subject to scrutiny should any candidate challenge its fairness. Reasons for rejecting any candidate's application must be shown at each stage of the process. If there are no appropriate candidates, an employer may decide to readvertise the post, perhaps bringing in an external recruitment agency to identify a wider pool of candidates. An existing member of staff may be invited to fill the role (this may be a temporary promotion) until a suitable candidate is appointed.

The most commonly used method of selection is an interview by a group of people, including managers and HR representatives. To ensure equality, all interviews for the same post should be allocated the same amount of time, and each candidate should be asked the same core questions, although supplementary questions may vary according to the individual candidate. The structure of the interview is common. The candidate will be introduced to each member of the interview panel and asked an opening question such as 'why do you want this job?' It is at this point that the candidate has an opportunity to demonstrate their knowledge of the organisation and their potential contribution. A successful opening contribution is likely to include three to four main points where the focus is on the organisation rather than the individual. An opening response relating, for example, to the candidate's own desire for promotion leaves the panel with fewer opportunities for further interaction with the candidate.

In some posts, particularly senior or management roles, the interview may begin with the candidate giving a pre-prepared presentation on a topic agreed in advance. The presentation topic will be the same for each candidate and is an opportunity for candidates to demonstrate to the panel their ability to think both strategically and in detail. Again, a presentation comprising three to four main points, each with an accompanying powerpoint slide, will provide a good structure and enable the panel to distinguish between candidates. The presentation may then open up into a discussion about why the candidate is applying for the post.

The next stage of the interview is likely to be a technical discussion, including experience of dealing with specific issues or solving problems. This provides an opportunity for the panel to understand more of the candidate's experience and for the candidate to elaborate on the information in their job application. It is useful for candidates to anticipate this kind of question and to have some examples in mind when they enter the interview. Planners may be invited to comment on a planning application or development site or to make some comments about the relevance of some specific current government policy for the location.

The last part of the interview is likely to relate to personal attributes. Here, the panel will be interested in the candidate's strengths and weaknesses and also their likely future career path and ambition. Again, it is useful for candidates to have some concrete examples of how these characteristics present, and how they address any weaknesses. The last part of the interview is likely to be the opportunity for the candidate to ask any questions of the panel. By this time, all of the main issues should have been covered, but the candidate will usually be given an opportunity to ask any further questions before the end of the interview, and further points may also be raised informally at a later stage. The interview usually concludes with the chair thanking the candidate and advising when a decision can be expected. Candidates applying for very senior jobs may be expected to wait for the panel to make its decision there and then.

Following the interviews the panel will undertake an analysis and assessment of the candidates. This will include reviewing all additional material such as psychometric tests (Toplis et al, 2005), application forms and references. This summing up and analysis may be undertaken by an HR professional who will not be directly involved in managing the selected employee and hence is seen to be more impartial. The panel may choose to eliminate some of the candidates from further consideration on the basis of this analysis and subsequent discussion. Reasons for this need to be clear and duly recorded. When the shortlist is reduced to two or three candidates, each panel member may be invited to give their assessment. If there is a tie between two candidates, the panel may call for further interviews or there may be a vote, with the chair exercising a casting vote. The panel may not have the final word on selection and may be making a recommendation that has to be considered by another group at a later date. Once a job offer has been made, there may follow a period of negotiation on salary and other conditions.

The main factors influencing selection on the basis of an interview are the way in which the candidate performs in this environment and the way in which the panel works together. The performance of the candidate at the interview may be more important than their job knowledge and experience (Huffcutt, 2011). Interview panels may be influenced by race, gender and age, even if these are explicitly excluded from questions and overt candidate appraisals (Alimo-Metcalfe,

2010). It is also possible for interview panels to recruit in their image or to recruit people similar to those who have undertaken the job before.

While an interview may be the main means of recruitment, it is common for more senior recruitment processes to include an assessment centre (Woodruffe, 2007). This may include exercises on numeracy and 'in-tray' tests, that is, testing candidates' ability to deal with a range of real-life work scenarios. This allows any potential employer to evaluate the experience and skills of the applicant in dealing with competing priorities within a fixed period of time. The selection process may also include a technical interview or appraisal, particularly where candidates have been selected by external recruitment consultants. This may be conducted by an HR professional and a senior figure with experience relevant to the job advertised.

Some selection processes include psychometric testing (Toplis et al, 2005). These are used to understand an individual's personality and how they work under pressure. Some of these tests may be team-role related and attempt to identify how candidates will fit in with others. The most frequently used team-role test is that developed by Belbin (2010, 2012), who has argued that there is a relationship between the clarity and make-up of teams using team-role profiles and the performance of the team. The roles identified through this process are shown in Box 5.6. Some teams may require members with different roles, whereas others may be more effective if all team members have similar characteristics.

BOX 5.6: Belbin's team roles
- Plant
- Resource investigator
- Coordinator
- Shaper
- Monitor evaluator
- Team worker
- Implementer
- Completer finisher
- Specialist

Source: Belbin (2010)

Belbin's team role theory has gained much usage and has been corroborated in other research (Senior, 1997). The main challenge may be identifying which mix of roles best suits different types of activity. In planning, those processing planning applications may require a different mix of skills from those undertaking plan-making and research functions. The nature of the work cycle may require different leadership traits. Is it more important to have a 'resource investigator' in regeneration or infrastructure planning than in development management – or are both types of people needed in both teams as there are different requirements within them?

Once a candidate has accepted a job offer, they receive a contract of employment that sets out the obligations of the employer and the employee. For some jobs, employees may be required to comply with an employer's due diligence responsibilities; for example, employees who work with children or vulnerable adults must undergo a Criminal Records Bureau check. If candidates are disabled, there will be a workplace assessment and appropriate equipment and modifications made. All appointments are made subject to a probationary period, during which the employer can assess whether the employee recruited is suitable for the role. This is also an opportunity for the employee to gain advice or clarification about the job role if necessary. Probationary periods may be extended. Employees have legal protection against employer discrimination as soon as they start a job. The unfair dismissal (variation of qualifying period) Order 2012 grants access to other employee rights after two years in employment.

Discussion Box: **Recruitment issues**

- How far do jobs differ in practice? Does each job need an individual job description and person specification?
- Do planners need specific skills sets for different types of planning roles?
- Do planners require specific recruitment tests?
- Is the Belbin team role approach appropriate in planning teams?
- Is an interview the best way to recruit a planner?
- Do planning leaders and managers require any specific skills or experience?
- Do planning managers need to be planners?

Learning, training and development

Training

Employers are responsible for providing training for their employees. Basic skills training may include report writing and time management, while more specialist coaching may be required in handling the media or presenting evidence in planning inquiries. Training will also be necessary when new IT systems or process changes are introduced. Training may be provided internally or through external consultants, on a one-to-one basis or in group sessions.

While much training may be generic and available to all staff, there may also be individual training programmes. These may cover initial professional training and development and may be undertaken through sponsored day release. Employees may fund their own distance learning through the Open University or other education providers. Employees who have attained membership of a professional body may be supported in undertaking further specialist technical education e.g. for transport or historic buildings or attend a management course.

Support may be provided through coaching and mentoring (Clutterbuck, 2007). Coaching helps employees develop skills and improve their performance. It is possible to develop a coaching culture inside an organisation, and this may be seen as the opposite of a competitive culture. Mentoring is about sharing development experience over a long period of time. Mentors can support mentees by explaining how they have dealt with particular situations or problems in the past. The focus here is on career and personal development. Both coaching and mentoring may be provided inside the organisation or by external suppliers.

Specific employee training programmes may also be developed as part of an action agreed following a staff appraisal. If the employee is not meeting the standard required, a training programme may be used to provide specific support to improve performance. Specific programmes may also be offered on how to cope with redundancy.

An employee can request nomination for secondment to a different team or organisation as a means of widening their experience. Secondment can provide an opportunity to find out how other organisations work and may for example involve a swap between a local government and a civil service job, or a public and private sector role. A secondment may also be used to learn a new skill set or develop networks and contacts that are beneficial both to the individual and to the organisation.

Continuous professional development

Continuous professional development (CPD) is a requirement of professional and accrediting bodies. CPD is designed to ensure that professional practitioners keep up to date with developments in their area and continue to provide a good standard of service to the public and their clients. It is also geared towards promoting personal development on the job. In this case, the employee will need both an annual personal development and an action plan, and will record all the CPD activities undertaken during the course of a year. Each affiliated professional and qualifying body will specify they type and number of activities needed to fulfil the requirements of the assessment and action programme. Many professional bodies provide certificates for those who have attended qualifying CPD events and may carry out random checks on individual members.

One of the key issues for any individual undertaking CPD is assessing and prioritising personal development needs. (Megginson and Whitaker, 2003). It may also be difficult to undertake CPD because of the costs and the time involved. Externalising self-assessment is difficult and may require that individuals become 'reflective practitioners' where individuals learn from their own experience (Schon, 1983). Much of the debate about CPD is whether it should be provided by the individual or the employer. A member of a professional body such as the Royal Town Planning Institute has an individual responsibility for ensuring that they have met the CPD requirements although employers may provide CPD for their own purposes such as ensuring that they meet their own professional insurance obligations. CPD can be undertaken through reading or distance learning courses. Training support to meet assessed personal needs may also be raised as part of the employee's annual appraisal.

Talent pools

Some organisations have a strong focus on supporting the development of talent internally. Talent pools identify the skills, aptitudes and experience of staff through the use of self-assessment methods. A suitable job candidate may be identified internally through the talent pool, obviating the need to recruit externally. This is seen to be a positive employment practice and one that encourages staff retention (Walker and LaRocco, 2002; Yarnall, 2011).

Performance management

Employees are required to undertake tasks set out for them by their line manager. These will be broadly covered by the contract of employment, although day-to-day tasks are likely to vary. The ways in which these tasks are performed, and their quality, timeliness and effectiveness, will be part of that individual's performance profile. The way an individual works within a team may also be an important part of this performance approach. The culture and organisation of the work of the team or the organisation may also be an important contributor to an individual's performance.

Most organisations have performance management frameworks that formalise the criteria for objective assessment of individual employees within the organisation (Mabey et al, 1998). While these frameworks are devised to asses the effective use of the human resources of the organisation, they also are reliant on the performance appraisal methods of assessment and measurement used. Where these are qualitative, it is likely that there will be some employee and manager assessment of the completion of tasks against specific or general objectives. Where the measures used are quantitative, they may encourage specific work practices focusing on what is to be measured to the exclusion of anything else. This can mean a focus on planning applications performance or income generated and may encourage employees to opt out of wider shared tasks and responsibilities.

Performance appraisal is usually carried out once a year, perhaps with intermediate weekly or monthly discussions about progress. Where new tasks have been introduced or where the employee is struggling to meet defined objectives, these discussions are likely to be more frequent and accompanied by other support measures.

Poor performance can have a negative effect on an individual or team. First, a lack of appreciation or the absence of a mechanism to discuss work may result in employees becoming demotivated. If they lack support, employees may make mistakes that could be costly for the organisation. Lack of motivation may result in higher levels of sickness or absenteeism and can influence the whole team and its performance levels. Employees may deal with such a situation by 'hobbying', that is, by concentrating on those aspects of the job that they prefer and neglecting the rest.

Some employees are uninterested in promotion. They may be 'satisficing', that is, working at a level that suits them and does not vary much over time or respond to inducements to change, while maintaining a level of competence to ensure that they do not draw attention to themselves. Some people adopt 'presenteeism' habits to cope with a long hours culture, and stay at their desks beyond their contracted work hours despite having nothing to do. Another aspect of presenteeism is when employees leave signs that they are in the building – for example, by putting a (spare) jacket on a chair – when they are elsewhere.

Discussion Box: **Performance management**
- Is performance management important in planning?
- Should all planning organizations have a performance management approach?
- How should planning performance assessment be assessed?
- What support can be given to planners if their performance is found to be an issue?
- How are performance management and motivation linked in planning

---

Recruitment and HR in planning

The recruitment and retention of planners is strongly affected by the prevailing economic climate (Durning, 2007). At times or recession, the number of planning schemes being developed and submitted for planning consent reduces. At such times, planners may be made redundant or encouraged to take early retirement. This often results in a plethora of new planning consultancies as individuals use their redundancy or retirement packages to set up their own businesses or small groups of planners breaking away from larger consultancies. It is also difficult to recruit students on to planning degree and conversion courses during an economic downturn, as high levels of unemployment among planners serve to discourage potential entrants to the profession.

When the economy is more buoyant, the number of planners employed increases significantly. The position can move from one of high unemployment to one of a shortage of planners within a short period of time (Sykes, 2003), with employers reporting a dramatic change from 400 to four applicants for a single post within a year. A more buoyant market may also see more movement between sectors, with planners in the public sector being attracted to work in the private sector either in consultancies or on the client side of major retail or house-building organisations. Durning (2007) examined the ways in which local authorities attempted to retain their planners in a time of economic buoyancy and found that the main focus was on changing working methods. Providing opportunities for technical and administrative staff to undertake more of the planning process and the increased use of agency staff or recently retired planners with their own small consultancies were also important strategies.

Discussion Box: **Recruitment and selection of planners**

- Are technical assessments necessary for recruiting planners?
- Do planning teams benefit from having people who perform different roles?
- What are the key issues in managing individual performance?
- What is the best way to manage personal CPD requirements?
- Is the employer obliged to provide CPD?

Communications and reputation management

Both internal and external communication is important to every organisation. Every organisation communicates with its staff as part of its leadership and management role. Communication is also important for the organisation's relationships with its suppliers, customers, the wider community and government. Communication is particularly important to planning in terms of its central remit for consultation and engagement in plan making and development regulation. Adair (2009) identifies it as the most important management skill and states that communication in organisations should not be reliant on hierarchies but also use internal networks. Communication also requires listening skills, and leaders and managers should plan their approach to communication with this in mind.

Channel strategies

Most organisations will have developed a 'channel' strategy for communicating with their customers, suppliers and staff. This strategy is likely to include an analysis of audiences, their channel preferences such as telephone or email, and the times that may be most appropriate to contact them. This facilitates segmentation of the customer base which can improve the efficiency and effectiveness of communication.

Communication methods

Communication may be direct or indirect. Direct communication includes face-to-face, telephone, online and written communications, as well as advertising. Written communication will be in the form of letters or emails, and is used to confirm what is being communicated verbally, face to face or by telephone. Emails may be more casual that in tone that letters, but they have the same legal status. Reports tend to be detailed and official in tone, and often include research or supporting evidence to back up the information contained within them. Letters and reports may have several signatories, including other organisations, in order to impart a sense of their importance to the recipients. Other forms of direct written communication include newsletters and newspapers, which tend to be used for specific purposes such as an individual development. Organisations may go to great lengths to get free or paid media publicity for products or services.

Other forms of communication include advertising in the street or through other print media.

Telephone communication is less formal than written communication and may be used to negotiate or confirm matters, although it has largely been replaced by email or electronic text messaging.

Indirect communication takes a variety of forms, including sponsorship of events, publications and activities. Sponsorship is a form of advertising, and organisations use it to create positive links to causes or activities. Organisations use sponsored events to attract clients and use the opportunity to gain influence with them through soft social means.

Social media has an increasing role in indirect communications. An organisation's web presence can be promoted through online search engines or by advertising on the websites of related organisations. The majority of websites use cookies to track user interest and may also tailor specific advertisements to particular sites to encourage sales or the use of particular products. Organisations may also pay to advertise services or facilities through Twitter or on smart phones. Informal communication through word of mouth and social media has led to the phenomenon of viral marketing, whereby online communities discuss the relative merits of products and services, which can result in their success or failure. In Scotland, the radio has been used to communicate planning issues in more remote areas (Improvement Service, 2010c).

Some informal communication is subliminal or not fully discussed, for example, where individuals are recommending a product or service in which they have a vested interest. Nye (2004) has discussed the role and use of soft power, where countries use their legal systems, national culture and other means to act as a cultural influence on others.

Barriers to communication

There are a number of barriers to communication. In the case of organisations, these may be cultural or physical barriers. The messages distributed within the organisation may not be regarded as credible if individuals are not 'walking the talk' and their actions differ from the messages that they are trying to convey. The way employees interpret messages will depend on their experience of the integrity of previous communications. Moreover, there may be individuals within the organisation who have alternative, informal communication channels or access to additional contextual information that may contradict or qualify the official message. Physical barriers to communication may exist where an organisation is split between different locations or buildings, and this may encourage a silo mentality, where teams operate in isolation from each other.

External communications may fail to reach their target audience because of inappropriate channels of communication. If the target group is elderly people, and the means of communication involves a community meeting in the evening, the communication may fail because clients are unwilling or unable to go out at night. Messages sent through social media may fail to reach an elderly audience because of a lack of familiarity with new technology (Ofcom, 2014), while younger audiences are likely to less receptive to printed materials because of the ubiquitous use of social media among this group. Those who are the target of the message may not be users of the channels of communication selected. If the target group is elderly, they may not use new technology other than tablets (Ofcom, 2014) and not be willing to go out at night to meetings. If the target age group is young, then they may not read any printed material or newspapers and only use social media to communicate. Advertising via print media or television may also suffer from segmentation in the market.

Customer surveys and feedback

Many organisations use targeted surveys as a means of obtaining customer feedback on their goods and services. These may be undertaken at the time of the service delivery or at a later stage. Many organisations, particularly retailers and restaurants, offer prize draws in return for feedback and some companies, for example, those in the travel industry, make feedback available online for others to view. Customer feedback is also used at the point of purchase when goods and services are ordered online and provide a means by which organisations can improve what they are delivering. In some cases, organisations advise of the action that they have taken in response to customer feedback. Where there have been service breakdowns or problems, such as those in the NHS, then these feedback mechanisms have been shown to be ignored or subverted (Francis, 2013).

The differences between communication and participation

There is a strong focus on consultation and participation in the planning process. Consultation is undertaken during the planning application process, when neighbouring residents and businesses, parish councils and amenities representatives are asked to comment on scheme proposals. These comments are considered as part of the determination of an application. In some cases, the local councillor may be involved and request that the planning application be subject to wider scrutiny or considered by the full council. All local authorities will have formal statutory processes such as these.

The process of policy and plan making also requires consultation and demonstration of a more participative form of engagement. The Local Democracy, Economic Development and Construction Act 2009 placed consultation duties on all local authorities in England. In planning, such consultation must be undertaken at various key stages in plan preparation. Evidence of the process, comments and feedback must be presented alongside the plan or policy documents and the local authority is required to demonstrate how it has responded to comments. The processes are included in the statement of community involvement.

If the community does not agree with the plan or considers that its views have not been taken into account, it may request that a planning inspector consider the issue. In the planning system prior to 2004, this process was adversarial and all objectors could be heard. Since 2004, the system has moved to an inquisitorial one where the inspector will decide whether any points that are raised in objection should be heard and the test of the plan is its soundness against the legislation and government guidance.

Consultation requirements for planning applications vary according to their type and scale. Some cases involve statutory consultees, but in more local matters, consultees are defined by the planning officer. In the case of larger planning applications, the applicant is required to undertake consultation and submit this with the planning application (2011 Localism Act and 2012 NPPF [National Planning Policy Framework]). This system also operates for applications for development consent orders in England, which are made under the 2008 Planning Act for national infrastructure projects. In these cases, although the infrastructure projects are national in scope and are determined within a national system, the local authority is required to assess the quality of the consultation and community engagement that accompanies the application. This may lead to the local authority having to undertake its own community consultation to provide a comparison with that provided with the application.

The scale and complexity of larger planning applications also make them subject to environmental impact assessment (EIA), which is operated within an EU legislative framework. Under the EIA directive process, consultation is a requirement and this is undertaken within the framework of the Aarhus Convention. In 2014, the UK was found to be in contravention of this convention by the European Court of Justice (ECJ), through a failure to implement the EIA directives on public consultation. The main point at issue was the high cost of engaging in the process of major planning applications, which were considered to be too expensive. This is primarily a judicial process and the ECJ determined that the costs of doing so were prohibitively high for any community group or individuals wishing to engage with the process.

Discussion Box: **Consultation and participation**

▪ Is there any difference between consultation and participation?
▪ How can feedback be used to improve services?
▪ Should the same communication methods be used for all groups and issues?
▪ How do planning processes exclude people from participating?
▪ Will consultation undertaken by an applicant be the same as that undertaken by the local authority?

Marketing

Marketing is the means through which organisations promote their goods and services to potential customers. Initially, marketing focused on specific products and informing potential customers of their existence and key features. Over time, marketing has extended through ranges of products to entire brands. Brand marketing now also includes brand alliances though cross-marketing or joint schemes, for example, where certain newspapers endorse particular supermarkets.

Marketing also includes promotional activities. These might include special prices for specific periods of time, 'buy one, get one free' offers, or reduced rents or office floor space. Marketing activities may also include incentive schemes where customers receive free or reduced cost goods and services in return for brand loyalty. Marketing is also undertaken within the sector through trade fairs or corporate entertainment.

Retail organisations derive most of their income from existing customers, so much marketing activity is focused on this group and where possible increasing the amount of goods or services they purchase. This may take the form of tailoring products more closely to fit the needs or tastes of existing customers, perhaps through extending colour ranges, or, in the case of new technology where innovation is highly prized, introducing new models of smart phones, computer tablets or other electronic goods. This might extend to colour ranges or the introduction of new models in IT and telephony where innovation is highly prized. Organisations may also maintain relationships with existing customers through email alerts advertising special offers and added-value online services, including discounts and sale previews.

In planning, marketing might be seen to be primarily the activity of the private sector, where companies seek to increase the number of applications they receive from existing and new clients. This may be achieved though networking, winning an important case that may be replicable in other circumstances, having long-standing connections and making contact through another client. The marketing activities of planning consultancies may include hosting private sector clients at sporting and cultural events.

Those operating in the public sector must abide by agreed codes of conduct for public bodies (Nolan, 1995), which means that all such invitations have to be disclosed and acceptance recorded. and any acceptance has to be set out in register. Local authority staff are prohibited from attending an external hospitality event associated with a consultant who is involved in any planning issue relating to that local authority. In these cases, the only opportunity for the consultancy to market or promote the scheme is in an informal briefing meeting with councillors and officers before the planning application is submitted. Lawyers are likely to be present to advise on the appropriateness of the discussion (rather than any specific points on the scheme).

Potential applicants for a major planning scheme may wish to market its benefits to residents before the application is made. This may be done through leafleting, telemarketing or local exhibitors and/or meetings. Any favourable evidence in support of the scheme may be submitted with the planning application and any less supportive views may be addressed in the application submission.

Councillors and officers may wish to market public sector schemes such as town centre regeneration projects with partners from the private sector. This also needs to be undertaken in a controlled and competitive environment, subject to EU procurement legislation. Any planning application made by a local authority must be managed by specific regulatory conditions and there is no additional presumption in favour of approval.

Reputation management

The role of reputation management and its importance have grown over time. In the past, this might have been thought of as a central component of public relations but now the management and maintenance of reputation for an organisation, company or individual is seen to be of critical importance in its core values. In the private sector, reputation management is associated with brands that are intangible but have a positive value. Brands may also extend into the voluntary sector.

Reputation management can have a number of positive aspects. First, organisations may be regarded as partners of choice if their reputations are positive and they are seen to be capable of delivering contracts. A positive reputation may bring access to resources and esteem from those outside the immediate sector, although it may also bring distrust and disrespect from immediate peers. Having a good reputation enhances organisational morale and affects staff attitudes and behaviours (LGA, 2010).

In most cases, reputation management concerns the external perception of a single organisation but reputational issues may occasionally affect a whole sector. In the period 1997-2007, widespread distrust of local government by central government led to performance management regimens, controls over expenditure and increases in centralist targets (Blair, 1998; Pollitt and Bouckaert, 2011; Hood, 2011).

Reputation management is also important for individuals. All organisations are concerned with having leaders or at least spokespeople who are recognised and trusted by their partners and by members of the public. A breakdown in trust and confidence is a legitimate reason for the termination of a chief executive's contract. The ability to hold a good reputation can also help in any individual negotiation of a salary and terms and conditions of employment. A good reputation can also help an individual to negotiate a favourable salary and terms and conditions of employment.

Discussion Box: **Marketing and reputation**
- Should public sector planners market their services?
- In the private sector, what are likely to be the most effective ways to win more work from existing and new clients?
- Is the organisation's reputation important for attracting work and employees?

Conclusions

The resources used to employ planners will be the greatest costs in operating a planning service or consultancy. The ways in which planners are employed, their performance and how they work are all important elements of managing these costs. The employment of planners in all sectors is closely allied to the economy and the prevailing property market which fluctuates in a cyclical way. When the market is buoyant then having good HR management practices in the organisation may support retention of staff whilst finding ways of maintaining relationships with staff who are made redundant when there is less work may make it easier for them to return once the market turns upwards. As planners are highly networked, knowledge of the employer market is well developed between them and this knowledge may be significant at specific times. For those recruiting or applying for posts, this chapter has indicated some of the ways in which to engage in these processes effectively.

SIX

Managing resources for planning: finance and assets

Introduction

Finance is a key consideration for all organisations. The way in which an organisation is able to manage and attract finance is critical to its success in achieving its objectives. Finance forms part of the organisation's resource base and is accompanied by staff, land and buildings, equipment, intellectual property and reputation, all of which are capable of being assigned a financial value. Management of these resources may be direct or indirect and includes both day-to-day management as well as dealing with change and crises.

Financial resources have a number of roles within planning. First, there are the costs of a planning service or planning application to consider (BCCI, 2011a). Planning is an essential component of all capital investment in land and buildings and plays a central role in the country's national and local economies (PAS, 2014c; RTPI, 2014). Planning is used to support investment and also generates mitigating development contributions to be spent on infrastructure and facilities.

Accounting for financial resources

Accounting for financial resources is considered in two ways – the use of capital resources for long-term investment and revenue or current resources for day-to-day expenditure. Accounting for the use of resources must be undertaken according to legally binding standards. Until 2013, the accounting standards for the private and the public sector differed, as did those between nations. Since 2013, International Financial and Reporting Standards (IFRS) have begun to be introduced; these will be the same for all sectors and across a number of countries. In the UK, their implementation is due to be completed in 2017. Local government legislation was reformed by sections 1-7 of the 2011 Localism Act, allowing for the formation of local authority trading companies and other organisational structures.

Capital finance

Capital finance is concerned with funds put aside for long-term investment and not needed for the day-to-day running of the organisation. It includes physical resources such as land, buildings and equipment. Capital funding is applied to those assets that have a life longer than five years. Some capital assets, such as buildings, are expected to have a working life of 60 years and the lifespan for transport infrastructure can range from 25 to 90 years.

Organisations have to account for capital and the use of their assets separately from their revenue expenditure. They need to make a financial estimate of their asset values as part of these reporting processes. The size and type of assets is an important component in any organisation's ability to borrow to invest in new capital projects and may also be used as security for a loan. In some start-up or small companies, the founder of the company may use their own property – their house, for example – as security for a loan, in addition to other kinds of funding, including credit cards (Robb and Robinson, 2014). Organisations determine the ways in which their capital is deployed. In the private sector, organisations consider their performance against a series of accounting ratios, including the return on capital employed.

In the public sector, capital investment creates public goods that provide a rate of return to society and the economy (Helm, 2014). The methods used to examine the rate of return on capital employed in the public sector frequently depend on cost-benefit analysis (Layard and Glaister, 1994; Mishan and Quah, 2007) More recently, the links between capital investment, particularly in infrastructure, and the economic performance by nations and territories has become more significant (Cheshire and Magrini, 2000a; Duranton et al, 2011; Arrow and Kruz, 2013).

While buildings are provided through capital funding, property rental is charged to the revenue account. Ownership of a building can generate income through rents, an 'uplift' in value or use for production. The costs of running a building (facilities management), including repairs, maintenance, heating, lighting, cleaning and insurance, are charged to revenue. Running costs are frequently a key issue for the third sector organisations that may be able to raise enough funding for a new building but then have difficulty meeting its annual running costs. The strategy for managing running costs, including letting out the space, will be a key consideration in any grant application for funding improvements to buildings. These may also increase the value of the building or reduce costs through retrofitting energy-saving measures. Improvements to the fabric of the building may be considered as capital expenditure, while IT systems, services and training may be assigned either to capital or revenue budgets.

The professional costs for developing a capital project may be charged to the capital account before funding for the whole project has been finalised. Once the project is agreed, these costs will be transferred to the capital budget for the project. If the project does not obtain funding, it is possible to charge any abortive fees to the capital account. In planning, it is possible to appoint planners funded from the capital costs of a project or to develop a project using this approach.

The capital programme is also part of the formal accounting process. The organisation cannot commit to more projects than it can fund and each project included within the capital programme has to receive formal commitment for its entirety or for specifically agreed stages. If a project falls behind or cannot be progressed, it can be substituted with another project. Most capital programmes have schemes on a reserve list that may be 'shovel ready' once funding has been allocated.

Projects funded from capital budgets are more attractive than those using revenue funding. A capital project requires a small proportion of the funding for a project to be available in the first year, although there will need to be firm commitments and legal guarantees for the funding for the remainder of the project. The costs can also be spread over a longer period. Projects funded from revenue must be found in full in the year they are undertaken and may bring no investment benefits to the organisation. Capital expenditure is usually defined as investment in that it creates a beneficial return equal to or greater than the cost of the investment over the medium to long term. Revenue expenditure may be reclassified as capital at the end of the financial year if there is capacity in the ceiling of the capital budget allocation for the organisation. Unspent revenue in the form of cash may be used for capital projects savings, purchase of goods and services or the reduction of local taxation levies and fees and charges. Unspent capital resources cannot be used for revenue purposes.

Organisations may fund capital projects from their balance or reserves. Most organisations prefer to raise some of the costs of a capital project from the markets, particularly when interest rates are low. Loans for capital expenditure may be raised from bonds or banks. In local government, loans can be raised from the Public Works Loans Board. The amount of loans that can be raised by any organisation will be determined by their loans-to-assets ratio, usually known as gearing or leverage. In the public sector, local authorities and health bodies are required to comply with prudential borrowing requirements agreed in 2003 and set out in the accompanying code (CIPFA, 2011). These set limits to borrowing amounts based on assets and existing commitments. Bonds may also be used in all sectors and some local authorities are grouping their loan requirements together to raise a larger bond, which is less expensive to manage and may be more attractive to investors. Some major infrastructure schemes are now being funded by bond finance such as the Northern Line underground extension at Nine Elms in London.

Revenue finance

The revenue or current expenditure account comprises inflows of revenue from sales, rents, licensing, contracted services or other payments such as investment interest or government grants. The outgoings from a revenue account include salaries, costs of production, some costs for rent, heating, lighting and cleaning of premises, training, marketing and some costs of borrowing finance. The revenue account is used to fund those business activities that do not have a long life and are paid in the present. In every organisation, the revenue income and expenditure is shown on the balance sheet, which has to be published as part of the organisation's accounts every year.

For practical purposes, revenue accounts are managed on a daily basis and the estimates of income and expenditure, together with the probable actuals – that is, income and expenditure against estimates – will also be closely monitored. These accounts are also profiled, as some organisations receive most of their income at certain points in the year but have their expenditure equalised throughout the year or at different peak periods. Where there is a gap between expected income and required expenditure, the organisation may have a cash-flow problem. This may be resolved though short-term bank financing or may result in the organisation being forced to close.

All organisations have other resources, such as their brand and the goodwill of their customers and client base. These resources may be monetised, perhaps at times of takeovers or mergers between companies, but they are not generally included within the balance sheet. Retention of the client base and name of a company may be a key issue in any takeover and it may be for this reason the take over is taking place.

The retention of a company's name and client base may be key issues in any takeover – and may even be the reason for the takeover.

Discussion Box: **Finance in the organisation**
- How can organisations increase their return on their assets?
- When is it better to rent rather than purchase property?
- Is it possible to charge salaries to the capital account?
- Why is the revenue budget important?

The role of finance in the organisation

Private sector

Finance has distinctive roles at differing points in an organisation's lifecycle. When an organisation is starting up as a business, it will need some working funding. This may be provided by a bank, charity, contractor or family and friends. Some types of business such as franchises may provide loans to those starting new businesses and the arrangements for these relationships may lead to tied goods being sold. Some organisations may provide funding to develop new supplier organisations, providing new businesses with a guaranteed level of purchase, usually on a diminishing taper over a fixed time period, in return for shares in the business. These may be known as 'sweetheart deals' (Bayou et al, 2011). This may not offer good value for money for the public sector or shareholders, although it may be a way of creating new businesses (Stiglitz, 2012). Individuals may fund start-up businesses with redundancy payments or money released from pension funds.

As business organisations grow and develop, the main source of income is expected to be the sale of goods, services and licences. Goods and services may be purchased singly or through long-term supply contracts. Licences provide a stream of income and may comprise a single payment or a fee per use. A business organisation will also have regular costs including salaries, workplace maintenance, insurance and taxation. For most companies, taxation is a major item of expenditure, covering employees, capital gains tax, corporation tax and value added tax. Companies that operate in more than one country may use transfer pricing arrangements to account for supplies or sales in the country that has the most advantageous tax rates rather than where they are sold, although there are now international initiatives to restrict this where possible (OECD, 2010).

Over the course of an accounting and reporting period, usually one year, a private sector organisation will expect to make a surplus. These surpluses may be applied in a number of ways. They may be provided as a dividend to a shareholder or owner, paid to employees or reinvested within the company. For companies operating in more than one country, there may be disincentives to moving revenue out of the countries where sales are derived, so surplus funds may be retained there. Companies making a loss may receive tax relief. Capital investment may also attract tax relief, as may certain types of research and investment expenditure.

Funding for hybrid organisations that straddle both the private and the public sector differs from that for private sector companies. Revenue income for utility providers, such as energy or water companies, is regulated through pricing by an independent regulator that also controls profits. These utility companies are required to fund future development of infrastructure, supply of service and maintenance from their pricing strategies, which has to be agreed on a regular basis (Brown and Sibley, 1986). The vast majority of utility investment will be funded by the purchasers of their services, although specific infrastructure investment may be funded by government.

Public sector

Central government is funded from taxation, loans (known as gilts) and some fees and charges. It also receives funding from the European Union and loans from the European Investment Bank for both capital and revenue purposes such as building infrastructure or skills support in areas of high unemployment. The bulk of taxation is generated through the economic activities of the country as well as regular tax payments, although there may be specific initiatives to generate income such as the auctioning of broadband licences (Gómez-Barroso et al, 2012) or selling gold reserves. Income may also be generated from fees and charges such as stamp duty on house sales. Apart from servicing the national debt and funding social welfare payments, one of the main costs for government is its employees. Some government departments, however, allocate funds to agencies and other bodies for investment in areas such as flood prevention, highways and housing. Traditionally, central government in the UK has not distinguished between current (revenue) and capital accounts, and all expenditure has been made from a single income pot. This has changed with the introduction of the IFRS and whole-government accounts (Heald and Georgiou, 2009; NAO, 2014).

Local authorities in the UK derive their income from a wide range of sources. First, in larger local authorities, the highest portion of income is a government grant, funded from taxation. This is based on a combined assessment of resident and daytime population, and social and economic need. The proportion of total income made up by the government grant is lower for smaller local authorities. Local authorities also receive income from council tax, a property tax that is set by each local authority and is moderated by the notional relative value of individual properties within value bands. Council tax increases are capped by the government. In addition to council tax, local authorities receive a portion of the business rates for their area. Local authorities also generate fees and charges from their services, including pre-application planning advice, specialist waste collections, parking and the issue of licences, for example for taxi drivers (Audit Commission, 2008). Some local authorities hold extensive property portfolios and will generate rents from use of these properties. They may be able to generate income through hiring premises for weddings, conferences and so on. Some local authorities also generate income from housing rents, an area of activity that is closely managed by the UK government.

Most local authority expenditure from the revenue account is for employees and their associated costs. Staff may provide corporate support or frontline services directly to citizens through social care or in schools. Until the early 1990s, the majority of council services were provided by staff employed directly by the local authority. Since the introduction of competition into the public sector through World Trade Organization agreements in 1976 (Morphet, 2013), however, there has been a shift to a mixed economy. Here the local authority retains overall responsibility for the service but engages another provider to deliver it. Such providers may be from the private sector, another local authority or a charity (Domberger and Jensen, 1997; Alcock, 2010; Billis, 2010b).

Third sector

Funding for charities and third sector organisations comes from donors, fundraising activities or grants for specific activities. Charities have begun to act more like business organisations in undertaking service delivery or providing consultancy services (Billis, 2010a; Harris, 2010). Many charities have a retail arm through charity shops, where they sell recycled and other goods. Most charities raise funds for specific objectives, for example, providing support for older people, children or arts activities. Charities are required to lodge their accounts with the Charity Commission. These are then published online in the same way as company accounts. Some charities, such as the National Trust, derive regular income from donated property through holiday rentals or visitor fees.

Charging and pricing for goods and services

Some business costs are fixed, while others are variable. Fixed costs are easier to control and are likely to be set for defined periods. These include energy, taxation and insurance. There will also be fixed costs in relation to the buildings used. Variable costs may include materials and some sources of energy supply. The costs of a business may also be subject to seasonal variations or weather, for example, in different types of food production.

Private sector

One of the key issues for any business is how to establish charges, fees or prices. The cost of providing goods or services is calculated on the basis of staff expenditure, overheads and materials plus a margin. This may be very different from the price that the market is prepared to pay. In certain sectors, such as clothing and technology, consumers may be prepared to pay a premium for new products when they first come on to the market, but once they become freely available the price inevitably comes down.

The costs of any business are based on the process of making goods or providing services. The cost price comprises the cost of supplying goods or services, including manufacture, delivery, marketing and commission on sales. It should also include a surplus or profit margin. Some organisations, for example retailers, transfer costs to the customer by cutting the number of in-store staff, offsetting poorer service and longer queues with slightly lower prices. Some furniture retailers expect customers to find their own goods rather than be offered assistance to locate and load them and retailers offering goods online may charge extra for loading items before dispatch.

An organisation's profits depend on sales and the extent to which costs are managed. Businesses that are heavily dependent on raw materials such as petrol may pre-purchase their expected requirements for the coming year though a futures market. Here the organisation hedges its bet against future price variation and although there is a risk that prices will fall, the organisation will have guaranteed its energy supply and protected itself against price rises. Other ways of managing costs include cutting energy consumption, minimising office space by allowing employees to work from home, and introducing positive working measures to reduce the number of days lost through sickness absence and staff turnover.

In some organisations, the cost of producing goods may have been sunk in development costs. Moreover, prices may be related to availability or a monopolistic supplier, particularly in the case of the pharmaceuticals and entertainment industries. Prices may also be manipulated to encourage the market, particularly among supermarkets through 'buy one, get one free' offers, temporary discounts or incentive-based loyalty cards. Some companies brand their goods as exclusive in order to exert higher prices and reinforce their image. This is particularly true for consumer goods but may also be the case with services and goods purchased by companies.

Prices are also set in relation to other suppliers. Retail companies may match the lower prices of competitors by refunding the difference between their own price and that of the rival brand, while others use comparisons to encourage trade. Some businesses have developed as comparison websites, claiming to provide the best quote for goods or services in any given set of circumstances while earning a fee from the successful companies for any sales made on their behalf. Some comparison websites are set up by suppliers with vested interests in companies whose goods and services they promote, while others, such as the Consumer Association, operated independently on a subscription basis.

In some sectors, such as the commercial rental market, it is common for providers to offer inducements such as lower rent at the beginning of the lease or rental period and then recoup these costs in higher prices over the remainder of the lease. A similar approach may be used in managing contracts. In this case, a contractor may begin by putting more effort and resources into providing the contracted service on the basis that once it is running effectively these additional resources can be withdrawn and the front-loaded costs offset.

Organisations such as retailers may introduce new products as loss leaders in an attempt to encourage future sales. Such inducements may equally be used when working with new clients or consultancies, where, for example, rates for services provided may be set at a levels that fall incrementally where further work is guaranteed. This practice may be used equally in consultancy as in the sale of goods. Rates for work can also be set where guarantees of more work will lead to lower day rates or tariffs being used. Some organisations may set very high rates in order to discourage an order, while others share pricing information to ensure that each obtains some business over time. Some groups of businesses may share information about pricing and ensure that each obtains some business over time. In the public sector, where cartel approaches are unlawful, there is no relation between cost and price. Ultimately, the price for goods or services must cover the organisation's costs and beyond this, prices are determined only by what the market will bear.

Pricing in planning consultancy

The pricing of work in planning consultancies depends on a number of issues. The first is the type of work and the nature of the client. Advising individual householders on planning applications attracts lower fees than corporate work, as individual jobs are likely to be small and householders are the group least willing and able to pay for this type of service. Where clients are companies or large organisations, fee levels will rise. Fees for work for single applications may be costed at an hourly or half-day rate. For long-term work or larger applications, fees may be agreed at a day rate or for at a fixed cost for the completed job.

The planning consultant may agree a fee for a piece of work that will cover the likely time to be taken although this may be distributed over a period of time when parts of the job are undertaken but not in a continuous way. It may include desk research, attendance at meetings or writing submissions. In some cases, clients may pay consultants a retainer to provide a continuing low level of advice, safe in the knowledge that the consultant will be sufficiently familiar with the job to deal with any major issues should they arise. Some organisations retain a single planning consultant to undertake all their work, whereas others, such as retailers, tend to divide their work between different planning consultants. In 2012/13, the largest planning consultancy generated nearly £22 million in planning fees (Sell, 2013).

Some situations require the services of more specialist consultancies, for example, in cases involving environmental, historic or transport issues, or for consultation or economic assessments. These may be for environment, historic or transport issues, for consultation or economic assessments. In these cases, consultants are likely to contribute less to the planning process but charge more for their services.

The third sector

In the third sector, pricing and charges depend on the service being offered. In charity retail, for example, where funds are generated though the resale of donated goods, prices are likely to vary according to the location of the shop and the prevailing incomes of likely purchasers. However, charities frequently remove some donated goods such as vintage clothing and books from the mainstream and resell them for higher prices where these items are in demand. In the UK, charities also receive the benefit of repayment of tax on donations. Charities request gift aid from donors and once the goods have been sold this can be reclaimed from the government, adding 25% to the value of the goods donated.

Where charities sell their services as part of a contract, they are likely to charge the same as companies in the private sector. This is a newer market (Billis, 2010a) and provides charities with extra income. It can also change the nature of the charity (Harris, 2010). Where charities sell one-off advice consultancy to another third sector organisation or to a company in the private sector, they may charge market rates unless the service is part of their core mission. While third sector organisations may be classified as being 'not for profit', this does not mean that they are not seeking to generate a surplus on their activities and using this to further their aims and objectives.

The public sector

The percentage of income derived by local authorities from fees and charges has steadily increased since 2000. In 2008, the Audit Commission, in a study entitled *Positively charged*, found that while only 20% of local authorities were using their charging powers to their full potential, over 25% of councils were generating more funding from fees and charges than from council tax. These rises may relate to the increased use of fees and charges, as well as the dwindling funding raised from council tax as a proportion of expenditure. However, the Audit Commission also found that charges were not generally informed by cost information and, in practice, fees and charges were likely to set be at lower levels when they were first introduced, and gradually increased. The charges applied by neighbouring authorities may also have some influence on charging levels. The study found that citizens were happy to pay the charges set by local authorities if, in doing so, this provided them with flexible services accessible at convenient times.

Generating income through fees and charges provides local authorities with some financial and service freedom. It also brings risks. First, where services are dependent on the market, including planning and licensing, staff may be cut when demand falls. Where fees and charges are used to fund or subsidise other services, such as home care or luncheon clubs, such services may be threatened if revenues decline. Also, as budgets are squeezed, there may be more pressure to allocate funding derived from fees and charges to the mainstream budget to offer other reductions. This may be the case with the community infrastructure levy (CIL). Unlike its precursor – section 106 contributions – CIL it is not tied to a specific development and once it has been collected, the local authority may choose how to spend it.

Another negative implication of charging for services is that it puts at a disadvantage those residents who cannot afford to pay. An inability to pay for the removal of bulky refuse, for example, may result in old furniture or broken electrical appliances being dumped in the street. Some residents will be unable to afford to use public transport or pay charges for sporting, social and cultural activities, although most local authorities apply discretionary discounts to specific groups, and in some cases the use of sports facilities is prescribed by GPs and funded by the NHS.

Local authorities in areas of severe economic disadvantage may decide not to charge for services, while others have a philosophical objection to charging, taking the view that public services should be free at the point of delivery. Moreover, a local or historical culture of free services will discourage local authorities from introducing or increasing charges, as this could lead to political unpopularity and harm their re-election prospects. Local authorities may not want to be the first in any area to charge for services because there is no culture of doing so. Finally, local authorities will be concerned that introducing or raising more fees and charges will lead to political unpopularity which may harm them in the next election. Unlike in the private and third sectors, most local authorities must have their charging structures formally agreed by councillors, together with any concessions for disadvantaged groups.

Some local authority charges are designed to cover their costs, such as special waste collections or the issue of licenses, while others may be token costs, for example, library services. Some local authority services are run by private or third sector companies on behalf of the local authority. In this case, the local authority may charge the contractor for running the service if an income surplus is likely to be generated. In most contracts, such as those for leisure and sporting services, the costs to the user are likely to be closer to the actual cost of providing the service, although the local authority may subsidise users through payments to the contractor.

Some local authority services generate more income than their costs, and this is particularly the case with parking. Local authorities may own car parks and levy additional charges for overstaying the parking period. They may also operate controlled parking schemes, whereby drivers use meters or pay for residents' parking permits. The use of parking to generate income for local authorities has been criticised by government ministers (HMG, 2013) as running counter to other policies such as town centre regeneration initiatives. The government has attempted to change the legislation on parking fines and fee levels, but essentially parking is a local matter and is generally used as part of a wider sustainable transport policy. This income may be used to improve public transport or road conditions, but may also be used to support wider council services.

Another key sources of revenue for local authorities is rental income from land and buildings used for industrial and commercial purposes. These include the use of land and buildings for industrial and commercial purposes. Some local authorities own convention centres and major visitor facilities. Some local authorities own convention centres, major visitor facilities and even airports, either directly or through their investment portfolios. Some local authorities own convention centres and major visitor facilities and even airports, either directly or through their investment portfolios. Other local authorities own their town centres including all the land and retail units and receive commercial rents. Some local authorities make a practice of purchasing plots of land dubbed 'ransom' strips, giving them the option to charge a premium to developers of neighbouring sites who may want to use the space to extend their development.

Local authorities use fees and charges as a means of changing residents' behaviour (Sunstein and Thaler, 2008; DfT, 2011). These initiatives may discourage long term commuter parking through charging scales, promote the use of car clubs, give residents discounts for healthy activities such as swimming and promote recycling and swapping of unwanted goods through freecyle as people change their behaviours rather than paying fees. Lastly, planning is one of the major ways in which local authorities generate income, both through the operation of regulatory services and contributions from developers. This is discussed further in the next section.

Discussion Box: **Charging and pricing**
- What considerations are there in sending a fee quote to a new client?
- Should people be charged for planning services when they are considering making a planning application?
- Should third sector organisations undertake consultancy at commercial rates?

Managing assets

Financial assets are an important consideration for all organisations. Some institutions, however, benefit from owning other assets, primarily land and buildings, but also patents, licenses and other protected measures that generate income through third-party use. These are primarily land and buildings but may also include patents, licenses and other protected processes that generate income through third party use. It is also possible to consider a monopolistic trading position or a brand as an asset, although it may be harder to assign a monetary value to them in an asset assessment, and, unlike other assets, they are less likely to be included on the organisation's balance sheet.

The ownership of assets may provide an organisation with the flexibility to undertake future development or protect it from future financial problems or economic downturns. In the public sector, ownership of land and buildings may enable the owner organisation to develop strategic proposals for town centres or other development, either solely or in conjunction with others.

Land

Land ownership may be attributed to historical or accidental factors, or it may be part of an organisation's trading strategy. In local government, for example, land acquisition and disposal has been influenced by different policies at different times. In the period before 1945, many local authorities acquired land for parks both within cities and in more rural areas, where large country house estates were frequently purchased to prevent their development for housing. After 1945, land acquisition was more purposeful, with a programme of local authority development for housing, transport and community facilities. The 1947 Town and Country Planning Act, together with the need for post-war reconstruction, encouraged large-scale development and urban remodelling. This involved local authorities acquiring land either by agreement or through compulsory purchase orders, especially when sites were being assembled for development. There was an incentive for local authorities to promote development, as each new building would generate local rate income that could be spent on local services. Some local authorities had a specific policy of purchasing land in their town centres (for example, in Bath and Woking) or over wider areas (in Birmingham). Some of the smaller local authorities had their land assets transferred to larger local authorities at the time of local government reorganisation in 1974. The current remaining pattern of land ownership by individual local authorities is somewhat random.

Many local authorities have a passive approach to land ownership, and opportunities to shift ownership or create larger sites with adjacent owners are not always pursued in a proactive way. Further there may be the potential to shift the ownership of land or to create larger sites with adjacent owners but these may not be pursued in a proactive way. In England, the Local Government Association (LGA) has run a series of initiatives that have encouraged local authorities to be more proactive in managing their land portfolios. In 2014, a register of all publicly owned land and buildings was published online. Local authorities in England have also been given more powers to develop their land assets through the 2011 Localism Act and some have taken this opportunity to establish house-building companies or establish joint ventures with private sector partners to develop their land holdings without losing a legal interest in the land.

Public sector organisations may purchase or hold land for long-term use, including land used by utility companies, universities and environmental agencies. This land might safeguard future development sites and give the public sector owner organisation the option to develop the site in the future. Some public sector and hybrid organisations have a strategic approach to land ownership. Social housing provider the Housing Association, for example, will have a pipeline of development sites in the same way as a private sector house builder.

In the private sector, land ownership is most likely to be planned and strategic. Holding land may have associated costs, particularly when it is purchased through loans. In some types of business, such as retailing, land may be purchased as a defensive measure so that other similar retailing uses cannot develop in the same location. House builders will also own land as part of their pipeline for development. They may also acquire options from landowners, giving them first right of refusal to purchase the land, usually at a pre-agreed price or using a pricing formula. These land options may or may not appear on the balance sheet.

Buildings

Public sector organisations are primarily engaged in delivering services. Frontline staff operate from public-facing buildings such as hospitals or schools, while back-office staff deliver local authority or government services such as tax and revenue collections and pension disbursement. The location of public-facing services, particularly hospitals, is critical for local communities. Since 2000, however, many public services have been digitised (Morphet, 2008), reducing the need for publicly accessible office accommodation while providing users with 24-hour online services.

The Varney review (2006) encouraged public sector organisations to consider the use of buildings in a more joined-up way in order to reduce the need for multiple sites owned by different public services in the same location. This led to some shared use of accommodation. In Surrey, for example, police services have been located in town halls and other public buildings. Amalgamating services into 'one-stop shops' is a more efficient way of serving local communities and has released buildings for other uses. Public sector organisations do not always manage their buildings actively, and there is a widespread belief among some authorities that retaining buildings is important to guard against future unforeseen needs. Buildings may be let out for short periods in these circumstances. A more active approach is the dual use by primary and secondary schools of the same building in order to deal with demographic peaks and troughs in the local population.

Private sector organisations are more likely manage their buildings actively, not least because all buildings have value as well as associated costs, such as maintenance and repair costs, insurance against damage, and heating, lighting and cleaning. Unless a building has the potential for long-term asset growth or use, the owner organisation may have an active disposals and acquisitions policy. In the public sector, as noted earlier, these regular costs may be off set by longer-term strategic needs.

Community assets

Community groups may be asset owners and local authorities are empowered to transfer the ownership of land and buildings to communities for less than their market value. In England, communities may seek to have specific facilities designated as assets of community value through the 2011 Localism Act although these powers will only be brought into use when the owners of the asset intend to sell (Sandford, 2013). These powers are being used to maintain pubs and other community facilities, including football grounds. Communities nominate the assets to their local authorities, which must maintain a community assets register.

Other assets

Other assets include IT equipment and machinery comprising significant vehicles and other transport rolling stock. Such assets will be included in the balance sheet, although their value will depreciate each year and a replacement fund may be established to renew them over fixed-term periods. This may also apply to office furniture and equipment.

Intangible assets may include patents and licenses that generate income from those who use them. This form of asset is most common in industries such as pharmaceuticals and IT where a considerable element of the cost is the development of new products and these costs are set against income from those that are successful. Income from brands may also be generated from franchised businesses such as hotels, restaurants and cafes, where the franchiser establishes the whole business for the franchisee to own and run. In the UK, some pubs are run this way, although the look and feel of each pub will vary and they may be tied to a particular brewer or supplier.

Financial resources derived from planning

Direct income: planning applications

Direct income is income paid by a service user for at least a portion of the cost of provision of the service. Public sector planning income is derived from fees and charges at local authority and national level. At the local authority level, there are three ways in which fees may be charged to generate income. The first is associated with the submission of planning applications. These fees are currently set nationally, although in England there has been a proposal to abolish centralised control (LGA, 2014). Local authority fee income will increase at times of economic growth, both as a result of the volume of applications submitted and the scale of developments, with higher fees related to larger schemes. In many local authorities, these fees are used to offset costs for parts of the planning service, so that in a recession, when fee income drops, staff levels are reduced.

Since 2000, there has been an increase in the number of local authorities charging for pre-application advice, where planning officers discuss proposals with applicants prior to formal submission. Before 2000, pre-application meetings had been open to all applicants free of charge. In the case of larger applications there may be a Planning Performance Agreement (PPA) and it is also possible that applicants will fund a full- or part-time planning officer to deal with their application within the local authority. In parts of the country where there is a focus on attracting development, developers may be exempt from paying pre-application fees. Likewise, applications involving listed buildings or developments within conservation areas are often exempt from pre-application fees, although there may be charges associated with other types of specialist development. There may be charges for more specialist services although applications that are for listed buildings or within a conservation area may be exempt.

The costs of other parts of the development management service, such as those associated with specialist services and administration, may also be offset against pre-application and application fees, although it is more likely that they will be found from other local authority income sources. While fees and charges for staff and documents may support budgets for planning within the local authority, they have their critics. There will be concerns that developments submitted through a PPA or those that provide funding for staff will be favoured as a consequence of the higher fees payable. This compromises one of the key principles in the planning process – that of equity. Those in favour of this type of funding argue that any local authority may be overwhelmed by a large planning application and not have adequate resources to deal with it, but this does not address the criticism.

Direct income: developers' contributions

Planning also generates income for local authorities through contributions from developers, either directly and through the CIL. These contribution methods operate on similar principles but differ in some respects. Developers' contributions relate to the development in question and are made under contract as part of the planning application consent in England through section 106 of the 1991 Planning Act. In Scotland, the requirements for developers' contributions are set out in Circular 1/2010. These agreements may also provide facilities and infrastructure through unilateral undertakings made by the planning applicants. Specific requirements for access on sites are included within section 278 agreements under the Highways Act 1980 in England. Contributions can be made in cash or in kind.

Contributions from developers are required when a planning application is significant or large enough to have an impact on the area beyond the defined site. The local authority dealing with the planning application may negotiate contributions from the applicant to mitigate these effects. The benefits that are negotiated may be on the site or in the surrounding areas and may include improving social, recreational or cultural facilities. They may also include training and support to the local community in terms of accessing the jobs that might be available in the new development, as was the case with the Olympic Park in London and the Bull Ring development in Birmingham.

Contributions are based on a balance between the extent of mitigation required and the value of the development. In order to assess a reasonable level of contribution for a particular development, planners – or in some cases consultants – will undertake a development appraisal (Isaac, O'Leary and Daley, 2010). Development appraisal methodologies are based on the value of the development once completed and take into account the costs of the development, including land, construction and profit. However, these methodologies do not necessarily work in practice (Crosby et al, 2010; Byrne et al, 2011; Coleman et al, 2013). Negotiations are expected to be transparent, although this is not necessarily always the case.

All planning proposals submitted to the local authority will be required to consider the needs of local community (Crook et al, 2006, 2008). The areas most commonly cited as potential contribution beneficiaries include open spaces, play areas, affordable housing, landscaping, and social facilities including health and education, albeit that the latter two are fully funded by the state. These considerations are in addition to those that might be regarded part of the main delivery of the development, including flood prevention, highways and wider environmental issues.

Overall, developers understand the principle of mitigation and regard the negotiation for contributions as part of the process in obtaining planning consent. In some cases, the assumption is that an offer of a new school or swimming pool as part of the development will make the local authority councillors determining the application more pre-disposed towards it. Also, because there is an established process of negotiating contributions in many local authorities, developers factor the costs of these contributions into the proposed development. In some cases, communities and developers prefer to use developer contributions to provide schools rather than affordable housing even though education is funded by the state, as such facilities may make developments more attractive both to purchasers and existing communities.

Direct income: community infrastructure levy

The CIL was introduced by the 2008 Planning Act in response to two key issues. The first was that developers had regarded the negotiation of planning contributions as a lottery. They wanted to have some system of calculating contributions for a development before submitting a planning application. CIL has to be adopted through a formal process in each local authority and is based on different development types and on the floor area of the completed development. The local authority will set the charges for all or parts of the local authority area. Some local authorities may decide not to implement CIL at all, or may only do so in smaller areas of their authority (Lord, 2009).

The second reason for implementing CIL was that practices for negotiating developers' contributions across the country varied considerably, and in some areas no contributions were collected at all (Crook et al, 2008). It was considered that a general application with a common approach would help local authorities be more systematic and simplify the negotiation and bargaining process. The new approach was further encouraged by government commitments to remove the potential for developers' contributions on the same scale as previously and thus forcing local authorities to use CIL.

The process of setting CIL depends on the list of local authority requirements for infrastructure set out under the section 123 of the 2008 Planning Act. Unlike a section 106 agreement, there is no requirement on the local authority to spend any CIL income either on the development on which it was levied or on any development included on its infrastructure list. While local authorities have to publish their income and expenditure from CIL, there is no legal pressure to spend this income within a set period. For applicants, non-payment of CIL is a criminal offence.

Since the implementation of the CIL regime, a number of issues have emerged. The first is that the level of CIL is still subject to viability tests for larger developments and in practice this may still be negotiated. Second, some applicants have been concerned that, unlike the section 106 system, CIL raised from their applications is not tied to their schemes and therefore does not enhance the marketability of their developments. Third, there are concerns from local groups that funding raised for infrastructure is not being spent in the appropriate areas. The government has introduced a scheme where neighbourhood planning areas can receive 25% of the CIL levied on developments in their area. This has encouraged more neighbourhood planning activity.

Managing income from planning in local authorities

The income generated from planning within the local authority may be considerable. Some local authorities have implemented governance arrangements for the use of CIL funding, although one study (LGA/PAS, 2013) found that in practice this was still a work in progress. The study indentified the corporate programme and Infrastructure Delivery Plan (IDP) that accompanies each local authority's local plan can be a starting point for this approach, which should focus on delivery rather than collection of funding.

While the fees from planning applications may be offset against staff costs, the contributions generated through developers' contributions and CIL may support other sources of funding available in the local authority. While this is generally understood, the income from planning has not, in practice, been clearly shown on local authorities' balance sheets or capital accounts and this may cause some problems. First, planning's role is not recognised. Second, the funds generated from s106 may become lost within the local authority balances. Third, the funds may not be used to support the projects identified though the planning process, either in the local plan or on an individual site. Some local authorities, such as the Royal Borough of Windsor and Maidenhead, overcome this issue by producing an annual report demonstrating the amount of income they have brought into the organisation as well as the wider investment that has been supported though the planning process.

Indirect income from planning

While direct funds generated by planning may be counted and be shown within a local authority's accounts, indirect funding generated by planning is more likely to be hidden and not assessed. There are at least three ways in which this type of funding is created. The first is through the plan making, including the preparation and publication of the IDP. The IDP provides information on committed public sector investment and supports local investor confidence (Morphet, 2013). Second, the quality of place created through design and development decisions has a significant impact on investment (Carmona and Sieh, 2004) and other issues such as mental wellbeing which can reduce pressure on mental health budgets (Buchanan and Partners, 2011). Third, the speed of the planning process may encourage more investment in the local authority. Although sites may be less expensive in other local authority areas, the speed of the decision-making process will be traded against the costs of delays by developers.

In a study of the value of planning by Adams and Watkins (2014) identified the ways in which planning adds value to society by shaping and regulating markets to improve places and the economic confidence shown in them. The authors also identify the role of planning in providing market stimulus where demand is low. Here planning can provide support to site assembly and embolden potential investors through master plans or demonstrations of other investment intentions. Finally, the study identifies planning's role in the development of capacity in places that can help to accommodate change.

Plan making and infrastructure delivery planning

Local plans have an important role in directing future development and investment. From 1991 to 2004, local plans were largely passive – that is, once completed and adopted, they were delivered by organisations other than the local authority. The major change in 2004, through the Planning and Compulsory Purchase Act, was to include spatial planning in the plan-making and delivery process. This placed an obligation on local authorities and their partners to promote and implement spatial planning in local plans. This change in philosophy and culture has yet to be fully adopted. Plans that identify new development sites for housing and business have the potential to generate more income for the local area, including the local authority and local businesses. Without active local plan policies, small centres and villages may not be sustainable and the development of specific sites can do much to keep local services alive.

In England, Wales and Scotland since 2004, local authorities have been obliged to include IDPs in their local plans (Morphet et al, 2007). The IDP brings together the investment projects from a variety of public sector and hybrid organisations including utilities, transport authorities, government agencies, health and education sectors, other local authority departments and housing associations. Even when the UK was in deep recession from 2007 to 2011, IDPs have proven to be effective, with central government investing approximately £40 billion in capital programmes (Morphet, 2011b, 2013).

The inclusion of IDPs in local plans has the potential to create confidence both in local communities and investors. IDPs also provide clear information about where future investment will be made. They support the local planning process but do not comprise a 'wish list' or a list of potential projects. Rather, they represent committed projects over a three- to five-year period, thus providing greater certainty. They include projects across the whole local authority area rather than those associated only with new development. New development on major sites is likely to require a certain amount of additional infrastructure, and existing residents are likely to be resentful of new developments that do not provide inclusive facilities.

Local plans must demonstrate their ability to focus and capture the benefits of existing infrastructure projects through a test of deliverability, as set out in the National Planning Policy Framework for England and Wales 2012. These projects, together with income generated through developers' contributions, can make a significant contribution to an area's future. In some local authorities, there is now a centrally led approach to bringing together such funding with the local authority's own funding.

Discussion Box: **Generating income from planning**
- Does society value the income and investment derived from planning?
- How much is good design worth?
- When is it helpful to offer community benefits as part of a planning application?

Conclusions

Finance and resources are an intrinsic part of the planning process; managing and generating resources for organisations, communities and individuals are essential societal outcomes of a planning process that is framed by the state. Territorial and spatial relationships between land and buildings and the infrastructure that supports and connects them are the key elements of planning. Planning contributes to these processes directly and through the influence of wider planning practice. The economic resources generated through planning are as important as the societal and environmental outcomes that contribute to the quality and value of places and national and local wellbeing. Leadership and management in planning are central to making these outcomes effective.

SEVEN

Managing planning processes

Introduction

A major part of public planning practice is concerned with regulation. This is undertaken through processes where there is a requirement for fairness and transparency. This requires a more system led approach which is complaint with administrative law through which regulatory practices and decisions may be challenged through Judicial Review. Other parts of planning including plan-making in the public sector and planning applications and scheme work in the private and voluntary sectors are project-based and are not subject to the same kinds of legal challenge. They comprise single activities, although multiple activities may be undertaken for the same client. Management in the public sector is more complex. Planning practice here embraces processes and projects. Moreover, there is an onus on public sector organisations to operate in democratic environment, which brings additional responsibilities for openness and accountability. While planners in all sectors are primarily engaged in major or complex applications, the responsibility for planning decisions in the public sector takes place within a framework established by democratically elected councillors and then delegated to the local authority officers to exercise on their behalf.

Determining planning applications requires that a fair process is followed within the time and budget allowed. Each element in the process must be tracked and monitored to ensure that deadlines are met and quality outcomes achieved (Adams and Tiesdell, 2013). Each planning application includes consultation and environmental assessments. A failure in the process leaves open the opportunity for legal challenge within complaint procedures, such as through the Ombudsman or through judicial review.

Leading planning application processes

Processing planning applications in the public sector is carried out primarily under the leadership of an individual who reports to the head of the service. While much of the focus is on the quality and performance of the management of these processes, there is also a need for leadership.

Public sector reform

The introduction of the Citizen's Charter in 1991 was accompanied by improvements in the management of the regulatory and delivery processes associated with public sector planning applications (Pollitt, 1994). Similar process reforms have been introduced across OECD countries in other areas affecting consumers and citizens, including the use of information and communication technology to provide and improve government services (Pollitt and Bouckeart, 2011). Against this backdrop of process improvement, changes and efficiencies in planning have included e-delivery systems, performance management and businesses process re-engineering.

While management has always been a major concern in the public sector, it has traditionally been treated as an administrative activity – that is, one of implementing decisions by politicians in line with agreed processes. Despite the tendency of central government to place more emphasis on effective policy and decision making, the prime concerns of local government were dwindling resources and centralised powers in the post-Thatcher era. This was accompanied by concerns that the public sector was dwindling and losing control in the wake of the move to open up more public services to competition. The birth of new public management (NPM) (Hood, 1991) changed the framework of the debate. NPM focused on change, improvement and performance management as key components of public service. Rather than objecting to competition as anathema to public services, it embraced it as a means of service improvement (Pollitt and Bouckaert, 2011).

It is possible to see the relationship between NPM with the work of Osborne and Gaebler (1992) and the subsequent approaches to neoliberal tight-loose frameworks of greater freedom and localism within performance management regimes (Brignall and Modell, 2000). The principles set out by Osborne and Gaebler provide a link to the reforms of the public sector implemented by the UK Labour government, particularly in England between 1997 and 2004. Initiatives such as best value (DoE, 1997) encouraged the use of competiton in local authority services through a more nuanced regime than the top-down approaches of the previous Conservative administration (Morphet, 2008).

Targets were also set in education for literacy, numeracy and science outcomes at key stages, school and local authority performance was published against identified standards. This culminated in the publication of 198 national performance standards in England (HMG and DCLG, 2007) focusing on outcomes and processes. These measured planning outcomes against the number of net additional homes provided (National Indicator [NI] 154), the number of additional affordable homes delivered (NI 155) and the number of planning applications processed against target timeframes (NI 157). These targets were abolished in 2010, although the process target remains and is the subject of regular reporting. Indeed, central government has powers to intervene where performance falls below target (DCLG, 2013c).

A second, parallel, strand of activity in public management concerned internal reform. While external performance standards prevailed overall, the means of achieving improvement and change were becoming increasingly localised and were identified as an issue of concern within the public sector. The Audit Commission, set up to audit and review sub-state public sector practices in 1991, had an increasing role in demonstrating how individual local authorities had improved their performance and encouraging others to consider the same kinds of approaches to change (ODPM, 2004a). Best practice, pilots and pathfinders were all used as means of promoting change in local government. By 2004, the focus moved towards one of whole-organisation change through local public service agreements in England that were contracts for performance improvement between local and central government (Boyne and Law, 2005; Sullivan and Gillanders, 2005). This approach was much criticised (James, 2004) and eventually the promised local government 'freedom' from central government micro-management was achieved in 2010, when the Audit Commission was abolished. Local authority performance management has since been led by the sector, primarily through peer reviews. In Scotland, these approaches have been encapsulated within single outcome agreements, which are negotiated between public sector bodies and the Scottish Government around defined objectives and targets.

Part of this reform involved the introduction between 2000 and 2005 of a major set of transformational initiatives within local government in line with EU support for e-government. Planning was one of the main public services included (Morphet, 2008). Under this initiative, local authorities received funding for transactional web services, one-stop shops and 24-hour service access. This meant that planning applications and related material that previously could only be accessed by attending local authority offices were now available online. It also provided online information on the planning process for interested parties, along with details of the consultation process. This public-facing approach was supported by back-office improvements, such as improved workflow processes enabling files to be accessed simultaneously and projects to be tracked and managed in real time.

The most significant element of the introduction of NPM was the focus on reform and improvement through the use of research and evidence (Andrews and Boyne, 2010). This was associated with the moral foundation of public services and, by extension, public service management, which has justified the existence of the public sector and shielded it from attack from neoliberals intent on dismantling the state. These changes also focused on consumers rather than the providers of public services (HM Government, 2007, 2009).

Leading the development management team

What are the key issues in leading and managing a team responsible for planning application processes? First, standards must be set, including the quality of the outcome as well as the speed and accuracy of the process. These standards must be incorporated within the team's planning and administrative practices. Next, the methods used to assess the achievement of these standards must be incorporated in the process systems. The client must be identified, be it the local authority, the line manager, the wider community, the applicant or a combination of these. The needs and aspirations of clients vary and it is important to understand how these work together.

The leadership skills involved in the planning process may also include project management, particularly in dealing with appeals against refusal of planning consent. These may be major activities, requiring expert support from lawyers and consultants. Such assistance will be a major factor in the budget. The level of appeals in each local authority varies. Refusal decisions are primarily made by councillors on the advice of their planners. In some local authorities, development is a hotly contested political issue and councillors may find it preferable to refuse planning consent, leaving decisions to the planning inspectorate. If an appeal is successful and development permitted, the decision can be 'blamed' on the government in future election campaigns. Any overturned refusal decisions then become the responsibility of central government, distancing the local authority from unpopular developments. If a planning application is refused on these rather than planning policy grounds, the local authority runs the risk of having to pay damages to the applicant from the planning budget. Many local authorities use performance indicators to track the number of appeals against national averages and inform local practices.

Process management in planning: development management

The submission of planning applications to a local authority for determination is a fundamental part of the planning system. Much of the planning activity in the private sector supports planning application submission or the representation of objectors. The planning application process is conducted through many stages and has legal requirements for appropriate assessments. The planning applicant is guaranteed that this process will be conducted fairly, in a transparent way and within an expected timeframe. This allows for expected planning application costs to be included in the project budget.

Within local authorities, development management (known formerly as development control) is the practice of determining planning applications and associated permissions. As Enticott (2006) points out, while much local authority activity has been exposed to competition, planning has been protected, despite frequent government criticism of planning performance. However, some local authorities have sub-contracted parts of their planning services, including householder applications and appeals, to consultants, although ultimate responsibility for the process remains with the local authority.

Planning regulation is set within a legal framework that operates at the local level. While there is little or no discretion in the interpretation of legislation reinforced by the national Planning Inspectorate (PINS), local determination is permitted for planning applications that are delegated to planning officers on behalf of the council and for those handled by councillors.

There are, however, restrictions on who can participate in planning applications determined by councillors. First, planning decisions may only be made by non-executive councillors who do not have an executive decision-making role in the local authority (DETR, 2000). Second, decisions cannot be taken by councillors who have a personal interest in the application, defined as a family or business connection with any aspect of the application (Nolan, 1995).

All planning applications determined by councillors must be considered at a public meeting, where planning officers present a report on the application together with any objections, and make a recommendation for its approval or rejection. Supporters and objectors to the scheme are given the opportunity to make their views known to the planning committee made up of the councillors as part of the determination of the application. Any ward councillor for the area in which the application is located may request to speak about the application. The committee then discusses the application and then makes a decision. If the decision is contrary to the planning officers' recommendation, the councillors must provide the planning grounds that will be used in any appeal against this decision.

Failure to manage this process appropriately can have specific consequences. A procedural irregularity, including a failure to provide all the necessary information and analysis, may result in a judicial review of the planning application process. This is undertaken within a special planning court that may overturn the decision of the local authority if it finds that processes have not been fairly undertaken. The second recourse is to refer the case to the local authority Ombudsman, who can investigate whether the process has been fair and recommend action, including the payment of compensation. The Ombudsman cannot make binding recommendations, however, or reverse decisions.

The public as citizens or consumers?

It is important to identify the client when considering the development management process. While community interests may be used as a basis for negotiation, the rights of the development applicants as consumers must also be considered. As Powell and colleagues (2010) identify, taking a consumer perspective suggests a freedom in selecting the regulating authority that is not there in practice – the site is located within a specific local authority's administrative area. Their responsibilities towards the customers of the planning service who are not the clients for its operation can create pressures. Since 2000, there has been a central government focus on the applicant and process performance (Carmona and Sieh, 2004).

> Discussion Box: **who is the client when determining a planning application?**
> ▪ Is the community the client for a planning application?
> ▪ How can you balance national and local policies when considering a planning application?
> ▪ Is the environment a client in the planning application process?

The quality versus quantity debate

Within the planning profession there has been a major debate about the competing objectives of quality and quantity in the determination of planning applications. Before the advent of performance management, planners argued that a quality decision required time and that a performance-driven approach would lead to worse decisions. One of the key ways of managing processes to address the quality versus quantity issue is through quality assurance (QA) and total quality management (TQM). Jablonski (1991) defines TQM as 'a cooperative form of doing business that relies on the talents and capabilities of both labour and management to continually improve quality and productivity using teams' (p 4). This includes three key elements – participative management, continuous process improvement and the use of teams. QA involves working to an agreed approach followed by a review by another team member or manager. There is an assumption that processes and work can always be improved, and that this continuous improvement needs to be undertaken in a cooperative and positive environment.

There are those who take the opposite view – that is, that TQM and QA are unnecessary and that the professional should be trusted to provide advice that obviates the need for external quality assurance processes. Nevertheless, risk management and professional indemnity assurance obliges all professionals to work within a quality framework of some kind in order to meet due diligence requirements.

The government has introduced a range of initiatives to speed up the planning decision-making process within local authorities have also been introduced. These include delegation, where planning officers may determine applications within a councillor-approved framework. In the past, all planning applications were determined by planning committees comprising councillors, so the introduction of delegation has had a major influence on the process. The application process has also been accelerated through permitted development rights, whereby certain building works and changes of use may be carried out without the need for a planning application. Here a planning application is required but a whole class of development is given development rights rather than requiring an individual planning application. A third initiative to expedite the process is the prior notification scheme, whereby advance notice of an intention to undertake a certain type of development precludes the need for a planning application. The fourth initiative involves improved IT and workflow systems.

The Audit Commission (2006) found that the emphasis on speed in decision making on planning applications was having a detrimental effect on the quality of the outcome, which may prove to be a legacy of this approach in the long term (Morphet, 2007). A mechanistic approach can lead to focusing on the process rather than the individual application or its unique setting – even in streets with rows of similarly designed houses, it is always apparent on closer inspection that there are differences that have accumulated over time. In their research on the performance models used in development management, Carmona and Sieh (2004) argue for a systematic approach to incorporating design and quality into the development management process in a more explicit way. By this measure, local authorities could incorporate quality objectives into planning processes to add to the value of developments and improve community and stakeholder confidence.

The development management process

The development management process requires overall leadership and management as well as attention to the component parts of the process, as follows.

Stage 1: pre-application advice

Local authorities have different approaches to pre-application advice. In some organisations it is a free service, while in others it is free to some applicants but charged to others. Applicants may request advice informally by telephone, email or in person, or through a formal pre-application meeting.

Variations in practice may be based on management decisions. Some local authorities provide advice online, while others potential applicants to speak to a planning officer. Some provide advice on-line whilst others require potential applicants to speak to a planning officer. In some local authorities, initial advice is provided by customer-facing administrative staff, while in others duty planners are available at set times to speak to potential applicants in person or on the phone. The Planning Advisory Service (PAS and BPF, 2014) found that a duty planner system was popular with applicants seeking planning advice. In some local authorities, the only option is to speak with a planning officer on the phone at a set time. In some local authorities, potential applicants may phone but only receive an automated phone message which may invite the caller to leave a message or request them to phone at another time or could inform them of when the officer will be available to speak with them. Applicants may seek a meeting in the local authority offices or on the proposed development site and before an application is submitted these meetings are agreed based on local procedural rules set by managers. The process for conducting meetings is based on local procedural rules set by managers, and the meeting must take place before the application is submitted.

Again, it is possible to identify different approaches towards advising potential applicants. The practice of providing duty officers to provide advice suggests that a local authority has designed its service with users in mind. By contrast, local authorities with a more internal focus are more likely to allocate planners' time to processing submitted applications than discussing potential applications. This could be described as a producer-focused approach.

A more proactive approach to pre-application discussions may have a number of positive implications, as shown in Box 7.1. Providing pre-application advice in a more systematic way reassures potential applicants. It shows the planning service and local authority in a positive light. A failure to provide advice may result in more planning application refusals. The Planning Advisory Service and the BPF

(British Property Federation) have identified 10 commitments for pre-application advice, which are set out in Box 7.2.

BOX 7.1: Reasons for providing pre-planning application advice
- Reduces the number of telephone queries later in the application process
- Improves the quality of planning applications submitted by allowing more discussion and negotiation on the application before it is submitted
- Reduces the likelihood of the application being refused
- May improve the design, layout and quality of the application
- Promotes development and growth, as applicants supported by the process are less likely to seek development opportunities in other local authority areas
- Formalises processes and relieves pressure on planners so they can engage with applicants in a positive way

BOX 7.2: 10 commitments for effective pre-application advice
Pre-application discussion should be:

1. a cooperative process between all participants;
2. timely and proportionate;
3. at the appropriate level;
4. good value for money;
5. with the appropriate people;
6. open;
7. developing deliverable solutions;
8. enabling councillors to be involved;
9. engaged with the community;
10. recorded.
Source: PAS and BPF (2014)

Stage 2: submission and registration of planning applications

A planning application needs to be validated before being registered after submission. This involves verifying the application form, accompanying plans and assessment documents, design and access statement and appropriate fee. Research has shown that over 50% of planning applications are submitted with some errors and cannot be immediately registered (Alexander, nd; IEWM, 2014).

Government has attempted to improve this process through the introduction of an electronic planning application form, 1APP, and providing opportunities for applicants to submit electronic applications through a government-run planning portal (www.planningportal.gov.uk). Local authorities were asked to manage their local processes (DCLG, 2010) and in 2013 the government imposed a seven-day limit to validation processes.

Local authorities undertake this validation and registration process in different ways. In some local authorities, all or most of the process is undertaken by administrative or technical planning support staff. In others, it is undertaken by planning officers. In some local authorities, validation and registration can be completed on the day of submission; elsewhere, it may take a week. These are important issues when the planning application process is undertaken within a specified timeframe. Some local authorities begin time monitoring only once the application has been registered. Delays at this stage can increase cost for the applicants and reduce confidence in the local authority. As a consequence, applicants may make their applications elsewhere.

All parts of the process can be managed more effectively, particularly at the point when planners or technical staff delegate tasks to administrative support staff. Variations in the percentage of planning work undertaken by support staff in local authorities suggest that there is potential for delegation to be managed differently and more cheaply, enabling planners to spend more time on core activities. This releases time to planners for their core activities. In some local authorities, the administrative tasks associated with planning have been retained by professionals concerned about job cuts or professional demarcation.

Stage 3: identifying areas for neighbour consultation

All valid planning applications are subject to a consultation period, so that the views of local people and businesses likely to be affected by the proposed development can be sought. This process is known as neighbour consultation. Once the site has been assessed, the local authority sends neighbour notification letters or emails to all adjoining neighbours. Consultees are given a fixed time period within which to respond. After notification, the consultation process may be taken forward by support staff. In some local authorities, the roles and responsibilities associated with this part of the process are pre-determined, while others define them on a case-by-case-basis.

Stage 4: undertaking assessment and statutory consultees

Local authorities also have a statutory duty to consult with other departments and agencies as part of the application assessment process. Assessment and consultation are conducted simultaneously and are at the heart of the planning application process. This stage also includes a site visit by the case officer, who may inspect several sites on the same day, making time management an important consideration. The management of site visits can be an important time management activity. Planning officers who use their own vehicles for site visits may claim fuel allowances. Otherwise, pool cars and bicycles or taxis are provided, or officers may be issued with a travel card for public transport. Elsewhere, there may be pool cars, the use of a departmental travel card, pool bicycles or a taxi service to undertake site visits. Some local authorities combine site visits with posting site notifications, which, if practical, may be more efficient than undertaking tasks separately.

Stage 5: preparing an analysis, report and recommendation

There are set procedures using electronic templates for analysing planning applications are preparing subsequent reports, and, where appropriate, recommendations for approval. Automated systems enable planning officers to build up their reports gradually. Some local authorities place a limit on the length of a report or require a summary report. At this stage, managers may check reports on a random basis, or may sign off all work regardless of the scale of the development or the experience of the planning officer. Delays can frequently occur at this stage.

Stage 6: making a decision and issuing planning consent or refusal

A confirmation letter is issued as soon as a decision has been made. Many local authorities prepare and print the letters prior to the decision-making meeting so that they can be signed and dispatched immediately.

Stage 7: agreeing conditions

Once consent has been granted, the development is monitored to ensure that the applicant fulfils the associated conditions. Most planning consultancies use conditions trackers to ensure that the work is undertaken appropriately, as failure to do so may reduce the resale value of the development. This is a major source of work for planning consultancies. In local authorities, fulfilment of planning conditions may be less assiduously monitored. This may affect the credibility of the planning service in the eyes of the local community, whose support for a development may have been based on specific conditions being met.

Stage 8: implementing the planning consent

The completion of any planning application process is when the development has been completed. Many developments fail to be implemented after consent has been granted. There are many reasons for this. One is that planning consent increases the value of a development, so that a developer may choose to sell the site rather than develop it once planning permission has been granted. Second, extant planning consents can increase the value of the company, so scheme implementation may be delayed to boost end-of year accounts and shareholder confidence. Third, developments are at the mercy of the market, and an economic downturn may affect a developer's ability to attract sufficient investment to implement the development. Delay may occur because the applicant is focusing on a development elsewhere. There may also be delays with associated aspects of the development, such as infrastructure investment from third parties or the local authority.

Implementation is an important part of the planning process. Planners may need to devote considerable time and resources to follow up key consents and identify any implementation problems. Delays affecting housing developments are a particular concern for local authorities, as non-implementation will have a significant effect on supply and demand. In some cases, the local authority may intervene by investing in a stalled development or buying it outright, although since 1990 this approach has become less common. Before 1990, these were traditional roles for most planning authorities but are a minority approach now as many local authorities regard their planning responsibilities as regulatory functions rather than as a mechanism for improving its locality. This proactive approach to planning has been lost from local authority practice.

Organising development management

Case officers

Applications are updated daily, with key dates monitored closely so that critical deadlines are met. Managers need to consider whether any difficulties in meeting deadlines are associated with poor performance or time management, or with volume of work. Under-performance may be tackled by training, coaching or mentoring, allocating different tasks, or moving the individual to a different team. Another approach may be to move the individual to a different type of work or to a different team. If all this fails then there may need for formal capability approaches that can lead to the termination of their contract. A failure to improve may trigger formal disciplinary measures.

Team organisation

Each planning case officer will be managing multiple planning applications all at different stages, at any one time and this work can be organised in different ways. In some local authorities, work may be allocated on the basis of geographical area, building on team members' familiarity with the locality so that site visits are more efficient. Within area teams, there may be a further geographical split or demarcation between those planners undertaking more complex or larger planning applications and those undertaking the rest. In some authorities, less complex planning applications may be grouped together and given either to experienced planners or more junior members of staff.

In some local authorities, administrative support for planning functions is centralised, with staff managed by an administrative or technical team leader. In others, support staff work directly within planning teams. Some authorities may provide specialist planning teams for particular areas, particularly where these areas are undergoing major development changes. Another method is to use a project management approach to planning applications, where the local authority assembles a group of experienced planners, including those with specialist knowledge, appropriate to the detail of the scheme. This has the advantage of expediting internal processes.

Another approach is to have separate teams for specialist areas, such as heritage, conservation and archaeology, minerals or waste. The use of such teams will depend on the character and functions of the individual authority, including the quantity of listed buildings in its remit. The number of local authority conservation and heritages officers fell by 33% between 2006 and 2013, and 25% of local authorities had no specialist conservation staff at all in 2013 (IHBC, 2013). This creates more pressure on remaining planners.

Group leaders

Planning processes place considerable pressure on managers, planning application case loads of their own. Those managing development management teams are unlikely to have had any specific management training and may have learned most of their management skills on the job, particularly if they have moved between different local authorities. A system that works well within one planning authority may founder in another. Best practice may be encouraged by peer visits between teams in different local authorities, or by peer reviews, where individuals in similar jobs share experiences and scrutinise each other's roles. This provides the basis for change and improvement. Peer reviews may be undertaken for specific issues such as business growth (PAS, 2013c). An overview of the peer review process is shown in Figure 7.1.

Quality management

Those who manage regulatory processes must ensure their quality and compliance. These processes include statutory consultation, environmental assessment and consultation with service providers and specialists. Quality assurance also applies to planning application assessments. Is policy being applied consistently by all planners across all types of application, for example?

Process based management is rule-based and means that there is reduced provision for decisions taken by individuals in specific cases. This is a particular issue in planning, where each location is unique. The requirement to be able to replicate the same judgement for similar planning applications is a key element in any administrative process, however, a failure to demonstrate that due process has been followed in planning applications may lead to requests for judicial review.

Figure 7.1: Process overview for peer challenge

1. Once the peer challenge has been commissioned

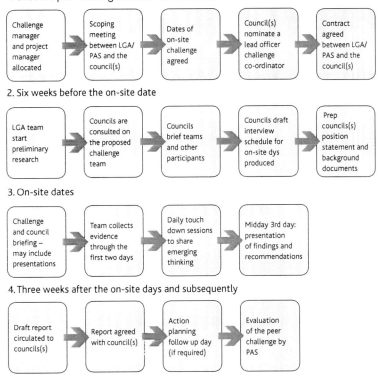

2. Six weeks before the on-site date

3. On-site dates

4. Three weeks after the on-site days and subsequently

Source: PAS (2013c)

Enforcement

Developments that breach or fail to apply for planning consent or are subject to local authority enforcement procedures. Breaches of planning legislation may result in the developer being prosecuted or the development being demolished. Planning enforcement may be managed proactively or reactively. Developments that attract complaints will not necessarily contravene planning consent. In cases of contravention, planning managers must consider the extent of any demonstrable harm before initiating enforcement action. Even then, planners will usually encourage the developer to submit a retrospective planning application. Even then, there will be a strong encouragement to submit a planning application. Complaints are likely to be more common in affluent areas. Enforcement practices have been a longstanding issue in planning as they can be difficult to resolve and may require considerable staff resources (Prior, 2000) although McKay and colleagues (2003) found that a coordinated approach and training could make a difference.

> Discussion Box: **Managing planning processes**
> ▪ What is the most important aspect of the development management process?
> ▪ Does speed of process affect quality?
> ▪ Who should be responsible for registering planning applications – planners or administrative support staff?
> ▪ How does development management contribute to local economic and community confidence?

Government and the planning process

Since 2002, central government has been concerned with perceived inefficiencies in the planning application system, and their detrimental effect on development and investment. This concern has been compounded by external pressure from the OECD and the EU (André, 2011; CEC, 2014). The government-commissioned Barker reviews on housing (2004) and planning (2006) were an attempt to identify the role of planning in the housing land market.

The government has promoted a series of measures to speed up the planning process. Some studies have considered improvements to the whole process, while others have considered specific elements of it, such as increased delegation (ODPM and LGA, 2004). The Audit Commission (2006) considered whether the planning system was fit for purpose, given the government's aspirations for it. The findings of the study and its recommendations have been repeated by subsequent reviews – namely, that there is a need for more pre-application discussion and better community engagement.

Another approach to tackling inefficiency was the introduction of planning delivery grants (PDGs) as part of the government's Comprehensive Spending Review 2000 (HMT, 2000). These were designed to encourage local authorities to support a new planning regime that came into force in 2004. In practice, however, the funding was used to improve development management. There was a focus on existing failures in the planning system rather than process reform (Smulian, 2009), and most of the funding was used to employ more staff to work within existing practices. Resources were used on quick-fix measures to improve performance rather than longterm investment in IT systems and staff training. The introduction of PDGs also enabled local authorities to reduce core funding for planning services. It was anticipated that this would lead to a resource crisis in due course (Addison and Associates with Arup, 2006a). Further, the use of PDGs did not help to assuage private sector criticisms of the planning system (Addison and Associates with Arup, 2006b).

The Killian Pretty review (DCLG, 2008) was set up by government to consider the costs of the planning regulation process and its effects on the economy. It focused on the potential for modernising the English planning application process and argued for a more 'proportionate' response, through simplified processes. As a result, the definition of planning became more proactive, emphasising development management rather than development control (DCLG, 2009). The government's definition of development management is shown in Box 7.3.

BOX 7.3: Definition of development management

Development management is a positive and proactive approach to shaping, considering, determining and delivering development proposals. It is led by the local planning authority, working closely with those proposing developments and other stakeholders. It is undertaken in the spirit of partnership and inclusiveness, and supports the delivery of key priorities and outcomes.

DCLG (2009, p 7)

Other government initiatives to improve the planning process include a review of pre-application discussions (PAS and BPF, 2014). While pre-application advice has always been seen as a confidential process, allowing applicants to discuss alternative approaches before formal submission, it is recognised that discussions should be recorded for the benefit of all parties, and this is becoming a more formal part of the process. This also suggests that councillors should be part of the process, although there are legal obligations on the conduct of such sessions. As things stand, councillors may only seek information at this stage and cannot provide express an opinion in case this leads to a charge of pre-determination before all information has been received and analysed.

Discussion Box: **The government's role in development management**
- Why should the government be concerned about the speed of processing planning applications in local authorities?
- Could the government do more to support local authorities in development management?

Different approaches to process improvement

In addition to these government sponsored initiatives, some local authorities are using management tools to improve the effectiveness and efficiency of their development management processes. These include the following.

Business process re-engineering

Business process re-engineering (BPR) aims to make services more accessible to the public and integrate them with back-office systems (Weerakkody et al, 2011). BPR requires that each separate stage in the process is listed and mapped – usually on a single (long) roll of paper – by members of the team delivering the service. This includes how long each task takes, how many people are involved and how tasks are achieved.

The first part of the process involves identifying potential areas for change. Any elements of the service identified as redundant can be removed quickly. Other parts of the service may need more consideration and resources for improvement.

Various studies have considered the role of BPR in planning processes. One of these, undertaken by the Planning Advisory Service (PAS, 2008), featured a group of local authorities working together to redesign their planning services through BPR. It found that using BPR in development management services to make them more efficient and effective required a focus on four key elements, as shown in Box 7.4.

BOX 7.4: Development management: key focal points from BPR
- Examining aspects of the process to identify its worth to the whole
- Data quality
- System quality and updating
- People – a focus on the tasks they undertake
- People – a focus on the tools they use to improve processes

Source: PAS (2008)

The study also found that clearly defining the required outcomes from the development management service, including design quality and sustainability as well as speed in determining individual applications, was important. Identifying the factual content rather than relying on assumptions or preconceptions about the process was also critical to improvement. The study found that improvement was dependent both on leadership and staff engagement. Poor performance was accompanied by low morale among planners and support staff. Finally, the study found that process mapping and identification of individual roles within each task improved staff engagement with the improvement outcomes.

A second study of the application of BPR to development management was sponsored by central and local government (Planning Advisory Service, 2008). This study was undertaken by four local authority pathfinders. Each had a different way of organising their development management teams, including by area and scale of application. All had the same issues at the start of the study, including inadequate resources for the volume of work undertaken, leaving staff feeling under constant pressure. Second, all local authorities identified the degree of change in the operational and legal environment as causing pressure on the process. Third, all wanted to be more customer focused.

The methodology used was established though the National Process Improvement Project (NPIP) and the stages in the improvement process method are shown in Figure 7.2.

In undertaking this BPR approach, the four pathfinder local authorities found a number of common issues emerging. The first was to ensure that the scope of the project was well defined – that is to include all the activities and people involved in the planning regulatory process. The second was to ensure that influential stakeholders were involved from the outset. Another key challenges was to cost the current approach to development management using an activity-based costing method (DCLG, 2008). The results were then benchmarked for each of the key elements of the process and the results are found in Table 7.1. These differences may be due to methods of costing, but they demonstrated the relative differences in costs between the different parts of the process as well as between different local authorities.

Figure 7.2: NPIP process method

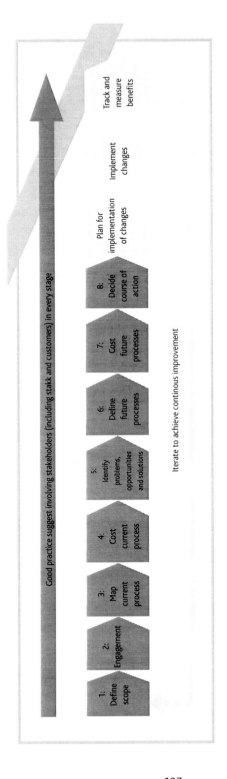

Source: The Local Government National Process Improvement Project, Transforming Local Planning Services Using Business Process Improvement Techniques, available at www.valueadding.com/images/stories/CaseStudies/NPIPPlanning.pdf accessed 4th March 2015

Table 7.1: Comparative sub-costs for development management processes

Sub process	Cost driver	Pathfinder A	Pathfinder B	Pathfinder C	Pathfinder B
Receipt	Applications received	£7	£8	£5	£8
Validation	Acknowledged	£12	£43	£39	£47
Other admin tasks	Applicatons received	£12	£9	£12	£53
Evaluation	Applications decided	£48	£87	£106	£96
Delegated applications	via delegated	£49	£52	£75	£95
Committee applications	Applications decided	£4	£17	£13	£17

Source: RCOE (2008)

The assessment and implementation of the process changes was undertaken using project management methodology. This included allocating a project owner, appointing a project manager, developing a detailed business case, planning implementation and undertaking risk assessment – all of which were deemed important by the pathfinder authorities. Another feature of the change process was to develop a view of 'what will be' for the future of the processes as well as mapping 'what is'.

Inevitably in a study of this kind using pathfinders, pilots or front runners, there is a 'halo' effect, where those undertaking the work are enthusiastic and supportive of the aims of the project and may be atypical of the rest. Even so, support for a project does not necessarily make it easier to undertake. Also the difficulties encountered provide good learning examples for others and as with all change episodes this is the narrative of a journey. Despite having pathfinder status (a measure of good practice), 27% of those participating identified their senior managers as the second major barrier to the project, as opposed to budget and IT (32%) and other staff (11%). Political pressures, at 4%, were shown to be the smallest obstacle to undertaking the BPR project. In one case where senior managers were identified as a barrier, the chief planner signed off all reports even when they were prepared by experienced staff. Elsewhere, planning applications submitted electronically were subsequently processed as hard copies rather than being managed through the IT system (Smulian, 2009).

Lean thinking

A variation on BPR is lean thinking (Womack and Jones, 2010). This was developed by Toyota and is based on five principles, shown in Box 7.5. It has been used in a variety of public services, including health (Jones and Mitchell, 2006) as shown in Box 7.6. Radnor and Walley (2008) identified issues that have to be addressed when transferring lean thinking from manufacturing to government. When this occurs, they argue that there is a danger of an overemphasis on the tools of lean thinking rather than seeing this as part of a wider change approach. Radnor and Johnston (2013) found that in UK central government there has been a focus on using lean thinking for internal processes and cost-saving without any external enhancement for citizens. This is in direct comparison with BPR, which focuses on improving backoffice processes to improve user experience.

BOX 7.5: Lean thinking principles

1. *Specify value* – as defined by the customer or user
2. Identify *value stream* – all the actions required to deliver product or service
3. Map and manage the process *flow*
4. Encourage customer or user to *pull* product or service rather than push
5. Deliver what customer or user wants – *perfection*

Source: Womack and Jones, emphasis in original (2010, p 10)

BOX 7.6: Using Lean in a public sector organisation

- How to improve flow to eliminate waste and reduce delays
- How to get things right first time, thus improving quality and lowering costs
- How to empower staff, motivate them to sustain results
- How to make good decisions using evidence that learning by doing gets results, quickly

Source: NHS: www.institute.nhs.uk/quality_and_value/lean_thinking/lean_thinking.html#sthash.ouNIl7qf.dpuf

Shared services

In some areas, there has been a move to share services between neighbouring local authorities, or between local authorities and private sector organisations. In Barnet (Kochan, 2014), all the environmental services within the local authority have been brought together to form a joint enterprise company with a private sector service provider. The company runs the local authority's internal planning service, but its main focus is to win contracts from other local authorities.

While shared services may be more efficient, they may also be more difficult to manage and scrutinise, particularly where there is a lack of clarity over responsibility and leadership. While they may create economies of scale, there can be confusion about what is included in the arrangements or who is responsible if the service goes wrong. These issues may be compounded when the shared service is then commissioned or purchased by a local authority from a third-party provider, whether that provider is in the public, private or third sector. Hammond (2011) has proposed a clear governance model and for all such arrangements, including democratic oversight and scrutiny of the services provided.

Fasttrack

Some local authorities, such as Sefton, Bristol and Doncaster, run fast-track accreditation schemes, where accredited agents submit planning applications in accordance with a code of practice that guarantees quality and helps speed up delivery. With over 50% of submitted planning applications found to contain errors (IEWM, 2009), the fast-track system aims to obviate the need for checking applications at the point of registration. Any agent found to have submitted an invalid planning application is prohibited from using the fast-track system for a given period, usually a year. As agents use fast-tracking to support their business, it is in their interest to ensure the quality of applications. It can also help the local authority in spending less time checking for errors on applications and then having to liaise with applicants prior to submission.

Lessons learned from major infrastructure development

In 2006, with the prospect of hosting the 2012 Olympic Games in London, the UK developed a new approach to major infrastructure planning. This was followed by the development of a national infrastructure planning system through the 2008 Planning Act.

The London Olympic Games and Paralympic Games Act 2006 contained specific provisions beyond those contained in existing planning legislation in order to help facilitate delivery of the Games. These included the ability to accept parameter plans for site designation where the precise site could not be determined until ground conditions were understood. This innovation also permitted a second innovation through the use of 'slot in' applications, obviating the need to resubmit planning proposals in the event of changes to the original plans. The third innovation was for partial consents, used to speed up permissions for developments such as bridges over rail lines. In these cases if the planning committee could not agree the whole scheme, it permitted the key elements required to use the rail development slots that had been booked with Network Rail and the rest of the proposals were considered at a later date when the planning application had been resubmitted.

The Planning Act 2008 signified another key change in the UK's approach to national infrastructure planning, identified as an area of high priority by the EU (CEC, 2013; Morphet, 2013). Under the Act, infrastructure policy is identified by different government departments and approved by parliament. When a planning application is submitted and accepted, there is a guarantee that the determination will be made within a year. Planning applications are managed and determined by the Planning Inspectorate which does not have to consider the basis for the individual project. Hearings may be short and focused around specific issues. Much of the work on the application is undertaken at pre-submission stage within a set timeframe for overall determination. The process is similar to that for a PPA, with the applicant paying for the service. The overall approach has been extended to industrial and commercial developments through the Growth and Infrastructure Act 2013. As there are no national policy statements for industrial and commercial development unlike those agreed by parliament for specific infrastructure then this may need further parliamentary policy in due course.

> Discussion Box: **Improving planning processes**
> ▪ Why should a planning manager be concerned with improving services?
> ▪ Is it possible to improve a service without involving those delivering it?
> ▪ What difference can IT training make in service delivery?
> ▪ How would you lead a development management improvement project?

Conclusions

As a central feature of planning, the practices associated with planning regulation and processes are an essential concern of its leadership and management. As this chapter has discussed, planning processes can be managed though continuous improvement approaches but may also need more specific and dedicated reviews from time to time. These may occur when new technology is introduced or financial pressures lead to a re-examination of processes. The introduction of changes in the definition of development and associated processes by central government also mean change and these may be accommodated over time without any reconsideration of the processes. Active leadership and management of planning processes are an essential feature of their effectiveness.

EIGHT

Managing planning: projects, plans and programmes

Introduction

Most planning activities – including the delivery of plans, planning applications, planning appeals, inquiries and examinations, and research and monitoring – require a project-based management approach. This chapter discusses the project management method, and in particular its application to planning. Projects are transitory activities that are intended to have lasting effects through the implementation of change or the identification of future change (Boltanski and Chiapello, 2005). In planning practice, plan making has frequently been regarded as a process (Kitchen, 2007), where contributing activities have no defined ends, only defined points of contribution. This fluid approach may be a reason why plan making is slow and inconclusive. Research, monitoring and specialist studies have defined content parameters, dependencies with other activities and can also be defined as projects in their own right.

What is project management?

Project management is used to manage specific rather than continuous activities. It is used in managing the construction of buildings and bridges, and in landscaping, where the preparation and ordering of the individual elements are critical to the project's success. It is also used to manage the production of reports or submissions, organisational change or improvement processes, and court cases. Project management methods are designed to support delivery on time, on budget and within the objectives set. Projects are characterised as having a beginning, middle and end, and as being completed in stages.

A large project may comprise numerous smaller projects and may be considered as a programme where individual projects and their components are interrelated and interdependent. Examples include major infrastructure projects such as railway or metro systems, or an Olympic Park, but may also include housing or university developments that are implemented over a longer period. Programme management may be used for multiple projects being delivered in a similar way, such as a new chain of convenience food stores or a change of corporate identity. Finally programme management may be used for multiple similar projects managed in the same time frame for different clients.

Each project has a senior responsible owner (SRO) within the sponsoring organisation and an individual project manager. In plan making, for example, the SRO may be defined as the local authority chief executive and the group leader as the programme manager. The project manager is likely to be the team leader responsible for the plan. The organisation's ownership of a project is critical to its success.

Why use project management?

The decision to use project management may be determined by the scale or importance of a project. Where outcomes are funded by third parties, the project management approach can serve as the quality assurance and risk management function. Such projects need to be delivered within a defined time period, such as during the school holidays, or, in the case of public transport improvements, overnight. Project management is important when more than one project is being implemented simultaneously, or where one may be dependent on another, for example, where materials are required at certain point in construction works.

The scale of the budget for a project will be a key consideration in the decision about whether to use project managements as well as the scale of any potential risks. A history of previous project failures may suggest that trust and confidence can only be maintained if project management is used. Many projects are not delivered in time or on budget (NAO, 2011). Costs may overrun, and the final project may differ from that commissioned. The initial costs of the project may have been underestimated by error. In other cases, a more cynical approach is taken, for example where prohibitively costly projects are undertaken on the assumption that sufficient budget will be found once the organisation has committed to the project's completion.

What are the benefits of project management?

Project management ensures consistent and controlled project delivery and manages any unexpected changes that may occur during the project's development and implementation (Kerzner, 2013). Project management techniques may be used to develop a project before it begins and can include scoping (Arksey and O'Malley, 2005), development of a business case, project appraisal and early stakeholder engagement. All projects include risk assessment as part of their development. As well as identifying difficulties at the outset, project management also pinpoints key areas for decision making and allows for regular reviews of the project against the plan of work.

Project management is also set within a wider context. Projects are not ends in themselves; once completed, they will be used by those who may not have been responsible for their implementation. In these cases, projects will have commissioners or 'owners' who take responsibility for the project and its objectives, and for promoting its role within the wider organisation. Integration within the organisation is also critical. As the project is scoped, there will be an opportunity to consider who will be implementing the project and whether the outcomes will require new ways of working.

Those implementing new systems or working within new buildings are central to the process of design and project development. Their views as stakeholders, along with those of the users of any new facility, will inform the project board. The wider organisation, the community and other interested parties should also be involved in the project's development and implementation. Without this wider engagement, the project may fail (Bourne, 2011). At all stages of the project, communication between the project board, the delivery team and stakeholders is essential.

Project management is a means of capturing and sharing lessons learned in the course of the project. Project management may be used to capture experiences that will inform future project development and delivery. While project management is usually undertaken by those with some specialist training, its principles and approaches may be used by all managers. Project management creates a way of thinking about managing resources to achieve specific outcomes. Using a project management approach can lead to increased awareness and improved project skills across the organisation.

A key component of any project management process is the development of the critical success factors (CSFs) that assess the project's progress, the quality of its deliverables and overall success. The CSFs should be identified when the project is established. CSFs may also inform component parts of the project. CSFs generally needs to be SMART, as shown in Box 8.1.

BOX 8.1: SMART approaches to project management

S Specific

M Measureable

A Achievable

R Realistic

T Timely

Criticisms of project management

Project management has its critics. The first criticism is that it may stifle innovation in a project as it develops; second, it may lead to a lack of flexibility if objectives change. A third criticism is that it is too complex and rule bound, especially where project management focus takes precedence over the outcome. Another criticism is that it may be too formal and expensive. In practice, project management may not be able to bend to changing political objectives, whether within the organisation or external to it, and attempting to do so may cause the project to fail (Aritua et al, 2011). Further criticisms are that project management identifies potentially disruptive weaknesses within the organisation, and that it transfers the power of decision making from individuals to groups.

Who uses project management?

Project management is practised in the private, public and third sectors. In UK central government, project management is anchored in the use of Treasury business cases (HMT, 2011). Resultant projects are subject to Gateway reviews (HM Treasury and Cabinet Office, 2011). Without attaining a green or green/amber level of risk assessment, a project is unlikely to proceed further without change (ODPM, 2004c). Despite this intervention, however, many major projects have failed. The National Audit Office is responsible for overseeing any approved public sector projects, with parliamentary scrutiny provided by the Public Accounts Committee.

Project management is routinely used in local government and in the health service for major projects such as new IT systems and new buildings (NHS, 2011). In the private sector, project management may be used for development, organisational change and fulfilling client instructions.

Discussion Box: **Project management**
- What are the main uses of project management in planning?
- How does the senior responsible owner make a difference?
- Managing plans as projects or processes – what are the key differences?
- Do you need special training to act as a project manager?
- Do project managers need to be planners?

Using project management in planning

Project management in planning is used in the private, public and third sectors. as shown in Box 8.2. In the private sector, planning consultancies use project management techniques to manage clients' instructions, including planning applications and planning appeals, and to prepare specific specialist reports. Clients are likely to specify time parameters for their work and consultants will organise tasks to achieve this, including attempting to manage the local authority planning application process. With larger planning applications, timescales are determined largely by agencies and statutory consultees, and to a lesser extent the speed with which the applicant provides relevant information, such as supporting research or details of any project changes. The time taken to process a planning application may be in the hands of the scheme's promoter, who may not want to spend consultants' fees before specific stages are reached. Private sector consultancies tend to focus on the staff costs.

In the public sector, project management is used to manage major planning applications, often within a dedicated team. Plan preparation has traditionally been managed as a process. However, an increased focus on achieving specific stages in the planning process – such as evidence giving, consultation and stakeholder engagement – means that project management is a more appropriate methodology in this context. The Planning Advisory Service (PAS, 2013b, 2014b) has developed a project management tool and training for plan making for local authorities and neighbourhoods. However as yet the language and practices of project management in plan making do not seem to be well developed or embedded in the practices of local authorities.

BOX 8.2: The uses of project management approaches in planning activities

- To implement change, for example to introduce a new IT system in development management
- To implement performance improvement, for example, in the number of planning applications determined within eight weeks
- To manage a major planning application or appeal
- To manage a national infrastructure planning application submitted within the local authority area
- To prepare a local plan
- To undertake a specific study or assessment
- To manage the development of the infrastructure delivery plan and its subsequent implementation
- To undertake an annual monitoring report
- To manage public and stakeholder engagement within the local plan process
- To manage a public examination of a local plan
- To implement a policy project, for example, a conservation areas review, a vacant land study, or a housing capacity study
- To implement a capital project, for example a new building, or a traffic management scheme or park enhancement scheme
- To implement area-based improvement, for example, a town centre management scheme, a parish plan or estate improvements

---

Who is involved in a project?

A project will include the involvement of a number of different groups, each with a specific interest and role to play in its development, completion, implementation and use.

A client or sponsor organisation

The client or sponsor organisation leads the project and is likely to be funding a major part of it. While a project may be promoted by a department or branch of an organisation, the responsibility for it lies with the organisation as a whole. The organisation also decides when the project will begin, and is responsible for all significant stage approvals.

Senior responsible owner

The senior responsible owner (SRO) is the person within the organisation who takes responsibility for the project. They will represent the project to the board and through decision-making processes. The SRO may be a department head or board member for the part of the organisation within which the project is located but is unlikely to have day-to-day responsibility for the project, other than to attend and possibly chair project board meetings.

Project management board

Project governance is critical. The project's management board is likely to comprise representatives of the key delivery organisations, stakeholders and possibly service users. The project board is frequently chaired by the SRO. There may also be sub-boards responsible for parts of the project or groups of stakeholders, and a sounding board that includes experienced individuals from outside the project who are able to provide impartial, independent advice.

Project manager

Each project will have a project manager, regardless of the label attached to the role. The project manager assesses the project's progress against agreed timescales, anticipates problems and deals with delays, maintains partnerships and oversees the whole project. Individuals responsible for component parts of the project will report to the project manager and deliver regular progress updates. Project managers will supervise any necessary changes to the project.

External consultants are frequently used as project managers as they can support the team with specialist knowledge and experience, help make a project more credible and mitigate potential risk. Consultants provide additional capacity to the project team or can backfill staff members who have been drafted to work with the project team. Extra capacity can also be used to allow internal staff the opportunity for temporary secondments to project teams. While it may more expensive to use external experts than to employ staff directly, consultants tend to be more flexible and are contracted only for the duration of the project. In addition, there are fewer employee costs, such as pension contributions and leave, associated with temporary staff so any short-term expense is offset by longer-term savings.

Consultants may be employed for organisational reasons. It is easier for a consultant to deal with difficult internal issues and to broker change. In planning, consultants may be used to provide an independent stance in any dealings with the local community (Loh and Norton, 2013). The programme officer appointed for the plan examination acts as a project manager and is recruited externally for this reason. Consultants provide an independent view to management about the potential strengths and weaknesses of the leading organisation and the project staff. Consultants are often used for organisational restructuring projects as they have no interest in potential redundancies or promotions.

There are a variety of reasons for leading projects from within the organisation. Internal project managers know the organisation, its staff and cultures. They can lead projects in ways that make them more attuned to existing methods. Internal project managers have greater knowledge of the culture and how issues are viewed through the organisational lens. It is less expensive to employ an internal project manager and using internal project managers is less invasive and more credible to the rest of the workforce. It also demonstrates that the organisation that is capable of leading projects. However, internal project managers may be less experienced than consultants and may find it difficult to assert any leadership or authority with more senior members of staff (Kerzner, 2013).

Stakeholders

Stakeholders are the principle customers and users of the project outcomes, which are known as deliverables. Stakeholders encompass people in the organisation who are affected by the project or may be dependent on the project for an undertaking of their own. Stakeholders also include those outside the organisation who will be affected by the project, for example customers or suppliers.

Users

Users include all those inside and outside of the organisation with an interest in the project. Where the project outcome is a new hospital building, for example, the medical and administrative staff, patients, their families and volunteers will all be users of the new facility. There also may be a wider set of users, including the emergency services, primary healthcare providers and potential retailers and third-party services. The users should be engaged in the project at various stages in the process, including objective setting, design and delivery. Users may be involved through a variety of methods, including focus groups, visits to other facilities, surveys, interviews or social media. The views of the users need to be recorded and reported at all stages of the project. Without a credible voice, users may become hostile towards the project. Online social media has been used to great effect in planning consultation in remote communities in Scotland, with Twitter, Facebook and blogs used in conjunction with mainstream channels of communication (Improvement Service, 2009b). Here the management of the social media as part of the usual mainstream channels of communication was found to be most effective in engaging users.

Sounding board

Sounding boards are used to elicit views on a project and its progress from those who have some interest or wider knowledge and experience. They have no central involvement or decision-making remit in the project, but are part of a wider quality assurance process. The sounding board will not be centrally involved in the project or decision making but are part of a wider quality assurance process.

As Bijlsma and colleagues (2011) found, their input adds to the quality of the decision-making process where projects are well run.

Project management methods

While all project management methods contain similar elements, some organisations will have a strong preference for a particular methodology. Two systems are discussed here: PMBOK and PRINCE 2. The PMBOK method was developed by the Project Management Institute (PMI, 2000). It is a US-based approach that incorporates ISO 21500, an international standard for quality management in projects. PRINCE2 (PRojects IN Controlled Environments, version 2) is used by the public sector in the UK and is required for projects funded by government.

   While PMBOK is based on general principles, PRINCE2 focuses on specific projects or programmes. This difference has influenced the language associated with each method, with PMBOK's 'phases' contrasting with PRINCE2's 'stages' (Wideman, 2002). While PMBOK provides an overview and general approach to project management, PRINCE2 encompasses the management, control and organisation of a project. The two methods are discussed in more detail in the next section.

Using PMBOK

The PMBOK method of project management has a number of phases, as follows.

Phase 1: purpose

PMBOK focuses on the purpose of a project, defined as being central to its success. The project's aims are also important and are linked with stakeholders and users as well as with the organisation as a whole.

Phase 2: scope

Once the objectives of the project have been identified, the scope of the project – what is and is not included – is agreed. The scoping process identifies core elements that are essential to project delivery as well as optional extras that may benefit the project but are not part of its central purpose. Maintaining focus on the core objectives of any project is a challenging task.

   The scoping process may be undertaken by the board or with users and stakeholders. The scope of the project is agreed by the SRO and is finally set by the project board. A key risk in any project is 'scope creep', which is defined by PMBOK as 'adding features and functionality without addressing the effects on time, costs and resources or without customer approval'. This is where it is easy to add additional features or project outcomes not included in the original objectives.

The danger of scope creep is that projects can become weighed down by extra elements that divert attention away from the main objectives (Giezen, 2012).

Phase 3: time

A key issue in project management is the amount of time that the project will take. If the project stands alone, there may be delivery factors to consider. Where a project is part of a larger programme or sequence of projects, time is critical. The time allocated to a project is also important in managing costs. The number of staff engaged on the project, external contract costs or other projects or organisational operational rules may all provide time limitations and constraints on project completion times.

The amount of time allocated to a project is derived from the work programme and the identification of milestones. Project milestones represent critical points in the project's development or delivery and may indicate when specific decisions need to be taken about further directions or allocations of funds. In central government project management, milestones are accompanied by project gateways or assessments, and the project may be curtailed if the relevant stages not been completed on time and on budget. In cases where projects are given priority over other aspects of an organisation's work, this focus on milestones may monopolise resources to the detriment of existing activities (Yaghootkar and Gil, 2012).

Phase 4: cost

Project development involves identifying costs. It is common to add a further 10% to the project budget as a contingency to cope with unexpected changes. The cost appraisal for delivering a project, and the ongoing running costs for the resulting new facility or process, may influence the choice of delivery method. The development and design of a health centre, for example, may influence the subsequent running costs through centralised reception services or the number of consulting rooms available. Another consideration will be the way in which the project is funded, whether through existing resources, a loan, a public–private financing arrangement or the creation of a joint company. Some costs 'rules of thumb' are shown in Box 8.3.

BOX 8.3: Some cost 'rules of thumb'
- Each employee costs twice their salary once on-costs such as tax, insurance and accommodation are taken into account
- Each full-time employee works effectively for the equivalent of 220-200 days a year when sickness, leave and training are taken into account
- The actual IT costs and timescales will be double the estimated costs
- Each project has a 50% chance of delivering on time and on budget

Source: Nokes and Kelly (1988)

Phase 5: quality

As each project is developed and then implemented, it will need quality assurance that is objectively assessed. Once completed, all projects are subject to objective quality assurance as a legal requirement, through both an internal and an independent, external audit. There are a variety of quality assurance tools available to organisations, one of the best known being total quality management (TQM), which was developed by author and management consultant W. Edwards Deming (see Box 8.4).

BOX 8.4: Definition of TQM

Total quality management is a management approach centered on quality, based on the participation of an organisation's people and aiming at long-term success (ISO 8402:1994). This is achieved through customer satisfaction and benefits all members of the organisation and society.

In other words, TQM is a philosophy for managing an organisation in a way which enables it to meet stakeholder needs and expectations efficiently and effectively, without compromising ethical values.

Source: Chartered Quality Institute (www.thecqi.org/Knowledge-Hub/Resources/Factsheets/Total-quality-management)

Quality management is an important means of managing and ensuring hat quality standards are met. The use of a quality management system during a project's development and delivery will help reduce risk-based costs such as insurance.

Another approach to quality management is quality audit, where projects are assessed against specific criteria including policies, procedures and requirements. It may also include an evaluation of delivery methods and an assessment of the success of the project in meeting its objectives.

There are a number of reasons for a project's failure to achieve quality standards. First, the sponsor's requirements may not have been fully expressed or understood. This emphasises the need to fully explore the project at the scoping stage. There may also be problems if the sponsor's requirements are understood but cannot be fully delivered. In this case, an achievable, but sub-optimal, solution may be identified. A worst-case scenario would be a lack of honesty about the shortfall between the project specification and the ability to deliver. Problems such as these may be not explicitly identified at the project scoping stage and may emerge later in the project. They are not necessarily overlooked but are not openly discussed or resolved. Quality and delivery may also be compromised by requirement changes during the course of the project, as a result of newly apparent outcomes or external factors such as changes in funding, legislation or political leadership of the sponsor organisation. This may happen because the sponsor changes their specification once they see additional or more beneficial outcomes through the development of the project or there may be changes within the external environment such as funding, legislation or political leadership of the organisation.

Problems may also arise – either immediately or in the long term – if work is not completed on time or to the required standard. This may bring problems later as will any decisions by the delivery partner to deliver in a different way as they may consider that they know better than the sponsor. Conflict between the delivery partner and the sponsoring organisation may also be an issue. Any opposition to the core objectives of the project or to those engaged in its delivery may cause disruption or delay.

Phase 6: human resources

Those given the task of implementing the project must have appropriate skills. This may mean recruiting staff for short periods to undertake the work or using contractors or consultants to undertake specific tasks. Staff training for the final implementation stage is also important. Training may be undertaken in stages, from initial familiarisation to continual use of new systems once they are fully available. If training is undertaken too early, and users are unable to apply new skills immediately, they tend to forget what they have learned. People learn better from each other and the most effective training, particularly for IT systems, is undertaken on a one-to-one basis, where short sessions for specific projects or applications may be more effective than group training.

Phase 7: communication

All projects need a communications plan that identifies the audience and their degree of engagement. The communication plan should be aligned with project milestones and use methods of communication that are appropriate to the message and the audience. A key component of the communications plan is the use of stakeholder feedback to influence the project. Without this feedback and influencing loop, those engaged in using the project or the stakeholders and project users may consider that their views are not being taken seriously. Any proposed changed to the project also need to be communicated.

Using PRINCE2

Prince 2 has the same features as PMBOK but has developed these into a system which also incorporates project change and the role of project owners and stakeholders. It provides a means of managing longer, more complex projects and is also commonly used in the public sector where there is a need to demonstrate transparency and change control to a wide range of institutions including Parliament.

Stage 1: outline business case

In PRINCE2, an outline business case (OBC) is a central requirement of any project. This may follow on from a strategic business case and an economic appraisal, which would identify both the reason for taking action and the best means of achieving it (Flanagan, 2013). The OBC includes a full statement of needs and objectives, that is, what the project aims to address and why. The second component of the OBC is an options appraisal. This compares the relative merits of different ways of delivering the project using criteria such as effectiveness, cost, likely implementation time and risk assessment. It also includes a benefits realisation assessment that analyses the ways in which the project will be implemented and how the defined outcomes will be reached.

The most detailed PRINCE2 guidance for UK public sector organisations is contained in *The green book: Appraisal and evaluation in central government* (HM Treasury, 2011). It is supported by other guidance including the Five Case Model, which identifies why business cases are a critical element of project definition and delivery (Box 8.5).

BOX 8.5: Why is the business case important?

The business case in support of a new policy, new strategy, new programme or new project must evidence:

- that the intervention is supported by a compelling *case for change* that provides holistic fit with other parts of the organisation and public sector – the 'strategic case';
- that the intervention represent best *public value* – the 'economic case';
- that the proposed deal is attractive to the market place, can be procured and is *commercially viable* – the 'commercial case';
- that the proposed spend is *affordable* – the 'financial case';
- that what is required from all parties is *achievable* – 'the management case'.

Source: Flanagan (2013, p 8) (emphasis in original)

The Five Case Model is described by Flanagan as a 'framework for thinking' (2013, p 9) and includes some quantitative and qualitative evaluation processes to support this – the so-called 'five cases'. Each case is accompanied by a template set out in a toolkit (Flanagan and Nicholls, nd) as follows:

1. **The strategic case.** The strategic case identifies the issue or problem to be tackled, the current position and the case for change. It needs to set out the financial implications, the costs and benefits, and the risks.
2. **The economic case.** The economic case addresses the financial aspects of the proposal within an analytical framework. It is likely to use methods such as cost benefit analysis (Mishan and Quah, 2007) and include an assessment of those costs and benefits that may not have quantifiable values, but have some role in the project. In the Green Book Model, the economic case will also indentify

the critical success factors and a preferred option within this case assessment, giving greater weight to this case than others, which represents its own interests.

3. **The commercial case.** The commercial case focuses on the procurement strategy, long-term pricing and running costs, and the way in which delivery may be achieved with other partners.

4. **The financial case.** The financial case focuses on the preferred option and the funding required, including its impact on the wider funding of the organisation.

5. **The management case.** The management case assesses the way in which the project outcomes will be delivered and any likely risks associated with this.

Flanagan (2013, p 28) summarises the core content of each of these cases, as shown in Box 8.6.

BOX 8.6: Five Case Model
Executive summary
Content

Strategic Case
Organisation overview
Strategy and programme spending aims
Existing arrangements
Business needs
Potential scope and service requirements

Economic Case
Critical success factors
Dependencies and constraints
Main options
Indicative wider public costs
Indicative wider public benefits
Risks
Preferred way forward

Commercial Case
Commercial strategy
Procurement strategy

Financial Case
Indicative costs
Funding arrangements
Affordability

Management Case
Programme management arrangements
Programme milestones
Programme assurance

Source: Flanagan (2013, p 28)

Once the cases have been evaluated, their relative merits and their interdependencies are considered. The relative weighting given to specific points, together with pressure from government or external organisations, can influence the evaluation outcome. There may be a political imperative to promote a particular solution and expedite the evaluation process, not least where government wishes to see a project start within its five-year term of office. There is also a danger that the organisation involved in promoting or delivering the project will influence the project assessment process in order to minimise the appearance of risks at this stage (Flyvbjerg, 2013). This may include an 'optimism bias', that is, an assumption that problems will be overcome throughout the project regardless of potential difficulties (Flyvbjerg, 2004, 2008; NAO, 2013).

Stage 2: project initiation document

The project initiation document (PID) is the contract between the project board and the project delivery team led by the project manager, and, as in any contract, both sides have obligations (Bentley, 1991). The PID contains a series of documents, including the OBC, the communications plan, the project delivery programme and the risk assessment. It also includes details of the responsibilities of the programme board and procedures for managing project changes. Any changes to the PID must be substantiated by progress and expenditure reports, and communicated to users, contractors and stakeholders.

The PID also links key milestones to programme deliverables. The milestones identify significant stages in the project and provide an opportunity to review progress and, if necessary, reassess the feasibility of the project. Stakeholders should be informed when each milestone has been completed, and key achievements may be accompanied by celebratory ceremonies or media briefings.

The PID also assesses progress against interdependent factors within the project or the wider programme. In the case of practical projects, there may be a need to ensure that planning permission has been granted by a specific date. Failure of one element could lead to wider failure, such as a delay in completing the project or additional costs.

Within PRINCE2, the PID follows a specific format (www.PRINCE2.com/downloads) that provides a logical pathway through the project. The template operates in real time and every change is noted both within the document and by dating the document. The PID is the responsibility of the project manager. The template contains guidance for users and may be applied in all types of project, even where the full PRINCE 2 methodology is not being followed.

Stage 3: communications plan

The PRINCE2 communications plan is similar to that in PMBOK, but the format and frequency of circulation of the PRINCE2 plan, and its accompanying reports, are clearly defined. Responsibility for these reports includes an assumption of ownership of the issues they contain. Project reports undertaken by the project manager are regarded as impartial. As with PMBOK, the communications plan should include provisions for incorporating stakeholder/user feedback.

Stage 4: risk assessment

Risk assessment is major element of all projects and is undertaken through systematic identification of individual risks. This is followed by an assessment of the risk's potential impact on the project. This is followed by an overall risk assessment for the project on a scale of 1-10, or, more frequently, through the use of a traffic-light system, where red indicates a high level of risk, green low and amber medium. Red/amber and amber/green indicate more nuanced categories of risk. These can be expanded by using red/amber and amber/green categories. One of the key benefits of the traffic-light system is that the use of colour enables the project manager and board to locate the risks immediately.

Once identified, risks are assessed for potential mitigation measures. What can be done to reduce the likelihood of the risk occurring or its impact on the project? Once the risk mitigation measures have been identified, it is usual to undertake a second risk assessment. Finally, each risk is assigned an owner, who takes responsibility for its management and mitigation. All risks, mitigation and ownership can be shown in tabular format.

The risk can partially met by mitigation but it is possible to take other approaches. Other ways of approaching risk mitigation include transferring the risk to a third party or taking out specific insurance. In some cases, risks are accepted as an inevitable part of the project. Chapter Nine discusses risk in more detail.

When undertaking a project risk assessment, there are a number of key factors to consider. First, is the approach suitable for the project under consideration? The risk potential increases if a project is not adequately reviewed before committing to a methodology and timescale for completion. Project risks may be associated with choosing the wrong approach, materials or design. There is also a need to consider the capital costs of building relative to ongoing maintenance costs. Risk assessment in relation to change management projects can be informed by previous successes and failures in the organisation. An organisation's culture, working processes and leadership style all have important implications for such projects and may contribute to their failure.

Governance arrangements are key to the way in which risk is managed. If a project is politically led, it may be driven forward regardless of commitment from operational staff. In such cases, any concerns raised via the project board may be underplayed or ignored, or the board may be reconstituted to remove objectors. Another response to criticism is to reform the board rather than to deal with the problems.

Discussion Box: **Using project management in planning**
- What role does project management have in planning in the private sector?
- What is the benefit of project management in plan making?
- Does project management have a role in planning in the third sector?
- What skills are required of a project manager in planning?
- Does a project manager in planning need to be a professional planner? What are the benefits and risks of not using a professional planner?

What challenges does project management face?

Whichever approach is used, project management remains a challenging task. First, people often find it hard to work together and change may be threatening to those who have previously operated within a stable environment. The success of any project will depend on the extent to which it is supported by the whole organisation. If one manager does not support the project, doubt may spread about the project's objectives.

Project management will come under scrutiny if a project is disrupted part way through by events that could have been predicted. Any such problems may serve to undermine the project and compromise its success. It is essential to think projects through and engage with all those involved, including those with reservations, so that all potential pitfalls are identified at an early stage. These issues can serve to undermine the project and its importance within the organisation and this may be a high risk to its success.

In the case of change management within organisations, some members of staff may see the project in the light of their own department or profession rather than the wider organisation. They may also regard projects in a relative light: What is being changed or favoured with a project? Who in the organisation is winning and who is losing? Failure to communicate with staff throughout a project's duration may result in a lack of understanding about the reasons for change, and any lingering conflict may cause long-term problems.

> Discussion Box: **Challenges for project management**
> ▪ Why do projects go wrong?
> ▪ What can cause scope creep?
> ▪ Why do projects overspend their budgets?
> ▪ How can stakeholders play an effective role in projects?

From project management to programme management

Programme management is the co-ordinated management of a portfolio of projects to achieve a set of business objectives. It provides the framework for implementing business strategies and initiatives and for managing multiple projects (CCTA, 1999). A programme may appear to comprise a set of unrelated projects, but in combination these projects aspire to a single outcome. A programme may include a set of building projects for a major piece of infrastructure such as a transport line or flood defences, or it may comprise a group of similar projects undertaken by one consultancy for a range of clients. Programme management may also be used in cases where many projects are being undertaken for one client.

Programme management involves managing multiple simultaneous projects that have some relationship to each other. The projects may have dependencies between them although they may be managed in different time frames. There are a number of considerations in managing a range of projects together, including the ability to view the programme as a whole and understand the contribution of individual projects to that programme. The projects must be managed together and although individual projects may have similar objectives, there may be differences in how outcomes are reached.

Programmes may be managed over longer periods than individual projects and may be subject to more pressure to change direction because of short-term political priorities or changes in the economic climate. Nevertheless, programmes need to be sufficiently flexible, and sensitive both to the internal effects of implementing individual projects and to the external operating environment. If a programme's objectives are no longer appropriate, the whole programme may need to be reviewed and, if necessary, refocused.

The programme support office comprises the project managers for individual projects and those with responsibilities across the programme as a whole, in areas such as finance, quality and stakeholder engagement. The programme manager has the role of integrating project operations and outcomes through robust management information systems, cross-programme monitoring and maintaining daily relationships with SROs and clients. Problems at project or programme level are raised with the programme manager in the first instance. Any issues that fall outside the programme manager's remit are raised with project and/or programme board. This may result in a change to the level of risk associated with the project.

Discussion Box: **Programme management**
- Is making a plan a programme or a project?
- Can programme management be used across a team or a department?
- Does a group of planners need programme management to support its work?
- To what extent are planning managers programme managers?

Managing planning as projects

Some planners have argued that plan making is an art rather than a science and that a project-based approach leads to problems in practice. Project prioritisation may be a political process, determining which issues are considered and how they are assessed (Kingdon, 2003). Plan making is framed by government guidance, although practice varies across a range of organisations and local authorities. The selection of priorities can have other bias, reflecting vocal communities or local politics. Plan making, unlike the development management process, is funded by taxpayers rather than through fees. This introduces a debate on the value of plan making and whether this type of public investment receives an adequate return on its investment. Adams and Tiesdell (2013) demonstrate that planning adds value and it is the attention to specific places that make the difference.

Plan-making practice in England has been problematic and each system reform has been driven by past delivery failures, particularly those involving delayed completion (Cullingworth and Nadin, 2006). Can the reasons for these delays be indentified? First, each process reform brings uncertainty, and nostalgia for the previous system (Morphet et al, 2007). Second, plan making is a political activity, advised by evidence. Its outcomes confirm or redistribute resources and these are complex issues at the local level. Third, considering plan making through the lens of project management demonstrates that the basic principles of scoping, resource allocation, commitment and certainty are rarely considered at the outset.

Despite a new plan-making system being introduced in England in 2004, fewer than 50% of local authorities had an adopted local plan by 2014. Why is this? The first reason can be attributed to the failure of government to explain the scale of the changes when the new system was first introduced (Clifford, 2013). Even a project set up to support the new approach was captured and reinforced by the culture of the existing system (Gunn and Hillier, 2014). A later study helped to diagnose this problem and action was subsequently taken to support the change agenda more openly (Morphet et al, 2007; DCLG, 2008).

Second, the planning delivery grants allocated to support the introduction of the new plan-making approach were hijacked by central civil servants to boost performance in development management. The third reason was the uncertainty created by change within the system, with further planning legislation for major infrastructure projects and developers' contributions introduced in 2008, a review of sub-regional planning in 2007 (HM Treasury, 2007) and a letter from the then opposition advising that the system would be abolished following the next general election if its party came into power (Spellman, 2009; Mathiason, 2009). These combined sources of uncertainty mean that an unwilling planning professional delayed implementation further.

Discussion Box: **Can plan making be improved?**
- Why are local plans delayed in local authorities?
- Would delays be avoided if private sector consultants prepared plans for local authorities?
- How could planning project methodology be improved?
- Would planning be more effective if all planners had some training in project management?

NINE

Sustainable management and risk

Introduction

Leadership and management in all organizations is concerned with sustainable practices and outcomes, that is managing with consideration for future generations.

The principle of sustainability has grown in importance since the United Nations (UN) Earth Summit conference in Rio in 1992. The extent to which organisations embrace sustainable management varies: it may be embedded within the organisation's culture, or it may be applied to specific actions. Sustainability may define the leadership of an organisation or it may be a compliance tool. Beyond this, corporate responsibility (CR) may be encouraged by shareholders, stakeholders and funders in all sectors where companies take responsibility for their impact on society (CEC, 2011). Finally, there is a strong relationship between planning, sustainability and risk management, whether in the context of environmental disaster management or employment practices. Not all risks are related to sustainability, however. This chapter considers all three issues, their relationships with each other and their role in planning leadership and management. All organisations, regardless of sector, must make a case for taking sustainable management measures above and beyond the statutory minimum. In the private sector, sustainable management may be of particular concern at various stages of the production and sales cycles (Holliday et al, 2002), for example in the choice of raw materials and energy used for production and in the logistics of delivering products to market. At each stage of the cycle, there are choices about methods used and each will have cost implications. The regulatory framework is set though international agreements and managed through large-scale trading groups such as the EU (Morphet, 2013). These regulations are informed by global bodies, such as the UN and the OECD.

While sustainable management may be a core value within an organisation, it may be compromised at times of economic recession (Butler, 2013) or when a business comes under threat from mergers or takeovers. In each sector, a business case has to be made to support the use of sustainable practices that extend beyond the regulatory minimum (Aigner et al, 2003). Views will inevitably vary between sectors. Some organisations will increase their sustainable management activity, while others will lobby for reduced regulation, arguing that sustainable management is harmful to their profitability.

Public and third sector organisations may align their core principles more closely with sustainable management than private sector organisations, but their business cases are still subject to scrutiny, not least where sustainable approaches incur more expense than other methods. This is a particular issue when managing public or donated funds, where accountability and transparency are of key importance. Moreover, public expectations of sustainable priorities may be higher in these sectors, although some may view them as a waste of money.

Sustainability throughout the business process

Introducing sustainable practices into the organisation

Organisations often find the introduction and application of sustainable practices challenging. First, the organisation's existing working practices may be effective without any consideration of sustainability. Second, there may be concerns about additional costs incurred from operating sustainably including those arising from the introduction of new working practices and the use of particular materials. Further, sustainability may be compromised when the business climate or economic environment is more challenging. Organisations may well comply with the minimum statutory requirements for sustainable management, but disregard the need for further action.

Some organisations, however, regard sustainable working as an opportunity (Oliver, 1997). This may include introducing more efficient working practices using web-based technologies, or attracting new customers by producing goods that are more sustainable. There may be opportunities for new designs for working practices. Retrofitting may also provide business opportunities. Some organisations may apply for accreditation for achieving quality standards in sustainable production or business processes. Independent accreditation such as this may give businesses a competitive advantage.

It may be easier for a business start-up than for an existing business to operate sustainably. New businesses may develop on the back of renewable technologies such as those for generating clean energy. Moreover, new businesses must comply with ever-more stringent regulations governing building and energy consumption standards. This may mean that initial costs are higher but operating costs are lower.

Sustainable working practices

In the public and voluntary sectors, organisations can operate more effectively by co-locating and sharing back-office services. The Varney review (Varney, 2006) found that this type of transformative approach reduces back-office costs and is more efficient for service users. There may be other benefits in co-locating services and facilities such as enabling organisations to provide onsite nurseries for employees which would reduce travel time for employees and be useful to look after the children of those visiting to access public services. Locating health and library or sports facilities together may support mutual objectives which are now recognised through social prescribing, where mental health can be improved by physical activity.

Organisations in all sectors are increasingly engaging their employees in promoting more sustainable working practices. Many organisations have green travel plans that support the use of public transport, car-sharing schemes and journey-to-work planning. On large development sites, green travel plans are now being extended to include construction workers. Employees may be able to work from home and use video conferencing technology to communicate with office-based colleagues. The introduction of wifi in public locations also facilitates more flexible ways of working, including during journeys on public transport.

Some organisations provide work hubs offsite to reduce employees' travel time or to preclude the need to return to the office in the event of offsite visits. Some organisations share multi-service hubs so that employees can 'hot-desk' – use any available workstation – on each other's premises.

A rise in the number of small, local supermarkets and shops located at travel termini has reduced the need for car journeys to out-of-town shopping centres and provides a greater number of pick-up points for goods ordered online. Goods may also be delivered direct to workplaces or to lockers at public transport nodes, thus reducing the need for redirection of undelivered parcels.

Sustainable web-based working

The use of web services in sustainable working practices is important in all three sectors. Web-based sales and marketing has changed consumer habits radically. The UK is now the largest online purchaser country in the OECD area (Hall, 2012), which has led to the closure of many high-street retail outlets. The use of on-line comparison shopping for goods and on price has also meant that new businesses can set up with lower market entry costs, because they have not had to provide shops or showrooms or distribute goods though third parties that will take a share of the profit, although there are higher security and authentication costs for payments from purchasers and a requirement for a reliable distribution chain and postal service. Despite the growth in online trading, the role of face to face events such as business fairs are increasingly popular. Online business does have an environment cost, however, as internet services require ever-increasing server capacity, adding to global CO_2 consumption.

Even where organisations do not use the web as a primary means of operation, they may still promote their business through a website. This provides the user with information about the organisation's services and products that is increasingly geared towards encouraging a financial transaction. Web media provides information about the organisation, its services and products and increasingly this has become transactional. The organisation may then capture personal information gathered during the transaction for direct marketing purposes. Theatres can then promote information to customers who have purchased tickets as direct marketing. Customer-facing organisations track user preferences and make suggestions to customers based on their past purchasing habits.

In the third sector, the use of social media to promote and collect donations has been made more common with the use of text message donations and other forms of easy giving. Public sector organisations increasingly provide service information online and may transactions, such as renewing library books or road vehicle licenses, are digital. Some public sector organisations provide individual online accounts for users and promote services through social media. In health, for example, the cost of missed appointments is being addressed though text messaging appointment reminders (Cabinet Office, 2010). The same approach is been used to remind people to take their medication. This has extended reporting faulty street lighting, dumped rubbish, reporting crimes or capturing major events on camera phones and having the facility to share them.

Using the web: the case of e-planning

Since 2000, local authorities have increasingly delivered planning services online. This includes regulatory processes such as making a planning application, tracking its progress, reviewing consultation responses and issuing decision notices. A national planning portal now enables users to submit planning applications online. It also provides free access to certain services, including reviewing evidence, providing comments and obtaining documents for plan making. All users have online access to planning services, although the standard of information presentation and ease of use of websites varies across local authorities. However there are still problems for the users of on-line services including being finding the information required, the use of different terms and web site structures. In 2013, only 32% of local authority websites were enabled to receive objections to planning applications compared with 72% enabled to pay a parking fine (Socitm, 2013). Online services are theoretically more efficient for local authorities as they reduce the number of telephone calls and visits from users, but only if the website is well managed and up to date (Socitm, 2014).

Discussion Box: **The sustainable organisation**
- Can all organisations be equally sustainable?
- Does sustainability require leadership?
- Which sustainable management practices are most useful?
- What are the main barriers in introducing more sustainable practices into an organisation?

Corporate responsibility

Corporate responsibility (CR), also known as corporate social responsibility, is primarily practised in the private sector, although both public and third sector organisations may also have a CR policy. CR is defined as 'actions by companies over and above their legal obligations towards society and the environment' and 'certain regulatory measures create an environment more conducive to enterprises voluntarily meeting their social responsibility (CEC, 2011, p 3).

In the UK, the government has not adopted a single definition of CR but borrows from those of the EU, the United Nations and the Organisation for Economic Co-operation and Development]] (2011) (OECD, 2011; BIS, 2013, 2014). In these definitions, CR is primarily assumed to be the domain of multinational companies, their responsibilities and the rest of the world (Jenkins, 2005). Essentially, CR is a form of corporate self-regulation, whereby an organisation monitors its compliance with legal requirements, ethical standards and international norms, and aims to have a positive impact on the environment and stakeholders. Organisations may embrace CR because there has been criticism of its past practices. In addition, they may be heavily reliant on suppliers in developing countries and want to demonstrate the quality of their own practices to distinguish them from other companies (Hemingway and Maclagan, 2004).

Although organisations have embraced CR, CR has its critics as well as its supporters. Welford (2013) argues that the agenda has been 'hijacked' as private sector organisations have narrowed the definition of sustainability to the environmental. Gray and Bebbington (2000) argue that environmental accounting has not been as successful or provided as much benchmarking potential as it could have.

What is the business case for CR in organisations?

While there may be an expectation that organisations should operate ethically and within the regulatory framework, why would they take their responsibilities further? First, operating within a sustainable framework may encourage an organisation to become more conscious of its business practices and therefore more efficient. Any organisation that has an overt policy to manage its energy consumption and recycle resources such as water and paper is likely to be good at managing other parts if its operation and potentially more efficient. A supportive chief executive is likely to embed CR into an organisation's corporate strategy (Carter and Greer, 2013; Mazutis, 2013). Some companies take CR further, and use it as a way of supporting and developing employees by providing opportunities for volunteering or secondment.

Benchmarking sustainable practices

One way of comparing different organisations' sustainable management performance is to use a benchmarking tool or environmental audit. Some of these are designed for certain types of organisation and others are for organisations within specific sectors. One example of a benchmarking approach is the FTSE4Good Index Series. This has been designed to measure the performance of companies that meet globally recognised corporate responsibility standards, and to encourage investment in those companies. FTSE4Good can be used in four main ways. First, it examines the performance of a company's potential responsible investment , financial instruments and fund products. Second, it acts as a research tool to identify environmentally and socially responsible companies. Third, it is a reference tool to provide companies with a transparent and evolving global corporate responsibility standard and lastly it can be used as a benchmark index to track the performance of responsible investment portfolios.

The FTSE4 Index is used by investors to identify companies with CR policies in order to minimise the social and environmental risks in their portfolios. Companies in controversial sectors tend to rank low on the index, which may encourage them to seek ways of improving their CR standards. Shareholders may be more interested in companies with sustainable practices that reduce costs, enhance brand status, attract more investment, and generate new sales, markets and products. Shareholders want to know whether these practices can attract more investors, open new markets, generate more sales or lead to new products. However, critics of the FTSE4 Index (Knox et al, 2005) suggest that it has encouraged companies to focus on their suppliers and customers rather than societal stakeholders. Curran and Moran (2007) showed that membership of the index had no beneficial effect on share prices. Potential employees, however, may review the ethical position of an organisation in relation to its reputation, working practices or sector when applying for jobs.

Discussion Box: **Corporate responsibility**
- Is CR worth adopting in an organisation?
- Can CR work in the public sector?
- What are the arguments for CR in an economic downturn?
- Should all organisations be required to report on their CR activities?

Understanding and managing risk

Definition of risk

Any choice of action includes identifying risk, which is most commonly held to mean a 'hazard' – something to be avoided if possible. Risk management covers all the processes involved in identifying, assessing and judging risks, assigning ownership, taking action to mitigate or anticipate risks, accepting risks where necessary and monitoring and reviewing progress against objectives or targets. There are differences in risk management in different sectors and in the way in which the costs of risk are allocated. In all sectors, some risk mitigation will be covered through insurance provided by a third party or by self-insurance.

The perception of risk is an issue that has engendered considerable debate and covers both risks that are socially constructed and those that are based on reality (Renn, 2008). Socially constructed models of risk are based on perceptions of danger that provide some grounds for concern but take on greater significance than experience suggests is realistic. Managing the perception of risk among communities and politicians is a key issue (Loosemore, 2006), particularly in areas at risk of flooding or earthquakes. Such incidents create rational fears on the part of the community. Risk management in specific locations may be tackled through a place audit and remediation method developed by the police and known as 'secured by design', although Minton (2009) is critical of the influence this has had on the design of new spaces. Conversely, areas of minimal danger, such as low crime incidence, can generate higher perceptions of risk because there is less experience of dealing with them (Foster et al, 2013). Such concerns may have a major influence on a population's mental health if residents fear leaving their homes after dark or going to certain areas for fear of being attacked (Park et al, 2011).

Why is risk assessment and management important?

Risk must be assessed and managed. Although Slovic (2000) has identified that the perception of risk can be greater than the reality, this perception is important and its inclusion within a risk management framework may raise awareness of potential problems for projects and processes. In considering ways of looking at risk, Hood and Jones (1996) identify two approaches. The first is based on a scientific approach that is rational and may be quantified, where risks are examined, quantified and set with in the context of probability theory. This method is used for construction projects or projects with a strong engineering component.

The second is based on a collaborative approach, where people accept risks within their organisation with their main concern being the extent of the organisation's resilience. Risk management is a core part of some services, particularly health services and those involving vulnerable children or adults. Some risks are greater at certain times for certain groups of people. For example, elderly people are more vulnerable during extreme hot or cold weather. In other organisations, risk may be about the costs of change or failure to change.

Much of the statutory requirement for risk identification and management in the UK is informed by EU and international legislation (Morphet, 2013). A failure to comply with this legislation may lead to claims of negligence. Organisations can insure against risks but they also need to demonstrate to insurers that their practices are compliant and up to date. Professional membership bodies provide quality assurance accreditation for minimum standards of competence. In some professions, there is no licence to practise without membership of the relevant body. Organisations and individuals can insure against professional negligence liabilities while professional bodies have the power to prevent their members from practising if they fail to meet the relevant competence standards. A further safeguard for employers is to compel employees in certain roles to undergo a criminal records check. This may apply to planners offering planning aid or planning education services within schools.

Failure to insure against risk may have serious consequences. Where an incident has led to a reduction in an individual's ability to work or threatened a community's livelihood through contamination, any assessment for loss of income may be undertaken over a long period of time to ensure that all the costs attributable to the disaster or incident have had an adequate period to be assessed. In the event of an incident leading to personal injury or land contamination, for example, it could take many years to assess the subsequent costs.

The wider role of risk management within planning

Risk assessment and management is part of the planning process. Risk assessment is undertaken on the development site, and covers, among other things, flood risk, water supply and underlying geology. Some conditions may require mitigation measures. In areas prone to flooding, for example, a developer may build housing with no ground-floor active use (RIBA, 2007) or use former extractive industry spoil storage sites for landscaping rather than built development. Some development is now assessed against enhanced risk assessments if it is close to gas or oil containers (HSE, 2011).

There may be economic risks associated with the location of a development, for example, where a retail development threatens the economic viability of a town centre, including its leisure, culture, restaurant and shopping facilities. Similarly, the economic viability of an industrial/commercial development will be compromised without adequate public transport links to the new site, and a lack of housing may be an economic disincentive to potential business start-ups (OECD, 2011). Other softer factors, such as a lack of skilled labour, may influence risk assessment. To overcome this, some planners have developed agreements that include conditions for training provision and labour selection as part of the planning approach (London Borough of Hounslow, 2008; Durham County Council, 2012).

Risk assessment is necessary for development proposals on previously used sites or brownfield land in urban or rural areas. Greenfield sites, that is sites that have never previously been developed, are more efficient for the developer, as infrastructure costs can be transferred to society but brownfield sites, that is re-use of previously developed land, is likely to be more efficient for society which has already sunk infrastructure investment into the location. Land use on previously developed sites may be an issue, with highly contaminated sites excluded from some types of development. The redevelopment of previously used sites for housing or schools may also be a local political issue (Clifford and Tewdwr-Jones, 2013). Local politicians may also face criticism for identifying sites for facilities opposed by local communities, such as waste or energy plants and prisons.

Some risks managed in planning – those associated with construction methods and use of materials or water, for example – are assessed by other professionals such as engineers or environmental scientists. All development proposals are considered within their context and are assessed for their impact on transport, air quality and public health.

Assessing specific risks in any proposed development is the responsibility of a designated regulator, guided by the relevant legislative codes and standards. These risks will vary according to the development but all will be subject to building control, and environmental health assessment within the local authority. Fire and rescue services are responsible for assessing risk in buildings for multiple occupation, and in public and commercial buildings. Other specialist regulators will be involved in transport developments and those involving waste or hazardous industrial processes. Some environmental risks are reviewed by government regulators.

Environmental impact assessment

Environmental impact assessment (EIA) is a formal approach to assessing the positive and negative effects of plans, projects, policies and programmes (Glasson et al, 2011). EIA is used around the world, and has been mandatory in the EU since its introduction in 1985. Since then, the system has been developed and amended (CEC, 2014b). EIA, together with strategic environmental assessment (SEA), provides embedded mechanisms for both the consideration of risk in any project and potential measures for its mitigation, which may be required as part of the planning process. The EIA can also indentify locations that are not suitable for development. Certain types of development proposal require an EIA on submission for consideration.

When to consider risk management

It is not always possible to eliminate risk entirely, in which case it is up to the project promoters to decide on acceptable levels of insurable risk. If a project is deemed too risky, it may not proceed.

For planners in practice, assessing and managing risk is part of the daily process. Organisations that fail to comply with risk management procedures are liable to prosecution, so managers must record all potential physical and social risks on a development site. These risks must be considered by all individuals who work on or visit the development. Physical risks may stem the condition of buildings, while social risks cover issues such as the incautious use of information, or inappropriate comments about applicants or colleagues on email or social media. This is a particular issue for local authority planners, as the Freedom of Information Act 200 gives anyone the right to request access to information recorded by a public authority. Where physical or social risks have been identified on specific sites these are recorded and this will be part of any decision to visit the site. These risks might be from site occupiers, who may not welcome an inspection, or the condition of the building. In addition to physical risks, the use of emails and social media need to be considered. Making comments about any colleagues or applicants in an email may lead to disciplinary action, as might any incautious use of information. These may be identified through Freedom of Information requests in the public sector.

Identifying risk

There are various points at which risk can be identified and assessed and these vary in different operational circumstances. Risk identification may be based on past experience or legislative compliance, and may be carried out by the project owners at the request of funders. Once identified, the risks are assessed according to the dangers they pose and the likelihood of their occurrence. While risk assessment processes are essential in built projects, they are less common in plan or policy making.

Risk levels and potential mitigations measures are commonly presented in tabular format. This information is then used to re-evaluate the project. These risk levels are included within a table which includes potential risk mitigation following which the risks are re-evaluated.

Joint risk assessment may be required at critical stages of the project's delivery where processes overlap. The project manager has responsibility for reviewing risk and reporting regularly to the project board. A project may be structured so that each interim stage requires approval before continuing, and failure to do this also constitutes a risk.

Some risks are difficult to assess but are considered as part of the risk assessment process. There are three types of risk in this category. The first type is defined by Popper's theory of falsifiability (1959), where one occurrence cannot guarantee a second. This may include first-time floods, or building or infrastructure failure. Popper's theory can be developed into theories and practices of unintended consequences whereby a combination of materials or circumstances may lead to an unpredictable outcome. Alternative scenarios and tests may be developed to identify these potential unintended consequences but this is not always possible. Organisations may respond to this by incentivising some actions through performance measures, leading to others being effectively reduced in importance. Margetts and colleagues (2010) explored some of the unintended consequences of policies in the public sector, although they found no 'law' of unintended consequences that may be applied universally.

'Unknown unknowns' (Rumsfeld, 2011) constitute the second type of ill-defined risk – namely, the notion that any activity, building or policy can be put at risk by something that has never been considered – a new factor. In these cases, risk may occur through a catastrophe or rupture (Zeeman, 1977). This may be enough to change expectations and behaviours, but in some cases these unknown unknowns go unrecognised for some time. However, according to the third type of risk, set out in the Kuhnian paradigm (Kuhn, 1962), there comes a point when their existence and effects must be recognised and taken into account.

Coping with risk

Risk 'aversion'

While many risks are tangible and easily identified, there may be other, more abstract, risks inherent in an organisation's culture. An organisation may be risk averse, for example, meaning that it does not welcome change and would prefer to let others take risks and bear the associated costs. Risk aversion may be found both in organisations that perform well and those that perform poorly (Hu et al, 2011).

Risk ownership

Risk ownership involves identifying the individual or individuals charged with demonstrating the fulfilment of risk assessment procedures, determining how risk will be managed and mitigated, and taking final responsibility for any risks incurred.

Managing risk

One of the key means of mitigating risk is through communication and working practices such as fire safety evacuation procedures, accident recording and examination of the kinds of problem that have occurred in other similar organisations.

Risk governance

Governance structures around managing risk are as important as identifying and mitigating risk. Risk governance may cover anything from fire risk management to energy availability and the management of natural resources. In some sectors, for example farming and retail, weather conditions may inform risk governance procedures. Many organisations establish compliance regimes for managing statutory risk assessment. The way in which risk governance operates depends on the culture of the organisation and the nature of its business. Renn (2008) has identified some key components that need to be considered in risk governance – the organisation's capacity, its political and regulatory culture, the actor network within the organisation and the social climate for risk – although he identifies the first two as being the most important.

Organisations may be responsible for managing risk in relation to individuals outside the immediate institution, for example, emergency services personnel. Emergency planning and disaster management procedures are also required for unexpected events such as flooding, transport disasters or outbreaks of contagious diseases. Organisations may be insufficiently aware of certain types of risk or may prioritise some risks over others. For example, in recent widely reported cases in some hospital trusts, hospital managers have been found to endanger the lives of patients rather than risk losing funding by failing to achieve performance targets (DH, 2010). Many such cases have been brought to light by whistleblowers. The endemic culture in the UK of disregarding whistleblowers, however, often results in their vilification.

Risk transfer

Risk transfer is a risk management strategy in which risk is shifted to an insurer by means of an insurance policy. Another form of risk transfer involves contracting out activities such as IT provision, or the management of a failing service to other organisations. Some organisations enter 'risk and reward' contracts with other institutions where the contractor takes on a larger portion of risk but receives a higher return as a consequence.

Risk acceptance

Organisations may accept residual or uninsurable risks. They may also be more willing to accept risk in cases where the overall outcome of a project is expected to be particularly beneficial. Here risk can also be managed and mitigated through training and communication.

Resilience in planning

The way in which risk is managed within an organisation or locality may be indicative of the organisation's resilience – that is, its capacity to absorb disruption or major threats and continue to function. The concept of resilience has grown to encompass multiple and conflicting meanings (Reid and Botterill, 2013). The term was initially used in psychology to mean the capacity to recover quickly from difficulties or shocks. In planning, resilience is frequently used in relation to environmental events such as flooding or earthquakes, or in social terms, in the context of anti-social activities such as terror attacks (Davoudi, 2012). Resilience is also used to describe an organisation's ability to absorb change. Berkes and colleagues (2003, p20) argue that 'crises can actually play a constructive role in resource management, forcing organisations to consider issues of learning, adapting and renewal'.

Resilience can be difficult to define in terms of how it affects individuals, communities or organisations. As Coaffee and Rogers (2008) demonstrate, it is easier for organisations to consider resilience in general terms than to apply it to existing practices or disaster management situations. Strengthening resilience incorporates a range of activities including the location and design of potentially hazardous sites such as power stations and airports, as well as less risky facilities within densely developed areas such as sport and entertainment venues and energy storage amenities. Such facilities must be designed to be efficient, but easily accessible and manageable in the case of an accident. In the case of major incidents such as serious transport accidents or terrorist attacks, responding organisations will need to rely on robust emergency planning and disaster management procedures. These include site management, traffic re-routing, liaison with health providers and the provision of temporary accommodation and facilities.

Many emergency scenarios will be rehearsed in advance. Local authority flood plans, for example, will involve identifying emergency accommodation such as schools and other community facilities, providing food, clothing and bedding, and co-ordinating volunteers. A major disaster can be a defining event whose legacy is difficult to shift. Coaffee and Rogers (2008) use the example of Manchester and its efforts to redefine itself for the 2002 Commonwealth Games following a bomb attack in the city centre in 1996.

A key consideration for governments and organisations is who is responsible for resilience planning? Is it an issue that is managed in the wider public sphere or is it a matter of personal responsibility? Zebrowski (2013) argues that the notion of developing resilient populations has become part of a neoliberal agenda for shifting responsibility from the state to the individual. This gives rise to the question of how far resilience is an additional or specific activity or how far it is part of the main task.

Many aspects of resilience are governed by legislation. In construction, safety compliance is managed through choice of building materials, design and means of escape. Development sites on fault lines or on land liable to flooding must comply with the safety requirements of the relevant EU environmental directives, and retrospective design measures may apply if new uses such as energy extraction emerge. These precautionary measures may require revision where there are first-time floods or new energy opportunities may emerge such as fracking. Whilst existing safety design measures may be adequate, these new phenomena may need new and more experimental approaches.

Too much regulation?

The two main drivers for regulation in the UK are the application of EU legislation relating to the environment, transport and trade as part of the Single European Market (Morphet, 2013); and the creation of new legislation addressing issues of social and public concern such as the Dangerous Dogs Act 1997 and regulations protecting vulnerable children and adults.

The volume of regulation is increasing, with governments and trade organisations becoming more and more concerned about the burden it places on business in particular. Successive reviews of regulatory regimes include the Hampton review of regulatory and inspection enforcement in 2004, which was followed by initiatives to ease the burden of existing legislation such as the Red Tape Challenge and the Better Regulation Task Force. The EU has also reviewed its approach to regulation (Monti, 2010) and has agreed to prioritise is effect on business when considering new legislation.

There are a number of ways to reduce the burden of regulation. The first is to abolish it completely. This happens on occasion, but it is more common for governments to reduce the number of regulatory returns and inspections required. Regulatory returns are prepared for regulators, essentially for supervisory purposes and may differ from returns prepared for internal use or shareholders. Another approach may be to move from a mix of self-regulation and external inspection to full self-regulation, although this could lead to concerns about accountability.

Many organisations are beginning to streamline regulatory processes, undertaking regulatory returns and inspections annually rather than at different stages throughout the year. There have been proposals for establishing Local Better Regulation Offices to foster a greater understanding between local authority regulatory services and the businesses they monitor. In planning, there have been calls for more collaboration between regulators at each stage of the process, particularly at the pre-application and consultation stages.

Discussion Box: **Risk evaluation and management**
- What are the key ways in which planning supports risk mitigation?
- What are the differences between risk assessment and EIA?
- Can risk ever be accepted?
- Should plans have risk assessments and if so what should they contain?
- How do you advise a client on risk?

The role of audit

All organisations must undergo financial audit – an independent, third-party examination of an institution's financial records and reporting activities – and this constitutes one aspect of risk management. This provides verification of records, processes or functions by those independent from the institution. The specific objectives of audit are shown in Box 9.1.

What happens if things go wrong?

Regulation notwithstanding, risk management is not totally foolproof. Accidents happen and in the event of damage, injury or loss of life, organisations may be sued for damages by those affected, including employees and visitors. Furthermore, those responsible for designing or approving a building or process may be sued for professional negligence. All workplace accidents in the UK are reviewed by the Health and Safety Executive (HSE) and other relevant specialist regulatory bodies, for example, in incidents involving fire, chemicals and major transport infrastructure. These regulators identify the causes of the accident and use their findings to develop prevention measures. In some cases, this will lead to a change in national or international legislation.

BOX 9.1: United Nations definition of the role of audit

- To independently identify information which is essential to develop an overall picture of the institution/local authority.
- To identify any weaknesses or administrative flows which otherwise would not be identified due to unwillingness or inability by insiders of the institutions.
- To identify strengths and weaknesses of the administrative structures in order to inform decisions on overall strengthening of the institution.
- To provide baselines on which reforms can be assessed.
- To provide the government (other governing bodies) and general public with credible information that result in public faith or trust of the institution and/or pressure for any reforms to address problems identified.

Source: Based on NAO (2015)

Risks in the workplace: the case of planning

All workplaces have risks. In planning, some of these risks are associated with proposed buildings and development sites. A procedure for examining risks and hazards in the workplace is set out in Box 9.2.

Discussion Box: **Managing personal risk**

- Is it important to take responsibility for personal safety?
- What responsibilities do you have for the safety of others?
- What risks might there be on a planning site visit?
- How can you prepare for managing personal safety?

Conclusions

Responsibilities for sustainability and risk management are key features of any leader and manager's role. They may not be explicit in the organisation of any organisation but they are an essential feature of daily practices and periodically need to be examined in a more transparent and focused way. Events and practices may suggest specific reviews and monitoring of specific events and the outcomes of internal decision-making also require reviews. Those leading and managing in planning need to ensure that sustainability and risk management are central components of an effective organisation.

BOX 9.2: Identifying hazards in the workplace

Step 1: Identify the hazards

In general

- Things around workplace e.g. slips and trips – cables, equipment, chemicals
- Operational practices, times of working etc
- Longer term hazards e.g. pollution, dust, asbestos in building

- Identify what has gone wrong before
- Have external check and review

Identifying the hazards in planning

Site visits

- personal attacks – guns, dogs, water hoses
- building conditions e.g. falling through floors, asbestos

Step 2: Decide who might be harmed and how

- Need to identify who might be harmed by each hazard
- Are some people more vulnerable at certain times e.g. during pregnancy
- Are some people visitors to the offices – do they know means of escape?

Step 3: Evaluate the risks and decide on precautions

- Need to do what is reasonably practicable
- Can you remove hazard altogether?
- Take out employer liability insurance – legal requirement for all companies
- Can you control the risk e.g. on site visits
    - go in twos
    - issue panic alarms
    - go with site supervisor
    - wear safety clothing e.g. boots, goggles
    - undertake health and safety training

Step 4: Record your findings and implement them

- Provides means of sharing information and adding comments
- Provides an action plan
- Can show employees that their health and safety is being considered
- Can be the basis of regular checks

Step 5: Review risk assessment and update as necessary

- Review regularly
- Keep an accident book (legal requirement) and review action plan after each entry to see if this could be avoided in the future
- Keep first aid kit near accident book
- First aiders
- Means of escape – keep clear

Source: Based on HSE advice on risk asseaament http://www.hse.gov.uk/risk/index.htm

TEN

Personal management in planning

Introduction

Planning is funded by civil society to regulate land use and support public investment within sustainable objectives. Planning provides an institutional framework and operational certainty for private sector investment. Planners are engaged in delivering the planning system. They occupy a number of roles that are primarily advisory rather than executive in nature. Planners certified by the Royal Town Planning Institute (RTPI) are bound by a code of professional conduct, which applies to members' professional activities and requires them to act with integrity and competence. Planners' professional status is defined by a Royal Charter in the UK (RTPI, 2012). Planners who do not adhere to the code may face disciplinary action. At worst, a planner may lose their membership and with it the designation 'chartered' town planner. Behaviour outside this code may be challenged and, in the worst case, professional planners may be removed from the membership of the professional body and, in the UK, lose the right to use the descriptor of a 'chartered' town planner.

Planners may have obligations to their employer, but does membership of a professional body confer an autonomous duty to society and to the practices of sustainability? RTPI members are required to undergo continuous professional development (CPD) to keep their skills up to date with changes in planning practice.

Planners operate within a political environment and for those directly employed in the public sector; this may give rise to pressures and tensions (Stocker and Thompson-Fawcett, 2014). Some commentators, like Kitchen (2007), have written extensively about this, while Kaiserman and colleagues (Ankers et al, 2010) created an imaginary and farcical local authority through which to explore the pressures of the public sector planner's role.

Self-management includes practical issues such as monitoring time-keeping, absenteeism and standards of work, and complying with confidentiality requirements. It also includes maintaining 360-degree relationships with colleagues, managers and clients. Some professionals may have personal ethical priorities, around the environment or social justice, for example, and work within organisations that are supportive of their views. Others may choose to work in a particular type of organisation in the public, private or voluntary sectors. Some professionals remain generalists, while others specialise in certain aspects of planning or professional practice and develop their career accordingly. Some professionals become managers of either specialist or wider functions.

Ethics in planning

The ethics of public policy are full of dilemmas, particularly for planners (Healey, 2010). Is it more important to preserve the environment than to create jobs (Rydin, 2011)? Is the provision of housing more important than saving local heritage buildings? How are strategic objectives identified within plan making or development decisions? Who is privileged or excluded as a result of these processes? Planning is about advising those who make decisions but this does not mean that planners sit on the fence. The nature of planning is that each case, albeit subject to wider policy and evidence-based considerations, is judged on its own merits, and planners always make a recommendation, no matter how difficult this might be.

Do such decisions require ethical judgement, however, or are they an integral part of professional practice? Would an ethical dilemma involve a situation where privileged information surrounding a decision is being kept out of the public domain? Such questions arise less frequently now that the Freedom of Information Act 2000 gives citizens right of access to information held by public authorities.

Bickenbach and Hendler (1994) argue that the process of weighing up evidence and policy in specific situations is what makes planning a profession. Further, it is this integrative and evaluative role that defines planners (Stead and Meijers, 2010) acting as boundary spanners (Williams 2002). Despite these tensions, society still depends on the planning system to create value and to deliver other social, environmental and economic goods. Professional are expected to uphold agreed ethical standards and adhere to a code of conduct, and a failure to do so may result in a charge of misconduct or loss of professional status. Ethical standards and codes of conduct are complementary but different, as Hendler (1991) argues, and there can be a separation between values and behaviours. Further, Hendler argues that professional codes may be ethically unsophisticated and that any aspects of a code are difficult to enforce.

In practice, planners advise their clients and it is on this basis that their ethical stance and conduct may be assessed. If a planner has a concern about a client, they may be able to refuse to undertake the instruction. This may be more difficult when the planner is an employee and there is a potential conflict between the planner's professional opinion and their duty to their employer. In these cases, there is no easy resolution, although the employer may provide some sympathetic management or additional information to help clarify a contentious situation.

Planning is a distributional activity and this is a key feature of its location within democratic frameworks and transparent processes. Campbell (2012) argues that the ethical dimension of planning has become more disaggregated as there is less common agreement on the role of planning. This may be because the ethical dimension was more commonly associated with planning in the public sector and the growth of planners in the private sector may now have shifted the balance away from this area. However, planning remains a publicly regulated activity and this regulation is framed by public life standards.

Discussion Box: **Planning's role in society**
- Is planning a public good?
- Could society manage without a planning system?
- Should planning operate within an ethical framework?

Professionalism

The nature of professionalism

Professionalism has grown since 1945 and has become the backbone of the service economy; its key concerns are shown in Box 10.1. Halmos (1970) argues that professionalism based on a Durkheimian personal service ethic has been important and has influenced professionalism with a moral purpose. In some cases, this has led to professionals taking moral control of agendas. However, against this there are arguments in favour of consumer and community-based determination of priorities for services and decision making that has partly been embodied in the concept of localism.

BOX 10.1: What is the nature of professionalism?

Professionals have power over the issues to be considered for attention:

1. what constitutes a 'problem' (definition);
2. what to do about a problem (goal setting);
3. how to do it (implementation);
4. how to evaluate what has been done (evaluation).

Source: Heraud (1979, p 8)

While the professional role is seen to have some positive features, it is also subject to a number of criticisms. In some cases, there is tendency for the professional to 'know best' what to do in a certain situation and this can discourage wider public debate on an issue. There may also be a sense of imbalance between the technical and professional competence of the decision maker. The decision maker will defer to the professional adviser on the grounds that they know best and are more competent to assess the issues associated with the decision. Anti-professional argument also suggests that professionals create institutions that reinforce their own status by 'cognitive exclusiveness over their professional expertise' (Bickenbach and Hendler, 1994, p 163). They can be accused of developing processes that have bureaucratic efficiency but are not tailored towards individual needs (Noordegraaf, 2013).

In this way, professionals come to hold positions of power in society – they are difficult to challenge and they separate themselves from others through their use of language, jargon and specific techniques that exclude others from the debate (Johnson, 1972; Hudson, 1978). This can create control through language within which these debates take place. Professionals may have their own agendas and only focus on those issues that they consider to be important. They are also viewed as being part of the establishment and more likely to support vested interests than wider community outcomes. This assumes that professionals are from higher social classes and that there is a class bias in their advice and practice.

The opposite of professionalisation is personalisation, where the consumer or user of the service creates the method of delivery that suits them best. In medicine, this manifests itself in the role of the expert patient, and in communities, individuals and groups may become very knowledgeable about aspects of the law and practice that are pertinent to their own situations. However, these debates are still framed by professional knowledge.

Discussion Box: **Professionalism**
- What powers do professionals have?
- What are the issues for professionals employed in public sector organisations?
- What are the likely tensions for a professional in the private sector?
- Can professionals ever offer independent advice?
- What happens if professional advice is ignored?

Planners as professionals

Planners offer independent advice to clients, however defined. In the public sector, this advice is transparent, while in the private sector it is confidential. In the third sector, levels of transparency are determined by the situation.

Planners gain professional status through education and supervised practical experience. Once qualified, planners are expected to keep up to date with current legislation and practice (Dubin, 1971). This is frequently translated into a more formal requirement to undertake a specific number of hours of CPD. Once appointed, a professional has a responsibility to promote the best interests of their clients within the context of professional standards and codes of conduct. Planners cannot provide advice outside these boundaries without compromising their professionalism. In addition to observing professional codes, planners will be expected to have professional indemnity insurance.

The public sector

Planning professionals work in a variety of settings and across all sectors. The challenges to planners vary in each sector and with the type of client. Planners working in the public sector may be uncertain about their 'client' – is it the employing organisation, the politicians who make the decisions or the community or environment? Vigar (2012, p 369) argues that there is a 'shrinking judgement space' for planners, particularly in the public sector. However, this judgement space may be similar to that of planners in the private sector where the client role is more clearly identified. In the reforms in local government in England in 2000 (Morphet, 2008), the split between the role of executive councillors and the rest of the councillors has provided more clarity and accountability in decision making.

While local politicians made decisions before the 2000 Local Government Act reforms on planning applications, the separation between the promotion of schemes by the executive and the quasi-judicial process for determining planning applications by non-executive members has resulted in the client role being identified more clearly. Further, the increase in delegated planning applications as a proportion of the whole has meant that the quasi-judicial process is used for much larger and important applications only and this again has separated the role of councillors from that of planning officers. As a consequence, the role of the planner in the public sector has not changed but has become more separate in its advisory role and the blurring of actions between councillors and planners has reduced.

Another approach to professionalism that has been proposed is collaboration where there is a partnership between the professionals and the community in an ongoing process (Heraud, 1979; Healey, 1997). Partnership may be a useful method of working where there is common ground on the objectives and there is a need to work through policy and delivery issues. However, McClymont (2014) argues that this is a process of decision making. The planner's professional role shifts when they are called on to provide advice on decisions to be made. Preparing for a decision in a collaborative and communicative way cannot remove the underlying (professional) responsibility of the planner in advising on the planning decision. Reasoned value or situated judgements are attempts at introducing transparency but they will inevitably include some weighting towards perceived societal, professional and/or localised objectives and goals. Each piece of advice will inevitably be framed (Goffman, 1974; Morphet, 2013). There is no dispute that planning has a major impact on people's lives (McClymont, 2014). What is less evident is the precise role of the planner in advising on discussions and framing decisions within a quasi-judicial framework set within a political context.

The private sector

Many planners work in a consultancy capacity where they are hired to undertake a specific instruction by a client. They may undertake multiple projects concurrently. This mode of professional working operates primarily in the private and voluntary sectors. In some cases, a multiple portfolio of clients and projects may lead to a conflict of interest for the planner. They may find that they have been asked to support a case for two opposing clients. In these situations, planners may operate a 'Chinese walls' approach, where two different parts of the company advise clients. There may be conflicts of interest for politicians with business or family connections with the private sector involved in decision making in planning applications. The standards of conduct for public life (Nolan, 1995) require all those engaged in making decisions and providing advice to declare their interests, whether real or perceived. This includes the interests of the individual and in the case of a conflict of interest, they must withdraw from that issue. Some planners work within organisations where planning is a contributory component of the organisation's activities but not its main focus. In these cases, the independence of professional planning advice may come under pressure from wider organisational interests.

Implementation

The link between the professionalism of planners and the implementation role of planning has been explored by Vigar (2012) and Hillier (2002), who argue that planners spend too much time on processes and not enough on the outcomes. The approach to constructing problems and how to deal with them through plans has been described as fantasy by Gunder (2014). He argues that the process of planning is normative and accompanied by an overt fantasy that plans are prepared with the tacit understanding that they are not real, and therefore could not be implemented. Plans are made to identify locations for investment and while their implementation has been a traditional professional planning role it is now more frequently undertaken by others. Plans identify the quantum of development needed and the locations best suited to sustainable delivery but all plans are open to investor challenge through the planning system.

Planning's role as a public good: the skills debate

The planning process is constructed as a public good throughout its operation. Planning applications demonstrate the contribution they are making to society through the provision of facilities, design, access and amenity. The notion of public good being embedded in the planning process is taken for granted, but a key tension is whether this should be the prime motivation of planners employed in the private and third sectors (Anderson and Pederson, 2012). This tension is particularly apparent where planning negotiations are focused on a development and its associated benefits. Even where the development involves the extension of a single house, planners will address issues such as townscape, design and choice of construction materials from the perspective of the public good.

While there is continual public debate about the role of planning and the costs that it places on development (Barker, 2004, 2006; HM Treasury, 2014), planning performs a number of roles for society and the country's economy. There has also been a parallel debate about the skills of planners and whether they are fit for purpose. Bickenbach and Hendler (1994) question whether planning has a moral mandate. Whilst recognising that planning has a distinct contribution to the public good, they also understand that planners work with others in larger organisations that have other objectives.

Discussions about skills reflect the changing importance that society has placed on planning during its evolution. The gap between planning education and the skills required for planning practice has frequently been criticised, although there is little evidence to support this criticism (Turok and Taylor, 2006). In the 1960s and 1970s, planners were criticised for a failure to work with communities and deliver effective change through consultation (Skeffington Committee, 1969). Planners were recognised as having a central role in understanding the redistributive effects of planning, and Eversley (1973) argued that this should be transparent. On the other hand, planners were credited with skills for strategic planning, introducing models and long-term forecasting for changes in population and growth (McLoughlin 1969; Lee, 1973).

In 1986, there was pressure from Margaret Thatcher's conservative government to abolish the planning system. This was met with opposition, however, from property developers, and those with financial and wider corporate interests. They argued that planning provided a consistent framework, which, despite criticisms, provided certainty in the operation and use of land and buildings and the application of locational determinants. The planning system was regarded as being open, maintaining value and promoting development.

This reinforcement of the planning system led to a consideration of the skills needed though the Nuffield report (1987). This emphasised an approach focused on development, and the Royal Town Planning Institute subsequently adopted as a priority the impetus to 'get things done'. In the 1990s, planning took an environmental turn, providing a means of using land efficiently and managing scarce resources (Rydin, 2011). By supporting specific developments in certain locations, planning promotes the sustainable use of infrastructure and land, enabling efficient access to places of work, public services, and cultural and shopping facilities.

The government continued to express concern over a perceived planning skills gap, which it saw as a barrier to achieving integrated development, improved design of schemes and being part of the development team (Egan, 2004). This concern was associated with both the establishment in 2004 of the Planning Advisory Service, a peer-supported improvement programme funded by central government but run by local government, and a skills competency framework for planners (PAS, 2013a). In their research for the Local Government Association on the so-called skills gap, Durning and Glasson (2006) found insufficient numbers of planners but little evidence of a lack of skills.

> Skills gaps (defined in this study as where the existing workforce has lower skill levels than necessary to meet organisational objectives) overall appeared to be less significant and the effect on service provision of these gaps was generally neutral (p 476).

A key question in this debate is whether the skills issue is one of personal development, initial professional education or employer responsibility. Moreover, with the debate focused primarily on the public sector, does it extend to the private and voluntary sectors? There has been considerable interest in encouraging all those engaged in place making to undergo skills training, although it is difficult to do this with volunteers and communities (Thomas and Littlewood, 2010; Farrell,

2014), although it is more difficult to require training and skills development in volunteers and communities.

> Discussion Box: **Planning skills**
> ▪ Is it possible to teach all the skills required for planning in initial professional education?
> ▪ Who should define the skills that planners need?
> ▪ Do the skills that planners use change over time?
> ▪ Should the government or the professional body determine the skills required in planning?

Planners' culture

Much of the debate about planning skills has been associated with the need for 'culture change' (Vigar et al, 2000; Shaw, 2006; Shaw and Lord, 2009). Inch (2010, p 360) argues that the skills gap is linked to 'identity regulation', suggesting that the prevailing planning culture inhibits the acquisition of new skills and the willingness to respond to change. What is unclear, however, is what constitutes planning culture, and, if such a culture exists, whether it is a unified concept among planners.

A common culture in a group implies shared values and objectives, as well as some binding norms generally created though a process of socialisation. This process may typically occur through professional planning education, carried by the ethos of the planning school (Thomas, 2012) where shared teaching and group work reinforces a certain perspective on problems, the use of a range of analytical tools and a means of using these to frame judgements. This may be developed in education and in practice (Durning et al, 2010).

Planners may appear to have a common culture in their approach to analysis and problem solving, but beyond this there may be differences. Managing process and projects, development management and plan making all embody different cultural practices, differences and misunderstandings. There are also different cultures in the private and public sectors, and between planning practitioners and academics (Campbell, 2014; Durning, 2004).

Calls for 'culture change' among all users of planning systems have become increasingly common in recent years. These have typically accompanied attempts to reform planning systems that have been viewed as incapable of realising the goals sought by central government policymakers. The idea of culture change has been embraced not just by governments seeking to manage reform, but also by a wide range of different user groups, including professional associations. In both Scotland and England, the notion of culture change has gained widespread support among different stakeholders. It has become a shorthand descriptor for the change in attitudes and practices that is required to realise the promises of planning reform.

In England, the culture change agenda was accompanied by the establishment of a specific team in central government and budgets funded from two Comprehensive Spending Reviews (2004 and 2007), which were aimed at encouraging changing practice alongside the introduction of a new spatial planning system. This approach was also accompanied by a pan-government Public Sector Agreement (PSA) target in 2007. This initiative was also supported by a 'personality' review led by Sir John Egan (2004). All of this appears to have led to little change, with local authorities using incentive funds to achieve planning application determination targets, purchase IT systems or employ staff on short-term contracts. It appears that little of the resource provided was used to introduce the spatial planning system.

Academic research has begun to examine the idea of culture change, tracing its roots from within the human relations school of management into the management of public sector reform initiatives (Clarke and Newman, 1997; du Gay, 2000). In planning, this has shown that culture change is regarded as a necessary process of change in the attitudes, skills and understanding of the system's users – the 'soft infrastructure' that gives meaning to the formal institutions of planning systems (Nadin and Stead, 2008; Shaw and Lord, 2009; Inch, 2010; Morphet, 2011b).

There is, however, a need to critically assess the idea of culture change and of culture governance more broadly (Bang, 2004), understanding it as a mechanism of coercive policy transfer (Dolowitz and Marsh, 1996) and a desire to manipulate actors' understanding of planning. This discourse is founded on the view that the existing culture of planning practitioners, particularly in local authorities, is a problem and in need of substantial change. Less attention has been paid to the role of national and local politicians, applicants and private sector planners. Implicit in this are images and understandings of what represents both good and bad planning. Indeed, given the tendency for the goals of planning reform initiatives to proliferate, there is a danger (and likelihood) that culture change may mean different things to different groups that have divergent understandings of what planning should seek to achieve. Despite this, however, the question of what culture change entails has rarely been explicitly debated.

Taken in these broad terms, however, it is incumbent on any group with an interest in a particular type of planning to advocate the culture within which planning goals might be achieved. Understood in this light, culture change becomes an important opportunity for organisations and individuals to reflect on the meaning and purpose of planning. Culture change may therefore be seen as an ongoing practice of interpreting and adapting to change, even in the absence of formal governmental initiatives.

Professional cultures also provide a strong context for action and deliberation. Gouldner (1957) identified two types of professionals – locals and cosmopolitans. Locals take as their reference the prevailing culture of the organisation that they are working in – the culture of 'going along to get along'. Cosmopolitans take a more outward-facing view, that external is always best. In practice, a mixture of both outlooks is important. In many organisations, the chief executive and their deputy will each take one of these roles – inward- or outward-facing. There can also be policy networks within professional organisations. Moreover, the implementation of new government guidance in local authorities may be influenced by existing respected policy networks among professionals or specialists.

The culture of the herd becomes important as a point of protection but may also lead to inappropriate action if guidelines are mis-interpreted. This method is sometimes known as 'phone a friend'.

On the other hand, planning culture may also be used as an excuse (Stead and Nadin, 2009) for rejecting top-down government reforms. As Davy (2013, p 222) states:

> Planners often ignore that their choices are the consequence of earlier decisions and will have consequences for situations that are neither properly anticipated nor deliberated in the planning process. Planners never operate in vacant spaces.

Discussion Box: **Culture change in planning**
- What does culture change mean to different actors in different contexts?
- What constitutes a (good) planning culture?
- How far is good planning culture related to concepts and practices of professionalism and professionalisation?
- How are conceptions of the good planning culture changed by shifts in governing ideology and governmental priorities?
- What is wrong with the existing culture of planning that means it needs to change?
- Who are the agents of culture change?
- What kind of attitudes/skills/knowledge are required to realise different types of culture change?
- How can effective culture change be realised? What are the tools and techniques of effective culture change?
- How effective is culture change in implementing planning reform?

Planning: who is the client?

One of the key issues in planning is the need to identify the client and to distinguish between different types of client in the public and private sectors. If there is a defined client, is the planner's role as a contractor, providing professional services, including advice and judgement, to the clients who make the decisions? The contractor could be the planning officer employed in a local authority or other public organisation, or a professional employed in a private or third sector organisation. In each case, the options for client identification have some similarities and differences.

Before identifying the clients in any situation, it is important to establish the range of roles that the client will hold. One definition of a client is the individual responsible for owning the solution, whether on behalf of themselves or the organisation they represent as a direct employee or as a consultant. The client's role is also to be accountable for the solution, either directly or as an intermediary. Where specialist consultants are used to undertake specific assessments or quality assurance, the lead contractor acts as the client for the work and is accountable for its quality and acceptance.

The roles and responsibilities of clients vary in each sector. In the public sector, the client for planning is the wider community that the local authority or agency serves. Here, democratically elected politicians identify priorities within a framework set by government legislation and policy. As each community differs by geography and prevailing priorities, so the responses to evidence through policy, regulatory decision making and implementation will also differ.

Clients receive their planning mandate indirectly through the electorate, with citizens effectively exercising choice over local and national objectives and priorities through the way they vote. In this way, politicians and local authority professionals act as proxy clients, interpreting and representing the views of the community (Alford, 2002). There are other considerations in the public sector, however, including the wider environment and sustainable legacy. These are long-term considerations beyond the reach of regular electoral cycles. Where planners work in large public sector organisations, the client group may comprise individuals within the organisation itself, such as managers or intermediaries responsible for the institutions wider requirements. In addition, a planner may regard their immediate line manager as their client.

In the private sector, the client will be whoever has instructed the contractors and the client will provide the brief. In this case, it is the planner's role to advise the client about how best to achieve their instructions and to identify potential difficulties. The client may be a developer, a land owner, a company, an individual, a community group or a public authority. Where the client is a company, the shareholders may be the ultimate client in the same way as the electorate or community in a local authority area, and the client will be acting on their behalf and interpreting and inter-mediating their priorities. In the third sector, the client is the organisation that has contracted the work. Here, the client presents its aims and objectives, which may involve people, places or wider social redistribution (Flyvbjerg, 2002).

Clients in the private and third sectors differ from those in the public sector in that they may not have any wider planning objectives beyond the immediate priorities they have identified. The development stage of a planning scheme, however, provides an opportunity for clients in all sectors to consider wider societal and environmental objectives. It may be that these wider objectives can be incorporated at no additional cost and to the benefit of the scheme itself.

By dint of their professional expertise, planners in the public sector may consider themselves capable of acting as the client. They may take the view that they are skilled in identifying what is important in any area or development and have the ability to determine the best outcome for the locality or the community. This is an understandable position, but may not reflect the reality of democratic decision making and the distribution of responsibility and power. However, as we shall see in the next section, the way in which analysis and assessment are undertaken to support decisions is a critically important process.

Professional advice and decision making

Providing advice to the client is the core activity in planning. The ability to evaluate all the elements and provide a balanced opinion is a critical element in this process. But how transparent is this advice, and to what extent is it influenced by past decisions, organisational culture and available time? Planners are required to have up-to-date knowledge of legislation and relevant legal judgements, as well as professional experience in their field. The consequences of any advice they give will have redistribution effects for over 60 years, which is the expected lifespan of any building.

As planners gain professional experience and are exposed to more complex decision making and a wider variety of situations, their knowledge and skills grow. Planners may also change sectors and interact with different clients in different ways. As Durning and colleagues (2010) have demonstrated, there are different stages in an individual's development, from novice, to expert novice, to novice expert and finally to expert.

Rule-based judgement

Rule-based judgement is characterised by the application of known rules – either legislation or legal judgements – measuring the client's proposals against these rules, and making a decision based on the projected outcome. A degree of interpretation will be involved as each case will be different, but clients may contest the outcome or push the rules to their limit in order to maximise the potential of their scheme. These rules are externalised and can be contested in their application, whilst any client might wish to attempt to push the boundary of existing rules and test whether any further changes can be made. Rule-based judgements are generally at the core of the development management process for assessing applications, and practice shows that these rules and their application are subject to interpretation, weighting and negotiation.

There is more variation in the application of rule-based judgements than is generally accepted to be the case, and such variations may be apparent between different local authorities or, at the national level, between planning inspectors. All planners use paradigms for decision making and these will be based on past experience, institutional cultures and personal values.

Evidence

Evidence is a central feature in the provision of planning advice. It has the virtue of being transparent and this means that it can be tested in public debates and legal settings. Evidence should be seen to be rigorous and collected in an unbiased way.

All evidence is likely to contain some bias, however. This is because, first, it is generally only collected where it is easy to do so. Firstly, evidence is generally only collected where it is easier to do so and may only measure the measurable.

Evidence relies on the right questions being asked. Second, some evidence, for example, that demonstrating economic growth or environmental considerations, may be given more weight than, say, evidence from the local community. Evidence collection also relies on the appropriate use of methodologies and the amount of funding available to undertake evidence studies. Lastly, it is vital that evidence is presented, however unequivocal, for example evidence of the consequences of building housing on a flood plain.

Community preferences

The collection of information on community preferences is generally viewed as being less rigorous and scientific than other evidence collection. This is because it is harder for individuals accurately to assess the impact of a future development than to evaluate past experience. In planning, community preference information – that is, residents' views about what they would like from a proposed new development – is collected in a variety of ways, including through surveys, discussion or focus groups, public meetings and online consultation. Even when presented with the wider benefits of a proposed development, communities may want to retain the status quo.

Community preference evidence only represents the views of those consulted. The area for decision involvement may be too narrow for the comments that the community may wish to make and some people may be excluded from the process altogether. Further, the views of the community may be discounted if there are concerns about the validity of the evidence collected. There are, however, more formal ways for residents to voice their opinions, for example, through neighbourhood and community plans, which may be made under the Localism Act 2011.

Political considerations

How far should political considerations be taken into account when a professional planner advises a client? Planners are not permitted to lobby decision makers, although they may seek support from politicians who are not involved in the decision-making process. Politicians are democratically accountable and represent the views of their electorate. Any planning decisions they make are in the public domain and are open to legal challenge. On planning matters, politicians may take a different view on a development compared with their political group. Planning decisions taken by politicians are in the public domain and open to legal challenge.

Government policy

Planning advice is provided within the context of government policy, which sets national priorities and objectives in areas such as the economy, housing and the environment. These may for the economy, in response to external requirements such as the provision of housing (André, 2011b; CEC 2013) or environmental events such as flooding. National policy is also has a focus on setting national standards of delivery and there are basic tensions between this, an antidote to a post code lottery for services and localism where local priorities are paramount.

Although in theory, incoming governments are unfettered by previous decisions and are free to make new policy and legislation, there are exceptions. In planning, for example, there is pressure from developers for continuity and certainty, and there are case law precedents for some planning decisions.

When advising clients, planners may be tempted to reinforce the role of government policy in localised decision making. In reality, however, national policy is open to interpretation in local circumstances, and in each planning application local conditions and the type of development proposed will have a strong weighting. It may be convenient for local politicians to suggest that they have had no choice but to make unpopular decisions in response to government requirements. Planners may also attribute any changes in the advice they give to clients to local decision making or political issues.

Discussion Box: **The basis of planning advice**

- What influences planners when they provide advice to clients?
- How can a planner weight the different issues that inform client advice?
- Would advice provided to a public sector client be different from that provided to a private sector client?
- How can the use of evidence be challenged?

Conclusions

Applying leadership and management in planning can be supported through the use of knowledge and skills that have been discussed in this book. Planners can benefit from training, continuous professional development, mentoring and coaching in the workplace. However, planners also have to take responsibility for developing their own leadership and management practice. Recognising and learning from the leadership and management of others is important whether effective or not. Understanding what has to be achieved and why is important for day-to-day activities and considering how to approach the tasks in hand rather than just following what has gone before is also important. Existing practice may be effective but analysing why this is the case and considering if it is fit for purpose might make it better. Effective leadership and management is a quest for improvement but not about instituting change for its own sake. Finally, effective leadership includes inquisitiveness about the future in order to benefit from the change it brings.

References

Ackroyd, S., Kirkpatrick, I. and Walker, R.M. (2007) 'Public management reform in the UK and its consequences for professional organisation: a comparative analysis', *Public Administration*, vol 85, no 1, pp 9-26.

Adair, J. (1987) *Effective teambuilding,* London: Pan.

Adair, J. (2003) *Action centred leadership,* Farnham: Gower.

Adair, J. (2009) *Effective communication* (revised edition), London: Pan Books.

Adair, J. (2010) *Effective strategic leadership* (revised edition), London: Pan Books.

Adams, D. and Tiesdell, S. (2012) *Shaping places: Urban planning, design and development,* London: Routledge.

Adams, D. and Watkins, C. (2014) *The value of planning,* London: RTPI.

Addison and Associates with Arup (2006a) *Evaluation of the planning delivery grant 2005-2006,* London: DCLG.

Addison and Associates with Arup (2006b) *The private sector perspective on development control in the context of planning delivery grant 2005/6,* London: DCLG.

AGMA (Association of Greater Manchester Authorities) (2011) Greater Manchester Combined Authority Order, Manchester: AGMA.

Aigner, D.J., Hopkins, J. and Johansson, R. (2003) 'Beyond compliance: sustainable business practices and the bottom line', *American Journal of Agricultural Economics*, vol 85, no 5, pp 1126-39.

Albrechts L. (2004) 'Strategic (spatial) planning re-examined', *Environment and Planning B* vol 31 pp 743-758

Alcock, P. (2010) 'Building the Big Society: a new policy environment for the third sector in England', *Voluntary Sector Review*, vol 1, no 3, pp 379-89.

Alcock, P. and Kendall, J. (2011) 'Constituting the third sector: processes of decontestation and contention under the UK Labour governments in England', *Voluntas: International Journal of Voluntary and Nonprofit Organizations*, vol 22 no 3, pp 450-469.

Alexander, S. (nd) *A revolution in planning*, PAS: London, http://www.pas.gov.uk/documents/332612/6011533/A+Revolution+in+Planning/70d27463-ba56-4394-a4c9-0dde97ebec4d (accessed 7th February 2015).

Alford, J. (2002) 'Why do public-sector clients coproduce? Toward a contingency theory', *Administration & Society*, vol 34, no 1, pp 32-56.

Alimo-Metcalfe, B. (2010) 'An investigation of female and male constructs of leadership and empowerment', *Gender in Management: An International Journal*, vol 25, no 8, pp 640-8.

Allmendinger, P. and Haughton, G. (2012) 'Post-political spatial planning in England: a crisis of consensus?', *Transactions of the Institute of British Geographers*, vol 37, no 1, pp 89-103.

Allmendinger, P., Tewdwr-Jones, M. and Morphet, J. (2003) 'Public scrutiny, standards and the planning system: assessing professional values within a modernized local government', *Public Administration*, vol 81, no 4, pp 761-80.

Amanatidou, E., Butter, M., Carabias, V., Könnölä, T., Leis, M., Saritas, O. and van Rij, V. (2012) 'On concepts and methods in horizon scanning: lessons from initiating policy dialogues on emerging issues', *Science and Public Policy*, vol 39, no 2, pp 208-21.

Anderson, L.B. and Pederson, L.H. (2012) 'Public service motivation and professionalism', *International Journal of Public Administration*, vol 35, no 1, pp 46-57.

André, C. (2011) 'Improving the Functioning of the Housing Market in the United Kingdom', *OECD Economics Department Working Papers*, No. 867, Paris: OECD Publishing.

Andrews, R. and Boyne, G. (2010) 'Better public services', *Public Management Review*, vol 12, no 3, pp 307-21.

Andrews, R. and Entwistle, T. (2010) 'Does cross-sectoral partnership deliver? An empirical exploration of public service effectiveness, efficiency, and equity', *Journal of Public Administration Research and Theory*, vol 20, no 3, pp 679-701.

Andrews, R. and Van de Walle, S. (2013) 'New public management and citizens' perceptions of local service efficiency, responsiveness, equity and effectiveness', *Public Management Review*, vol 15, no 5, pp 762-83.

Andrews R., Boyne, G. and Walker, R.M. (2012) 'Overspending in public organizations: does strategic management matter?', *International Public Management Journal*, vol 15 no 11, pp 39-61.

Ankers, D., Kaiserman, D. and Shepley, C. (2010) *Grotton Revisited*, London: Routledge.

Ansoff, H.I. (ed) (1969) *Business strategy*, Harmondsworth: Penguin.

Aritua, B., Smith, N.J. and Bower, D. (2011) 'What risks are common to or amplified in programmes: evidence from UK public sector infrastructure schemes', *International Journal of Project Management*, vol 29, no 3, pp 303-12.

Arksey, H. and O'Malley, L. (2005) 'Scoping studies: towards a methodological framework', *International Journal of Social Research Methodology*, vol 8, no 1, pp 19-32.

Armstrong, H. (1997) Keynote address, presented at Solace conference, Belfast, June.

Arrow, K.J. and Kruz, M. (2013) *Public investment, the rate of return, and optimal fiscal policy* (vol 1), Abingdon: Routledge.

ASC (Academy for Sustainable Communities) (2007) *Mind the skills gap The skills we need for sustainable communities*, ASC: Leeds.

Asheim, B.T., Moodysson, J. and Todtling, F. (2011) 'Constructing regional advantage: towards state-of-the-art regional innovation system policies in Europe?', *European Planning Studies*, vol 19, no 7, pp 1133-9.

Ashworth, R. and Snape, S. (2004) 'An overview of scrutiny: a triumph of context over structure', *Local Government Studies*, vol 30, no 4, pp 538-56.

AUDE (2013) *Annual report 2012-2013*, Cambridge: AUDE.

Audit Commission (2006) *The planning system: Managing expectations and capacity*, London: Audit Commission.

Audit Commission (2008) *Positively charged*, London: Audit Commission.

Auerbach, A.J. (ed) (2008) *Mergers and acquisitions*, Chicago, IL: University of Chicago Press.

Ball, M. (2011) 'Planning delay and the responsiveness of English housing supply', *Urban Studies*, vol 48, no 2, pp 349-62.

Balls, E. (2003) 'Foreword', in D. Corry and G. Stoker (eds) *New localism,* London: NLGN.

Bang, H.P. (2004) 'Culture governance: Governing self-reflexive modernity', *Public Administration*, vol 82, no 1, pp 157-190.

Barca, F. (2009) *An agenda for a reformed cohesion policy*, Brussels: CEC.

Barker, K. (2004) *Review of housing supply*, London: HM Treasury.

Barker, K. (2006) *Barker review of land use planning: Interim report – analysis*, London: HM Treasury.

Barlow Report (1940) Report of the Royal Commission on the Distribution of the Industrial Population Report, London: HMSO.

Barnes, I. and Preston, J. (1985) 'The Scunthorpe enterprise zone: an example of muddled interventionism', *Public Administration*, vol 63, no 2, pp 171-81.

Baron, A. and Armstrong, M. (2007) *Human capital management achieving added value through people*, London: Kogan Page.

Barrett, S.M. (2004) 'Implementation studies: time for a revival? Personal reflections on 20 years of implementation studies', *Public Administration*, vol 82, no 2, pp 249-62.

Baunsgaard, V. and Clegg, S. (2013) '"Walls or boxes": the effects of professional identity, power and rationality on strategies for cross-functional integration', *Organization Studies*, vol 34, no 9, pp 1299–325.

Bayou, M.E., Reinstein, A. and Williams, P.F. (2011) 'To tell the truth: a discussion of issues concerning truth and ethics in accounting', *Accounting, Organizations and Society*, vol 36, no 2, pp 109-24.

BCCI (Bank of Credit and Commerce International) (2011a) *Fact sheet: The planning system cost*, London: BCCI.

BCCI (2011b) *Fact sheet: The planning system complexity*, London: BCCI.

BCCI (2011c) *Fact sheet: The planning system consistency*, London: BCCI.

Beckert, J. (1999) 'Agency, entrepreneurs and institutional change', *Organization Studies*, vol 20, no 5, pp 777-99.

Belbin, R.M. (2010) *Team roles at work*, Abingdon: Routledge.

Belbin, R.M.M. (2012) *Management teams*, Abingdon: Routledge.

Belfast City Council (2013) *Belfast City Masterplan, 2013-2020*, Belfast: Belfast City Council.

Bentley, C. (1991) *Practical prince: A guide to structured project management*, Oxford: NCC Blackwell.

Benton, M. and Russell, M. (2013) 'Assessing the impact of parliamentary oversight committees: The Select Committees in the British House of Commons', *Parliamentary Affairs*, vol 66, no 4, pp 772-97.

Berkes, F., Colding, J. and Folke, C. (eds) (2003) 'Introduction', in *Navigating social-ecological systems*, Cambridge: Cambridge University Press, pp 1-29.

Best, J. (2006) *Flavor of the month: Why smart people fall for fads*, Oakland, CA: University of California Press.

Betjeman, J. and Games, S. (2009) *Betjeman's England: Betjeman's best topographical television programmes*, Edited and introduced by Stephen Games, London: John Murray.

Bevir, M. and Trentmann, F. (2007) 'Introduction: consumption and citizenship in the new governance', in M. Bevir and F. Trentmann (eds) *Governance, citizens and consumers: Agency and resistance in contemporary politics*, Basingstoke: Palgrave Macmillan, pp 1-22.

Bickenbach, F. and Hendler, S. (1994) 'The moral mandate of the "profession" of planning', in H. Thomas (ed) *Values and planning*, Aldershot: Avebury, pp 162-77.

Bijlsma, R.M., Bots, P.W., Wolters, H.A. and Hoekstra, A.Y. (2011) 'An empirical analysis of stakeholders' influence on policy development: the role of uncertainty handling', *Ecology & Society*, vol 16, no 1 (no page numbers).

Billing, Y. (2013) 'Women managers — and male norms? A comparison of some Scandinavian organizations over time', in M. Paludi (ed) *Women and management: Global issues and promising solutions*, Westport, CT: Praeger.

Billis, D. (2010a) 'Towards a theory of hybrid organisations', in D. Billis (ed) *Hybrid organizations and the third sector: Challenges for practice, theory and policy*, Basingstoke: Palgrave Macmillan, pp 46-69.

Billis, D. (2010b) 'Revisiting the key challenges: hybridity, ownership and change', in D. Billis (ed) *Hybrid organizations and the third sector: Challenges for practice, theory and policy*, Basingstoke: Palgrave Macmillan, pp 240-62.

Billis, D. and Glennerster, H. (1998) 'Human services and the voluntary sector: towards a theory of comparative advantage', *Journal of Social Policy*, vol 27, no 1, pp 79-98.

Birchall, J. (2011) *People-centred businesses: Co-operatives, mutuals and the idea of membership*, Basingstoke: Palgrave Macmillan.

BIS (Department for Business, Innovation and Skills) (2012) *Leadership and management in the UK: The key to sustainable growth. A summary of the evidence for the value of investing in leadership and management development*, London: BIS.

BIS (2013) *Corporate responsibility: A call for views*, London: BIS.

BIS (2014) Good for Business and Society: A government response to a call for views, London: BIS.

Blainey, S.P. and Preston, J.M. (2013) 'A GIS-based appraisal framework for new local railway stations and services', *Transport Policy*, vol 25, pp 41-51.

Blair, T. (1998) *Finding the way a new vision for local government*, London: IPPR.

Blair, T. (2010) *A journey*, London: Random House.

Blanchard, M. (2014) 'Planning applications', isurv, www.isurv.com/site/scripts/documents.aspx?categoryID=118 9 (accessed 14 May 2014).

Bloom, N., Propper, C., Seiler, S. and Van Reenen, J. (2010) *The impact of competition on management quality: Evidence from public hospitals*, Discussion Paper 2010/09. London: Imperial College London Business School.

Boezeman, E.J. and Ellemers, N. (2014) 'Volunteer leadership: the role of pride and respect in organizational identification', *Leadership*, vol 10, pp 160-73.

Bolden, R. (2011) 'Distributed leadership in organizations: a review of theory and research', *International Journal of Management Reviews*, vol 13, no 3, pp 251-69.

Boltanski, L. and Chiapello, E. (2007) *The new spirit of capitalism*, London: Verso.

Bouckaert, G. and Van Dooren, W. (2009) 'Performance management and management in public sector organizations', in T. Bovaird and E. Loffler (eds) *Public management and governance*, pp 151-64, Abingdon: Routledge.

Bouckaert, G., Peters, B.G. and Verhoest, K. (2010) *The coordination of public sector organizations: Shifting patterns of public management*, Basingstoke: Palgrave Macmillan.

Bourne, L. (2011) 'Advising upwards: managing the perceptions and expectations of senior management stakeholders', *Management Decision*, vol 49, no 6, pp 1001-23.

Bovaird, T. (2012) 'Strategic management in public sector organizations', in T. Boivard and L. Loffler (eds) *Public management and governance* (2nd edn), Abingdon: Routledge, pp 61-80.

Box, G.E., Jenkins, G.M. and Reinsel, G.C. (2013) *Time series analysis: Forecasting and control*, Chichester: John Wiley & Sons.

Boxall, P. and Purcell, J. (2003) *Strategy and human resource management*, Basingstoke: Macmillan.

Boxall, P. and Purcell, J. (2011) *Strategy and human resource management*, Third Edition, Basingstoke: Palgrave Macmillan, p 1.

Boxall, P., Hutchison, A. and Wassenaar, B. (2014) 'How do high-involvement work processes influence employee outcomes? An examination of the mediating roles of skill utilisation and intrinsic motivation', *The International Journal of Human Resource Management*, http://www.tandfonline.com/doi/abs/10.1080/09585192.2014.962070 #.VNYWv_msWPs

Boxall, P., Purcell, J. and Wright, P. (2008) 'Human resource management: scope, analysis and significance', in *The Oxford handbook of human resource management*, Oxford: Oxford University Press, pp 1-18.

Boxer, R., Perren, L., and Berry, A. (2013) 'SME top management team and non-executive director cohesion: Precarious equilibrium through information asymmetry', *Journal of Small Business and Enterprise Development*, vol *20, no* 1, pp 55-79.

Boyne, G.A. and Law, J. (2005) 'Setting public service outcome targets: lessons from local public service agreements', *Public Money & Management*, vol 25, no 4, pp 253-60.

Brandsen, T. and Pestoff, V. (2006) 'Co-production, the third sector and the delivery of public services: an introduction', *Public Management Review*, vol 8, no 4, pp 493-501.

Branson, A. (2014) 'DCLG plans to toughen "special measures" criteria', *Planning Resource*, 24 March, www.planningresource.co.uk/article/1286627/dclg-plans-toughen-special-measures-criteria (accessed 15 May 2014).

Braun, S. (2012) 'Effectiveness of mission statements in organizations – a review', *Journal of Management and Organization*, vol 18, no 4, pp 430-444.

Brignall, S. and Modell, S. (2000) 'An institutional perspective on performance measurement and management in the "new public sector"', *Management Accounting Research*, vol 11, no 3, pp 281-306.

Brindley, T., Rydin, Y. and Stoker, G. (2013) *Remaking planning: The politics of urban change*, Abingdon Routledge.

Broussine, M. (2012) 'Public leadership', in T. Bovaird and E. Loffler (ed) *Public management and governance* (2nd edn), Abingdon: Routledge, pp 261-78.

Brown, A. (2014) *The myth of the strong leader: Political leadership in the modern age*, London: Random House.

Brown, S.J. and Sibley, D.S. (1986) *The theory of public utility pricing*, Cambridge: Cambridge University Press.

Brownill, S. (1990) *Developing London's Docklands: Another great planning disaster?*, London: Sage Publications.

Buchanan, C., rmjm consulting, Tewdwr-Jones, M. (2011) *A review of the extent to which the spatial planning system supports the delivery of the government's health, wellbeing and social care objectives. Final Report*, London: Department of Health.

Burgess, E., Monk, S. and Whitehead, C.M. (2010) *How can the planning system deliver more housing?*, York: Joseph Rowntree Foundation.

Burgess, G. (2014) *The nature of planning constraints: Report to the House of Commons Communities and Local Government Committee*, Cambridge: Cambridge University Press.

Butler, R. (2004) *Review of intelligence on weapons of mass destruction: Report of a Committee of Privy Councillors HC 898,* London: HMSO.

Butler, S. (2013) 'Plan A must be woven into the fabric of our brand, says new Marks and Spencer chief', *The Guardian*, 8 July, p 15.

Byrne, P., McAllister, P. and Wyatt, P. (2011) 'Precisely wrong or roughly right? An evaluation of development viability appraisal modelling', *Journal of Financial Management of Property and Construction*, vol 16, no 3, pp 249-71.

Cabinet Office (2006) *World class public services*, London: Cabinet Office.

Cabinet Office (2008) *Excellence and fairness: Achieving world class public services*, London: Cabinet Office.

Cabinet Office (2010) *Applying behavioural insight to health*, London: Cabinet Office.

Cabinet Office (2012) *Civil service reform plan*, London: Cabinet Office.

Cameron, E. and Green, M. (2012) *Making sense of change management: A complete guide to the models, tools and techniques of organizational change* (3rd edn), London: Kogan Page.

Campbell, H. (2012) '"Planning ethics" and rediscovering the idea of planning', *Planning Theory*, vol 11, no 4, pp 379-99.

Campbell, H. (2014) 'Specialists and generalists: are there too many hedgehogs and not enough foxes?', *Planning Theory & Practice*, vol 15, no 3, pp 287-290.

Campbell, H. and Marshall, R. (2000) 'Public involvement and planning: looking beyond the one to the many', *International Planning Studies*, vol 5, no 3, pp 321-44.

Carmel, E. and Harlock, J. (2008) 'Instituting the "third sector" as a governable terrain: partnership, procurement and performance in the UK', *Policy & Politics*, vol 36, no 2, pp 155-71.

Carmona, M. (2009) 'The Isle of Dogs: four development waves, five planning models, twelve plans, thirty-five years, and a renaissance… of sorts', *Progress in Planning*, vol 71, no 3, pp 87-151.

Carmichael, L., Barton, H., Gray, S. and Lease, H. (2013) 'Health-integrated planning at the local level in England: impediments and opportunities', *Land Use Policy*, vol 31, pp 259-66.

Carmona, M. (2010) *Public places, urban spaces: The dimensions of urban design*, Abingdon: Routledge.

Carmona, M. and Punter, J. (2013) *The design dimension of planning: Theory, content and best practice for design policies*, Abingdon: Routledge.

Carmona, M. and Sieh, L. (2004) *Measuring quality in planning: Managing the performance process*, London: Spon.

Carpenter J. (2013) 'Special Service' *Planning* 13 December pp 16-19.

Carter, S.R. and Greer, C.R. (2013) 'Strategic leadership values, styles, and organizational performance', *Journal of Leadership and Organizational Studies*, vol 20, no 4, pp 375-93.

Cathcart, A. (2013) 'Directing democracy: competing interests and contested terrain in the John Lewis Partnership', *Journal of Industrial Relations*, no 55, no 4, pp 601-20.

Cave, S., Rehfisch, A., Smith, L. and Winter, G. (2013) *Comparison of the planning systems in the four UK countries*, SPICe Briefing 13/35, London: House of Commons Library, Scottish Parliament Information Centre.

CBI (Confederation of British Industry) (2011) *Making the right connections: CBI/KPMG infrastructure survey 2011,* London: CBI.

CCTA (Central Computer and Telecommunications Agency) (1999) *Guide to programme management*, London: CCTA.

CEC (Commission of the European Communities) (1999) *European spatial development perspective*, Brussels: CEC.

CEC (2001) *Directive 2001/42/EC on the assessment of the effects of certain plans and programmes on the environment*, Brussels: CEC.

CEC (2007) *Treaty of Lisbon*, Brussels: CEC.

CEC (2010) *Europe 2020 A European strategy for smart, sustainable and inclusive growth*, Brussels: CEC.

CEC (2011) *A renewed EU strategy 2011-14 for corporate social responsibility,* Brussels: CEC.

CEC (2013) Regulation 1303/2013 laying down common provisions on the European Regional Development Fund, the European Social Fund, the Cohesion Fund, the European Agricultural Fund for Rural Development and the European Maritime and Fisheries Fund and laying down general provisions on the European Regional Development Fund, the European Social Fund, the Cohesion Fund and the European Maritime and Fisheries Fund and repealing Council Regulation (EC) No 1083/2006

CEC (2014a) Council recommendation on the national reform programme 2014 of the United Kingdom, (2014/C 247/26) Brussels: CEC.

CEC (2014b) 2014/52/EU amending Directive 2011/92/EU on the assessment of the effects of certain public and private projects on the environment (2014/52/EU) Brussels: CEC.

CfPS (Centre for Public Scrutiny) (2008) *Ten questions to ask if you are … scrutinising how physical activity can be promoted through planning, transport and the physical environment,* London: CfPS.

Chapman, R.A. and O'Toole, B. (2010) 'Leadership in the British civil service: an interpretation', *Public Policy and Administration*, vol 25 no 2, pp 123-36.

Charbit, C. (2011) 'Governance of public policies in decentralised contexts: The multi-level approach', *Regional Development Working Papers*, 2011/04, Paris: OECD.

Charity Commission (2014) 'Becoming a trustee', www.charitycommission.gov.uk/trustees-staff-and-volunteers/trustee-role/becoming-a-trustee (accessed 16 May 2014)

Cheshire, P. and Magrini, S. (2000a) 'Endogenous processes in European regional growth: convergence and policy', *Growth and Change*, vol 31, no 4, pp 455-79.

Cheshire, P.C. and Magrini, S. (2000b) *Policies for urban growth, local public goods, spillovers and convergence/divergence: Some empirical and methodological answers*, Venice: Universita degli Studi di Venezia.

Child, J. (1997) 'Strategic choice in the analysis of action, structure, organizations and environment: retrospect and prospect' *Organization studies*, vol 18, no 1, pp 43-76.

Cini, M. and Borragán, N.P.S. (eds) (2013) *European Union politics*, Oxford: Oxford University Press.

CIPD (Chartered Institute of Personnel and Development) (2013a) 'Leadership factsheet', www.cipd.co.uk/hr-resources

CIPD (2013b) 'Job design factsheet', www.cipd.co.uk/hr-resources/factsheets/job-design. aspx (accessed 24 May 2014).

CIPD (2013c) 'Competence and competency frameworks', www.cipd.co.uk/hr-resources/ factsheets/competence-competency-frameworks.aspx (accessed 24 May 2014).

CIPD (2013d) 'SWOT analysis', www.cipd.co.uk/hr-resources/factsheets/swot-analysis. aspx (accessed 1 June 2014).

CIPD/Halogen (2014) *Employee Outlook*, London: CIPD.

CIPFA (Chartered Institute of Public Finance and Accountancy) (2011) *Prudential code for capital finance in local authorities*, London: CIPFA.

Clarke, J. (2007) ' "It's Not Like Shopping": Citizens, Consumers and the Reform of Public Services' in *Governance, Citizens and Consumers Agency and Resistance in Contemporary Politics* ed. M. Bevir and F. Trentmann, Basingstoke: Palgrave Macmillan, pp 97-118.

Clarke, J. and Newman, J. (1997) *The managerial state: Power, politics and ideology in the remaking of social welfare*, London: Sage.

Clausewitz, C.M. (1832) *On war*, https://archive.org/details/onwar00maudgoog.

Clegg, B. and Birch, P. (1998) *Disorganization: The handbook of creative organizational change*, London : Financial Times Pitman Publishing.

Clifford, B.P. (2006) 'Only a town planner would run a toxic waste pipeline through a recreational area': planning and planners in the British Press', *Town Planning Review*, vol 77, no 4, pp 423-55.

Clifford B. (2007) *Planning at the coalface: the planner's perspective survey – preliminary results: Executive summary*, London: Kings College Dept of Geography.

Clifford, B. (2013) 'Reform on the frontline: reflections on implementing spatial planning in England, 2004–2008', *Planning Practice and Research*, vol 28, no 4, pp 361-83.

Clifford, B. and Tewdwr-Jones, M. (2013) *The collaborating planner*, Bristol: Policy Press.

Clutterbuck, D. (2007) *Coaching the team at work*, London: Nicholas Brealey Publishing.

Coaffee, J. and Rogers, P. (2008) 'Rebordering the city for new security challenges: from counter-terrorism to community resilience', *Space and Polity*, vol 12, no 1, pp 101-18.

Cole, I. (2012) 'Housing market renewal and demolition in England in the 2000s: the governance of "wicked problems"', *International Journal of Housing Policy*, vol 12, no 3, pp 347-66.

Coleman, C., Crosby, N., McAllister, P. and Wyatt, P. (2013) 'Development appraisal in practice: some evidence from the planning system', *Journal of Property Research*, vol 3, no 2, pp 144-65.

Conrad, E., Cassar, L.F., Christie, M. and Fazey, I. (2011) 'Hearing but not listening? A participatory assessment of public participation in planning', *Environment and Planning C*, vol 29, no 5, pp 761-782.

Conservative Party (2009) *Control shift*, London: The Conservative Party.

Cooper, C.L. and Finkelstein, S. (eds) (2012) *Advances in mergers and acquisitions (vol 10)*, Bingley: Emerald Group Publishing.

Corry, D., and Stoker, G. (2002), *New Localism: refashioning the centre-local relationship*, London: The New Local Government Network.

Coulson, A., and Whiteman, P. (2012) 'Holding politicians to account? Overview and scrutiny in English local government' *Public Money & Management*, vol 32 no 3, pp 185-192.

Cox, E. (2014) *The future of England: The local dimension*, London: IPPR.

Craig, P. (2012) 'Subsidiarity: a political and legal analysis;, *Journal of Common Market Studies*, vol 50, vol 1, no 1, pp 72-87.

Crook, A., Henneberry, J., Rowley, S., Watkins, C. and the Halcrow Group (2006) *Valuing planning obligations in England*, London: Department for Communities and Local Government.

Crook, A., Rowley, S., Henneberry, J., Smith, R. and Watkins, C. (2008) *Valuing planning obligations in England: Update study for 2005-06*, London: Department for Communities and Local Government.

Crosby, N., McAllister, P. and Wyatt, P. (2010) *Fit for planning? An evaluation of the application of development viability appraisal models in the UK planning system*, Henley: Henley Business School.

Cullingworth, B. and Nadin, V. (2006) *Town and country planning in the UK*, Abingdon: Routledge.

Curran, M. and Moran, D. (2007) 'Impact of the FTSE4Good Index on firm price: an event study', *Journal of Environmental Management*, vol 82, no 4, pp 529-37.

Darley, G. and McKie, D. (2013) *Ian Nairn: Words in place*, London: Five Leaves Publishing.

Davies, J.S. (2004) 'Conjuncture or disjuncture? An institutionalist analysis of local regeneration partnerships in the UK', *International Journal of Urban and Regional Research*, vol 28, no 3, pp 570-85.

Davoudi, S. (2000) 'Planning for waste management: changing discourses and institutional relationships', *Progress in Planning*, vol 53, no 3, pp 165-216.

Davoudi, D. (2012) 'Resilience: a bridging concept or a dead end?', *Planning Theory and Practice*, vol 13, no 2, pp 299-333.

Davy, B. (2013) 'Planning cultures in Europe. Decoding cultural phenomena in urban and regional planning', *Planning Theory*, vol 12, no 2, pp 219-22.

DCLG (Department for Communities and Local Government) (2006a) *The private sector perspective in development control in the context of planning delivery grant 2005/6*, London: DCLG.

DCLG (2006b) *Developing the local government services market to support long-term strategy for local government*, London: DCLG.

DCLG (2006c) *Administrative burdens measurement: Final report*, London: DCLG.

DCLG (2006d) *Planning obligations: Practice guide*, London: DCLG.

DCLG (2008) *Activity based costing*, London: DCLG.

DCLG (2009) *Development management: Proactive planning from pre-application to delivery*, London: DCLG.

DCLG (2010) *Guidance on information requirements and validation*, London: DCLG.

DCLG (2011) *New homes bonus scheme*, London: DCLG.

DCLG (2012) *National Planning Policy Framework*, London: DCLG.

DCLG (2013a) *Case study on integration: Measuring the costs and benefits of whole-place community budgets*, London: HMSO.

DCLG (2013b) *Planning performance and the planning guarantee:*
Government response to consultation, London: DCLG.

DCLG (2013c) *Streamlining the planning application process: Consultation*
government response, London: DCLG.

Deas, I. (2013) 'Towards post-political consensus in urban policy? Localism and the emerging agenda for regeneration under the Cameron government', *Planning Practice & Research*, vol 28, no 1, pp 65-82.

De Jouvenel, H. (2000) 'A brief methodological guide to scenario building', *Technological Forecasting and Social Change*, vol 65, no 1, pp 37-48.

Depledge, D. and Dodds, K. (2014) 'No "strategy" please, we're British', *RUSI Journal*, vol 159, no 1, pp 24-31.

De Roo, G. and Porter, G. (2007) *Fuzzy planning*, Aldershot: Ashgate.

DETR (2000) *Statutory Instrument No. 2853 The Local Authorities (Functions and Responsibilities) (England) Regulations*, London: Parliament.

DfT (Department for Transport) (2011) *Behavioural insights toolkit*, London: DfT.

DH (Department of Health) (2010) *Report of the Mid Staffordshire NHS Foundation Trust public inquiry*, London: The Stationery Office.

DoE (Department of Education) (1997) *The principles of best value*, London: DoE.

Doherty, T.L., Horne, T. and Wootton, S. (2014) *Managing public services –implementing changes: A thoughtful approach to the practice of management*, Abingdon: Routledge.

Dolowitz, D. and Marsh, D. (1996) 'Who learns what from whom: a review of the policy transfer literature', *Political Studies*, vol 44, no 2, pp 343-357.

Domberger, S. and Jensen, P. (1997) 'Contracting out by the public sector: theory, evidence, prospects', *Oxford Review of Economic Policy*, vol 13, no 4, pp 67-78.

DRD (2014) *Regional development strategy building a better future*, Belfast: DRD.

Drucker, P. (1977) *The practice of management*, London: Pan.

Drucker, P. (2011) *Peter Drucker's the five most important questions self assessment tool: Facilitator's guide*, New York, NY: John Wiley & Sons; 3rd Edition edition.

DTLR (Department for *Transport, Local Government* and the *Regions*) (1998) *Modern local government in touch with the people*, London: HMSO.

DTLR (2001) *Planning delivering a fundamental change: Planning Green Paper*, London: DTLR.

Dubin, S.S. (ed) (1971) *Professional obsolescence*, London: The English Universities Press.

Dublin City Council (2011) Dublin City Master Plan, 2011-2017, Dublin: Dublin City Council.

Du Gay, P. (2000) *In praise of bureaucracy: Weber-organization-ethics*, London: Sage.

Duhr, S., Colomb, C. and Nadin, V. (2010) *European spatial planning and territorial cooperation*, Abingdon: Routledge.

Duranton, G., Gobillon, L. and Overman, H.G. (2011) 'Assessing the effects of local taxation using microgeographic data', *The Economic Journal*, vol 121, no 555, pp 1017-46.

Durham County Council (2012) *Local plan preferred options: Developers' contributions*, Durham: Durham County Council.

Durning, B. (2004) 'Planning academics and planning practitioners: two tribes or a community of practice?', *Planning Practice and Research*, vol 19, no 4, pp 435-46.

Durning, B. (2007) 'Changes in the recruitment and retention of professional planners in English planning authorities', *Planning Practice and Research*, vol 22, no 1, pp 95-110.

Durning, B. and Glasson, J. (2006) 'Delivering the planning system in England: skills capacity constraint', *Town Planning Review*, vol 77, no 4, pp 457-84.

Durning, B., Carpenter, J., Glasson, J. and Butima Watson, G. (2010) 'The spiral of knowledge development: professional knowledge development', *Planning Practice and Research*, vol 25, no 4, pp 497-516.

Eastleigh Borough Council (2013) *Local development framework*, Eastleigh: Eastleigh Borough Council.

Eckerson, W.W. (2010) *Performance dashboards: Measuring, monitoring, and managing your business*, Hoboken: John Wiley & Sons.

Eckert, P., (2006) 'Communities of Practice' in *Encyclopaedia of language and linguistics*, Amsterdam: Elsevier.

Edelenbos J.,Van Buuren J and Klijn, E-H (2013) 'Connective Capacities of Network Managers', *Public Management Review*, vol 15, no , p131-159.

Edmondson, A.C. (2011) 'Strategies of learning from failure', *Harvard Business Review*, vol 89, no 4, pp 48-55.

Edwards, J., McKinnon, A. and Cullinane, S. (2011) 'Comparative carbon auditing of conventional and online retail supply chains: a review of methodological issues', *Supply Chain Management: An International Journal*, vol *16, no* 1, pp 57-63.

Egan, J. (2004) *The Egan Review: skills for sustainable communities*, London: ODPM.

Einiö, E. and Overman, H. (2012) 'The effects of spatially targeted enterprise initiatives: evidence from UK LEGI', www-sre.wu.ac.at/ersa/ersaconfs/ersa12/e120821aFinal00166.pdf (accessed 15 May 2014).

Ellis, K.M. and Keys, P.Y. (2013) 'Workforce diversity and shareholder value: a multi-level perspective', *Review of Quantitative Finance and Accounting*, pp 1-22.

Elphicke, N. and House, K. (2014) *Review of local authority role in housing supply*, London: HMG.

Endacott, R., Sheaff, R., Jones, R. and Woodward, V. (2013) 'Clinical focus and public accountability in English NHS trust board meetings', *Journal of Health Services Research & Policy*, vol 18, no 1, pp 13-20.

Enticott, G. (2006) 'Modernising the internal management of local planning authorities', *Town Planning Review*, vol 77, no 2, pp 147-72.

Etzioni, A. (2014) 'Humble decision-making theory', *Public Management Review*, vol 16, no 5, pp 611–19.

Evans, T. (2011) 'Professionals, managers and discretion: Critiquing street-level bureaucracy' *British Journal of Social Work*, vol 41, no 2, pp 368-386.

Eversley, D. (1973) *The planner in society: The changing role of a profession*, London: Faber.

Eydeland, A. and Wolyniec, K. (2003) '*Energy and power risk management: New developments in modeling, pricing, and hedging*', (Vol. 206), Chichester: John Wiley & Sons.

Fang, L., Guangyu, Y. and Hailin, L. (2013) 'From organizational identity to mission statement: a research review and theoretical analysis framework', *Management Review*, vol 10, 012.

Farmer, S.M. and Fedor, D.B. (2001) 'Changing the focus on volunteering: an investigation of volunteers' multiple contributions to a charitable organization', *Journal of Management*, vol 27, no 2, pp 191-211.

Farrell, T. (2014) *The Farrell review*, London: DCMS.

Feeney, M.K. and deHart-Davis, L. (2009), 'Bureaucracy and public employee behaviour', *Review of Public Personnel Administration*, vol 29, no 4, pp 311-26.

Fell M., Smith, L., Keep, M. and White, E. (2014) *Shale gas and fracking - Commons Library Standard Note,* SN06073, London: House of Commons Library.

Fiedler, F.E. (1967) *A theory of leadership effectiveness*, New York, NY: McGraw-Hill.

Finch, J. (2009) 'Stevenage since the 1940s' in J. Finch et al (eds) *Humane readings: Essays on literary mediation and communication in honour of Roger Sell,* Amsterdam: The John Benjamin Publishing Company, pp 89-106.

Fishbein, M. and Ajzen, I. (2011) *Predicting and changing behavior: The reasoned action approach*, Abingdon: Taylor & Francis.

Flamholtz, E.G. and Randle, Y. (2012) *Growing pains: Transitioning from an entrepreneurship to a professionally managed firm*, San Francisco, CA: John Wiley & Sons.

Flanagan, J. (2013) *The Five Case Model: Supplementary guidance on the Treasury green book*, London: HM Treasury.

Flanagan, J. and Nicholls, P. (nd) *Public sector business cases using the Five Case Model: A toolkit. The templates*, London: HM Treasury.

Flyvbjerg, B. (2002) 'Bringing power to planning research one researcher's praxis story', *Journal of Planning Education and Research*, vol 21, no 4, pp 353-66.

Flyvbjerg, B. (2004) *Procedures for dealing with optimism bias in transport planning*, London: Department for Transport.

Flyvbjerg, B. (2008) 'Curbing optimism bias and strategic misrepresentation in planning: reference class forecasting in practice', *European Planning Studies*, vol 16, no 1, pp 3-21.

Flyvbjerg, B. (2013) *From Nobel prize to project management: Getting risks right*, http://arxiv.org/abs/1302.3642

Follett, M.P. (1942) *Dynamic administration*, New York, NY, and London: Harper and Brothers Publishers.

Foot, J. (2009) *Citizen involvement in local governance,* York: Joseph Rowntree Foundation.

Foster, S., Knuiman, M., Wood, L. and Giles-Corti, B. (2013) Suburban neighbourhood design: associations with fear of crime versus perceived crime risk, *Journal of Environmental Psychology*, vol 36, pp 112-17.

Forester, J. (2013) 'On the theory and practice of critical pragmatism: deliberative practice and creative negotiations', *Planning Theory*, vol 12, no 1, pp 5-22.

Francis, R. (2013) *Francis Report on the Mid Staffordshire NHS Foundation Trust Public Inquiry*, London: The Stationery Office.

Fraser, S. (2014) 'What makes a good leader?', Speech at Foreign and Commonwealth Office Leadership Conference, 12 May.

French, S.J., Kelly, S.J. and Harrison, J.L. (2001) 'Operationalising vision and mission', *Journal of the Australian and New Zealand Academy of Management*, vol 7, no 2, pp 30-40.

Friend, J.K. and Jessop, W.N. (1969) *Local government and strategic choice*, London: Tavistock.

Friend, J.K. and Hickling, A. (1987) *Planning under pressure: The strategic choice approach*, Oxford: Pergamon.

Frow, N., Marginson, D. and Ogden, S. (2005) 'Encouraging strategic behaviour while maintaining management control: multi-functional project teams, budgets, and the negotiation of shared accountabilities in contemporary enterprises', *Management Accounting Research*, vol 16, no 3, pp 269-92.

Gallent, N. and Robinson, S. (2012) *Neighbourhood planning: Communities, networks and governance*, Bristol: Policy Press.

Gallent, N., Morphet, J. and Tewdwr-Jones, M. (2008) 'Parish plans and the spatial planning approach in England', *Town Planning Review*, vol 79, no 11, pp 1-29.

Gatenby, M., Rees, C., Truss, C., Alfes, K. and Soane, E. (2014) 'Managing change, or changing managers? The role of middle managers in UK public service reform', *Public Management Review*, DOI:10.1080/14719037.2014.895028.

Geddes, M. (2006) 'Partnership and the limits to local governance in England: institutionalist analysis and neoliberalism', *International Journal of Urban and Regional Research*, vol 30, no 1, pp 76-97.

Gibney, J. and Murie, A. (eds) (2008) *Towards a 'new' strategic leadership of place for the knowledge-based communities*, Birmingham: University of Birmingham and Academy for Sustainable Communities.

Giezen, M. (2012) 'Keeping it simple? A case study into the advantages and disadvantages of reducing complexity in mega project planning', *International Journal of Project Management*, vol 30, no 7, pp 781-90.

Gimson, A. (2012) Boris: the rise of Boris Johnson, London: Simon and Schuster

Gladwell, M. (2006) *The tipping point: How little things can make a big difference*, New York, NY: Hachette Digital, Inc.

Glasson, J. and Marshall, T. (2007) *Regional planning*, Abingdon: Routledge.

Glasson, J., Therival, R. and Chadwick, A. (2011) *Introduction to Environmental Impact assessment* (4th edn), Abingdon: Routledge.

GLC (1976) *Greater London development plan*, London: GLC.

Goetz, K.H. and Meyer-Sayling, H.-H. (2009) 'Political time in the EU: dimensions, perspectives, theories', *Journal of European Public Policy*, vol 16, no 2, pp 180-201.

Goffman, E. (1974) *Frame Analysis*, Cambridge, Mass: Harvard University Press.

Goleman, D. (2006) *Emotional intelligence*, London: Random House.

Goleman, D., Boyatzis, R.E. and McKee, A. (2002) *The new leaders: Transforming the art of leadership into the science of results*, London: Little, Brown.

Golub, J. (ed) (2013) *New instruments for environmental policy in the EU*, Abingdon: Routledge.

Gómez-Barroso, J.L., Mochón, A., Sáez, Y. and Feijóo, C. (2012) 'Simulating digital dividend auctions: service neutrality versus dedicated licences', *Telematics and Informatics*, vol 29, no 1, pp 11-25.

Gomez-Mejia, L.R., Cruz, C., Berrone, P. and De Castro, J. (2011) 'The bind that ties: socioemotional wealth preservation in family firms', *The Academy of Management Annals*, vol 5, no 1, pp 653-707.

Gouldner, A.W. (1957) Cosmopolitans and locals: toward an analysis of latent social roles', *Administrative Science Quarterly*, vol 2, pp 281-306.

Gouldner, A. (1960) 'The norm of reciprocity: a preliminary statement', *American Sociological Review*, vol 25, pp 161–78.

Grange K. (2013) 'Shaping acting space: In search of a new political awareness among local authority planners", *Planning Theory* , vol 12, no3, pp 225-243.

Gray, R. and Bebbington, J. (2000) 'Environmental accounting, managerialism and sustainability: is the planet safe in the hands of business and accounting?', *Advances in Environmental Accounting & Management*, 1, pp 1-44.

Greasley, S. and Stoker, G. (2008) 'Mayors and urban governance: developing a facilitative leadership style', *Public Administration Review*, vol 68, no 4, pp 722-30.

Griffiths, R. (1986) 'Planning in retreat? Town planning and the market in the eighties', *Planning Practice and Research*, vol 1, no 1, pp 3-7.

Gunder, M. (2014) 'Fantasy in planning organisations and their agency: the promise of being at home in the world', *Urban Policy and Research*, vol 32, no 1, pp 1-15.

Gunn, S. and Hillier, J. (2014) 'When uncertainty is interpreted as risk: an analysis of tensions relating to spatial planning reform in England', *Planning Practice and Research*, vol 29, no 1, pp 56-74.

Gunn, S. and Vigar, G. (2012) 'Reform processes and discretionary acting space in English planning practice, 1997-2010', *Town Planning Review*, vol 83, no 5, pp 533-52.

Guy, C. (2000) 'From crinkly sheds to fashion parks: the role of financial investment in the transformation of retail parks', *The International Review of Retail, Distribution and Consumer Research*, vol 10, no 4, pp 389-400.

Hague, C. and Jenkins, P. (eds) (2013) *Place identity, participation and planning*, Abingdon: Routledge.

Hall, J. (2012) 'Britons are biggest online shoppers in developed world', *The Telegraph*, 1 February, www.telegraph.co.uk/news/uknews/9054400/Britons-are-biggest-online-shoppers-in-developed-world.html (accessed 4 May 2014).

Hallsworth, M. and Rutter, J. (2011) *Making policy better: Improving Whitehall's core business*, London: Institute for Government.

Halmos, P. (1970) *The personal service society*, Constable: London.

Hambleton, R. and Howard, J. (2012) *Public Sector Innovation and Local Leadership in the UK and the Netherland*, York: Joseph Rowntree Foundation.

Hamiduddin, I. and Gallent, N. (2012) 'Limits to growth: the challenge of housing delivery in England's "under-bounded" districts', *Planning Practice & Research*, vol 27, no 5, pp 513-30. Hammond, E. (2011) *Shared services and commissioning*, Policy Briefing 10, London: Centre for Public Scrutiny.

Hammond, E. (2012) *High street and town centre regeneration*, Policy Briefing 21, London: Centre for Public Scrutiny.

Hampton, P. (2004) *Reducing administrative burdens: effective inspection and enforcement*, London: HMRC.

Handy, C. (1993) *Understanding organizations*, (4th edition), London: Penguin.

Harris, M. (2010) 'Third sector organizations in a contradictory policy environment', in D. Billis (ed) *Hybrid organizations in the third sector: Challenges for practice, theory and policy*, Basingstoke: Macmillan, pp 25-45.

Harrison, J. (2013) 'Rethinking city-regionalism as the production of new non-state spatial strategies: the case of Peel Holdings Atlantic Gateway Strategy', *Urban Studies*, vol 51, no 11, pp 2315-2335.

Harrison, R., Mason, C. and Robson, P. (2010) 'Determinants of long-distance investing by business angels in the UK', *Entrepreneurship and Regional Development*, vol 22, no 2, pp 113-37.

Hartley, T.C. (2007) *The foundations of European Community law: An introduction to the constitutional and administrative law of the European Community*, Oxford: Oxford University Press.

Haughton, G., Allmendinger, P., Counsell, D. and Vigar, G. (2010) *The new spatial planning: Territorial management with soft spaces and fuzzy boundaries*, Abingdon: Routledge.

Haughton, M. (1997) 'Performance indicators in town planning: much ado about nothing?', *Local Government Studies*, vol 23, no 2, pp 1-13.

HBF (Home Builders Federation) (2014) *Barker Review a decade on*, London: HBF.

Heald, D. and Georgiou, G. (2009) 'Whole of government accounts developments in the UK: conceptual, technical and timetable issues', *Public Money & Management*, vol 29, no 4, pp 219-27.

Healey, J. and Newby, L. (2014) *Making local economies matter: A review of policy lessons from the Regional Development Agencies and Local Enterprise Partnerships*, London: Smith Institute.

Healey, P. (1992) 'A planner's day knowledge and communicative action in planning practice', *Journal of American Planning Association*, vol 58, no 1, pp 9-20.

Healey, P. (1997) *Collaborative planning shaping places in fragmented societies*, Basingstoke: Palgrave.

Healey, P. (2007) *Urban complexity and spatial strategies: Towards a relational planning for our times*, Abingdon: Routledge.

Healey, P. (2010) *Making better places*, Basingstoke: Palgrave.

Heclo, H. and Wildavsky, A. (1984) *The private government of public money* (2nd edn), London: Macmillan.

Helbron, H., Schmidt, M., Glasson, J. and Downes, N. (2011) 'Indicators for strategic environmental assessment in regional land use planning to assess conflicts with adaptation to global climate change', *Ecological Indicators*, vol 11, no 1, pp 90-5.

Helm, D. (2014) 'A credible natural capital policy: accounting, compensation and planning, 18 February 2014 presentation', Slides from a presentation at UBS Smith in the City event, www.dieterhelm.co.uk/node/1371 (accessed 4 May 2014).

Helms, M.M. and Nixon, J. (2010) 'Exploring SWOT analysis–where are we now? A review of academic research from the last decade', *Journal of Strategy and Management*, vol, 3, no 3, pp 215-51.

Hemingway, C. and Maclagan, P. (2004) 'Managers' personal values as drivers of corporate social responsibility', *Journal of Business Ethics*, vol 50, no 1, pp 33-44.

Hendler, S. (1990) 'Moral theories in professional practice: do they make a difference?', *Environments*, vol 20, no 3, pp 20-30.

Hendler, S. (1991) 'Do professional codes legitimate planners' values?', in H. Thomas and P. Healey (eds) *Dilemmas of planning practice. Ethics, legitimacy and the validation of knowledge*, Aldershot: Avebury, pp 156-67.

Heraud, B. (1979) *Sociology in the professions*, London: Open Books.

Herzberg, F. (1966) *Work and the nature of man*, Cleveland, OH: World Publishing.

Heseltine, M. (2012) Evidence given to the House of Commons, Business Innovation and Skills select Committee 11 December.

Hibbert, S.A., Hogg, G. and Quinn, T. (2002) 'Consumer response to social entrepreneurship: the case of The Big Issue in Scotland', *International Journal of Nonprofit and Voluntary Sector Marketing*, vol 7, no 3, pp 288-301.

Hibbert, S.A., Hogg, G. and Quinn, T. (2005) 'Social entrepreneurship: understanding consumer motives for buying The Big Issue', *Journal of Consumer Behaviour*, vol 4, no 3, pp 159-72.

Hillier, J. (2002) *Shadows of power: An allegory of prudence in land-use planning*, Abingdon: Routledge.

Hind, A. (2011) 'New development: increasing public trust and confidence in charities: on the side of the angels', *Public Money & Management*, vol 31, no 3, pp 201-5.

Hindmoor, A., Larkin, P. and Kennon, A. (2009) 'Assessing the influence of Select Committees in the UK: The Education and Skills Committee, 1997–2005', *The Journal of Legislative Studies*, vol 15, no 1, pp 71-89.

Hirsh, W. (2004) 'Positive career development for leaders and managers', in J. Storey (ed) *Leadership in organizations: Current issues and key trends*, Abingdon: Routledge, pp 225-48.

HM Government (2007) *Building on progress: public services*, London: Prime Minister's Strategy Unit.

HM Government (2009) *Putting the frontline first: Smarter government*, Cm 7753, London: HMSO.

HM Government (2013) *Consultation on local authority parking*, London: Department for Transport.

HM Government and DCLG (2007) *The New Performance Framework for local authorities and local authority partnerships: Single set of national indicators*, London: DCLG.

HM Government and LGA (2014) *Local public service transformation: A guide to whole place community budgets*, London: LGA.

HM Treasury (2003) *Productivity in the UK, 4: The local dimension*, London: HM Treasury.

HM Treasury (2007) *Sub-national economic development and regeneration review*, London: HM Treasury.

HM Treasury (2011) *The green book: Appraisal and evaluation in central government*, London: HM Treasury.

HM Treasury (2013) *National infrastructure plan*, London: HM Treasury.

HM Treasury (2014) *National infrastructure plan 2014*, London: HM Treasury.

HM Treasury and Cabinet Office (2007) *The future role of the third sector in social and economic regeneration final report*, Cmnd 7189, London: HMSO.

HM Treasury and Cabinet Office (2011) *Major project approval and assurance guidance*, London: HM Treasury.

Holliday, C.O., Schmidheiny, S. and Watts, P. (2002) *Walking the talk: The business case for sustainable development*, San Francisco, CA: Berrett-Koehler Publishers.

Holman, N. (2013) 'Effective strategy implementation: why partnership interconnectivity matters', *Environment and Planning C: Government and Policy 2013*, volume 31, no 1, pp 82–101.

Hood, C. (1991) 'A public management for all seasons?', *Public Administration*, vol 69, no 1, pp 3-19.

Hood, C. (2000) *The art of the state: Culture, rhetoric, and public management*, Oxford: Oxford University Press.

Hood, C. (2011) *The blame game: Spin, bureaucracy and self-preservation in government*, Oxford: Princeton University Press.

Hood, C. and Jones, D.C.K. (1996) *Accident and design*, London: UCL Press.

HoPS (2012) *Planning performance framework*, Glasgow: Heads of Planning Scotland.

Hosken, A. (2008) *The ups and downs of Ken Livingstone*, London: Arcadia Books.

London Borough of Hounslow (2008) *Planning obligations: Supplementary planning document to the Hounslow Local Development Framework Directorate of Planning, London Borough of Hounslow*, London: London Borough of Hounslow.

Howells, S. (2012) *Grow your own way: Taking a localist approach to regeneration*, London: Localis/LGA.

HSE (Health and Safety Executive) (2011) *HSE's land use planning methodology*, London: HSE.

Hu, S., Blettner, D. and Bettis, R.A. (2011) 'Adaptive aspirations: performance consequences of risk preferences at extremes and alternative reference groups', *Strategic Management Journal*, vol *32, no* 13, pp 1426-1436.

Huczynski, A. (2012) *Management gurus*, Abingdon: Routledge.

Hudson, K. (1978) *The jargon of the professions*, London: Macmillan.

Hudson, M. (2011) *Managing without profit: Leadership, management and governance of third sector organisations* (3d edn), London: Directory of Social Change.

Huffcutt, A.I. (2011) 'An empirical review of the employment interview construct literature', *International Journal of Selection and Assessment*, vol 19, no 1, pp 62-81.

IEWM (Improvement and Efficiency West Midlands) (2009) *Improving planning services using systems thinking*, Birmingham: Improvement and Efficiency West Midlands.

IEWM (2014) *How the other half grows*, Birmingham: IEWM.

IHBC (Institute of Historic Building Conservation) (2013) *A fifth report on local authority staff resources*, Tisbury: IHBC.

Improvement Service (2009a) 'Visioning exercise', case study, www.scotland.gov.uk/Resource/Doc/212607/0108902.pdf (accessed 1 June 2014).

Improvement Service (2009b) 'Use of online social media in planning consultations', case study, http://www.scotland.gov.uk/resource/doc/212607/0110727.pdf (accessed 3 February 2015).

Improvement Service (2010a) 'Stirling: visioning at whole council area scale', case study, www.scotland.gov.uk/Resource/0040/00400736.pdf (accessed 1 June 2014).

Improvement Service (2010b) 'Tayplan – visioning at the regional scale', case study, www.scotland.gov.uk/Resource/0040/00400732.pdf (accessed 1 June 2014).

Improvement Service (2010c) 'Using local media to promote planning awareness', case study, www.scotland.gov.uk/Resource/Doc/212607/0110413.pdf (accessed 1 June 2014).

Improvement Service (2014) 'Benchmarking project making planning costs clearer', 26 February, www.improvementservice.org.uk/news-and-features/news/benchmarking-project-making-planning-costs-clearer (accessed 27 April 2014).

Inch, A. (2010) 'Culture change as identity regulation: the micro-politics of producing spatial planners in England', *Planning Theory and Practice*, vol 11, no 3, pp 359-74.

Isaac, D., O'Leary, J. and Daley, M. (2010) *Property development: Appraisal and finance*, Basingstoke: Palgrave Macmillan.

Ishkanian, A. and Szreter, S. (eds) (2012) *The Big Society debate: A new agenda for social policy?*, Cheltenham: Edward Elgar Publishing.

Ivory, C. (2013) 'The role of the imagined user in planning and design narratives', *Planning Theory*, vol 12, no 4, pp 425–41.

Jablonski, J.R. (1991) *Implementing total quality management: An overview*, San Diego, CA: Pfeiffer.

Jacobs, H. (1989) 'Localism and land use planning', *The Journal of Architectural and Planning Research*, vol 6, no 1, pp 383-400.

James, O. (2004) 'The UK core executive's use of public service agreements as a tool of governance', *Public Administration*, vol 82, no 2, pp 397-419.

Jay, A. (1970) *Management and Machiavelli*, Harmondsworth: Penguin.

Jenkins, R. (2005) 'Globalization, corporate social responsibility and poverty', *International Affairs*, vol 81, no 3, pp 325-40.

John, P. (2014) 'The great survivor: the persistence and resilience of English local government', *Local Government Studies*, vol 40, no 5, pp 687-704.

Johnson, C. and Talbot, C. (2007) 'The UK Parliament and performance: challenging or challenged?', *International Review of Administrative Sciences*, vol 73, no 1, pp 113-31.

Johnson, T.J. (1972) *Professions and power*, London: Macmillan.

Jones, D. and Mitchell, A. (2006) *Lean thinking for the NHS*, London: NHS Confederation.

Jones, P. and Evans, J. (2013) *Urban regeneration in the UK: Boom, bust and recovery*, London: Sage Publications.

Jones S. (2014) 'Distributed leadership: a critical analysis', *Leadership*, vol 10, no 2, pp 129-41.

Joseph, J. (2013) 'Resilience as embedded neoliberalism: a governmentality approach' *Resilience: International Policies, Practices and Discourses,* vol 1, no 1, pp 38-52.

Kahn, K.B. and Mentzer, J.T. (1996) 'Logistics and interdepartmental integration', *International Journal of Physical Distribution & Logistics Management*, vol 26, no 8, pp 6-14.

Kaiserman, D., Ankers, S. and Shepley, C. (2010) *Grotton Revisited: Planning in Crisis?* , Abingdon: Routledge.

Kaplan, R.S. and Norton, D.P. (1996) *The balanced scorecard*, Boston, MA: Harvard Business School Press.

Kellermanns, F.W., Eddleston, K.A., Sarathy, R. and Murphy, F. (2012) 'Innovativeness in family firms: a family influence perspective', *Small Business Economics*, vol 38, no 1, pp 85-101.

Kempster, S., Higgs, M. and Wuerz, T. (2013) 'Pilots for change: exploring organizational change through distributed leadership', *Leadership and Organization Development Journal*, vol 35, no 2, pp 152-167.

Kerslake, B. (2014) *Reflections on reform*, Speech to Institute for Government, 25th September.

Kerzner, H.R. (2013) *Project management: A systems approach to planning, scheduling, and controlling*, Chichester: John Wiley & Sons.

Kihl, M. (1995) 'Integrating planning theory and practice', *Policy Studies Journal*, vol 23, no 3, p 551.

Killian, J. and Pretty, D. (2008) *Planning applications: A faster and more responsive system. Final report*, London: DCLG.

Kingdon, J. (2003) *Agendas, alternatives and public policies* (2nd edn), London: Longman.

Kitchen, T. (2007) *Skills for planning practice*, Basingstoke: Palgrave Macmillan.

Klasen, N. and Clutterbuck, D. (2012) *Implementing mentoring schemes*, Abingdon: Routledge.

Kletz, F., Hénaut, L. and Sardas, J. (2014) 'New public management and the professions within cultural organizations: one hybridization may hide another',

International Review of Administrative Sciences, vol 80, no 1, pp 89-109.

Knieling J. and Othengrafen, F. (2009) *Planning cultures in Europe*, Farnham: Ashgate.

Knox, S., Maklan, S. and French, P. (2005) 'Corporate social responsibility: exploring stakeholder relationships and programme reporting across leading FTSE companies', *Journal of Business Ethics*, vol 61, no 1, pp 7-28.

Kochan, B. (2014) 'Running planning services in a joint venture', *Planning*, 17 January, pp 18-19.

Koene, B., Galais, N. and Garsten, C. (ed) (2014) *Management and Organization of Temporary Agency Work*, Abingdon, Routledge.

Kornberger, M. (2013) 'Clausewitz: on strategy', *Business History*, vol 55, no 7, pp 1058-73.

Krugman, P.R. (2011) 'Increasing returns in a comparative advantage world', in *Comparative advantage, growth, and the gains from trade and globalization: A Festschrift in honor of Alan V. Deardorff*, Singapore: World Scientific Publishing, pp 43-51. Kruse, R., Gebhardt, J.E. and Klowon, F. (1994) *Foundations of fuzzy systems*, Chichester: John Wiley & Sons.

Kuhn T. (1962) *The structure of scientific revolutions*, Chicago, IL: University of Chicago Press.

Kunzmann, K. (2000) 'Strategic spatial development though information and communication', in W. Salet and A. Faludi (eds) *The Revival of Strategic Spatial Planning*, Amsterdam Academy of Arts and Sciences, pp 259-65.

Lambert, C. (2006) 'Community strategies and spatial planning in England: the challenges of integration', *Planning, Practice & Research*, vol 21, no 2, pp 245-55.

Lawless, P. (1996) 'The inner cities: towards a new agenda', *Town Planning Review*, vol 67, no 1, pp 21-43.

Lawrence, P.R. (2010) 'The key job design problem is still Taylorism', *Journal of Organizational Behavior*, vol 31, nos 2-3, pp 412-21.

Layard, P.R.G. and Glaister, S. (eds) (1994) *Cost-benefit analysis*, Cambridge: Cambridge University Press.

Leach, S., Hartley, J., Lowndes, V., Wilson D. and Downe, J., (2005) *Local political leadership in England and Wales,* York: Joseph Rowntree Foundation.

Leach, S., and Lowndes, V. (2007) 'Of roles and rules analysing the changing relationship between political leaders and chief executives in local government', *Public Policy and Administration*, vol 22, no 2, pp 183–200.

Lee, C. (1973) *Models in planning*, Oxford: Pergamon.

Lehrer, M. (2001) 'Macro varieties of capitalism and micros varieties of strategic management in European airlines', in P.A. Hall and D. Soskice (eds) *Varieties of capitalism: The institutional foundations of comparative advantage*, Oxford: Oxford University Press, pp 361–86.

Levitt, R. and Solesbury, W. (2012) *Policy tsars: Here to stay but more transparency needed*, London: KCL.

Levitt, S.D. and Dubner, S.J. (2010) *Freakonomics*, London: Penguin.

Lewis, A.E. and Fagenson, E.A. (1995) 'Strategies for developing women managers: how well do they fulfil their objectives?', *Journal of Management Development*, vol 14, no 2, pp 39–53.

LGA (Local Government Association) (2008) *Planning at the heart of government*, London: LGA.

LGA (2010) *New reputation guide*, London: LGA.

LGA (2013) *The general power of competence: Empowering councils to make a difference,* London: LGA.

LGA (2014) 'Capital assets', www.local.gov.uk/capitalassetseconomicgrowth (accessed 16 May).

LGA/PAS (2013) *Decisions, decisions: Governance and spending on CIL*, London: LGA.

Likert, R. (1961) *New patterns of management*, New York, NY: McGraw Hill.

Lindblom, C. (1959) 'The science of muddling through', *Public Administration Review*, vol 19, Spring, pp 79–88.

Linstead, S., Maréchal, G. and Griffin, R.W. (2014) 'Theorizing and researching the dark side of organization', *Organization Studies*, vol 35, no 2, pp 165–88.

Loh, C.G. and Norton, R.K. (2013) 'Planning consultants and local planning: roles and values', *Journal of the American Planning Association*, vol 79, no 2, pp 138–47.

Loosemore, M. (2006) 'Managing project risks', in S. Pryke and H. Smyth (eds) *The Management of Complex Projects a Relationship Approach*, Oxford: Blackwell, pp 205–12.

Lord, A. (2009) 'The community infrastructure levy: an information economics approach to understanding infrastructure provision under England's reformed spatial planning system', *Planning Theory and Practice*, vol 10, no 3, pp 333–49.

Lowndes, V. and McCaughie, K. (2013) 'Weathering the perfect storm? Austerity and institutional resilience in local government', *Policy and Politics*, vol 41, no 4, pp 533–549.

Lowndes, V. and Skelcher, C. (1998) 'The dynamics of multi-organizational partnerships: an analysis of changing modes of governance', *Public Administration*, vol 76, no 2, pp 313–33.

Lowndes, V. and Sullivan, H. (2004) 'Like a horse and carriage or a fish on a bicycle: how well do local partnerships and public participation go together?', *Local Government Studies*, vol 30, no 1, pp 51-73.

Lyons, M. (2007) *Place-shaping: a shared ambition for the future of local government*, London: HMT.

Mabey, C., Salaman, G. and Storey, J. (1998) *Human resource management: A strategic introduction*, Oxford: Blackwell Business.

Mace, A. (2013) 'Delivering local plans: recognising the bounded interests of local planners within spatial planning', *Environment and Planning C: Government and Policy 2013*, volume 31, no 6, pp 1133–46.

Machiavelli, N. (1513) *The prince,* www.gutenberg.org/ebooks/1232.

Macmillan, H. and Tampoe, M. (2000) *Strategic management*, Oxford: Oxford University Press.

Macmillan, L. and Vignoles, A. (2012) *Mapping the occupational destinations of new graduates: Research report*, London: Social Mobility and Child Poverty Commission.

Madden, A. (2010) 'The community leadership and place-shaping roles of English local government: synergy or tension?', *Public Policy and Administration*, vol 25, no 2, pp 175-93.

Malpass, P. (2000) *Housing associations and housing policy: A historical perspective*, Basingstoke: Macmillan.

Mangham I. (2004) 'Leadership and Integrity', in D. Storey (ed) *Leadership and organizations: Current issues and key trends*, London: Routledge, pp 41-57.

Margetts, H., 6, Perri and Hood, C. (eds) (2010) *Paradoxes of modernization: Unintended consequences of public policy reform*, Oxford: Oxford University Press.

Marlow, D. (2013) 'Turning over the stones: should cities pursue city deals, LEP growth strategies or whole place community budgets in pursuit of growth?', *Journal of Urban Regeneration and Renewal*, vol 6, no 4, pp 406-16.

Marshall, T. (2000) 'Urban planning and governance: is there a Barcelona model?', *International Planning Studies*, vol 5, no 3, pp 299-319.

Marshall, T. (2012) *Planning major infrastructure: A critical Analysis*, Abingdon: Routledge.

Maslow, A. (1954) *Motivation and personality,* New York, NY: Harper.

Mathiason, N. (2009) 'Leaked letter warns Tories to delay property developments', *The Observer*, 30 August, www.theguardian.com/business/2009/aug/30/conservatives-housing-property-delay (accessed 5 May 2014).

Mazutis, D.D. (2013) 'The CEO effect: a longitudinal, multilevel analysis of the relationship between executive orientation and corporate social strategy', *Business and Society*, vol 52, no 4, pp 631-48.

McAdam, R., Walker, T. and Hazlett, S. A. (2011) 'An inquiry into the strategic-operational role of performance management in local government', *International Journal of Public Sector Management*, vol 24, no 4, pp 303-24.

McCallum, D. (1979) 'The development of British regional policy', in D. MacLennan and J.B. Parr (eds) *Regional policy: Past experience and new directions*, Oxford: Martin Robertson, pp 3-42.

McClymont, K. (2012) 'Revitalising the political: development control and agonism in planning practice', *Planning Theory*, vol 10, no 3, pp 239-56.

McClymont, K. (2014) 'Stuck in the process, facilitating nothing? Justice, capabilities and planning for value-led outcomes', *Planning Practice and Research*, vol 29, no 2, pp 187-201.

McCrae, J. and Randall, J. (2013) *Leading functions across Whitehall*, London: Institute for Government.

McEldowney, J. (2003) 'Public management reform and administrative law in local public service in the UK', *International Review of Administrative Sciences*, vol 69, no 1, pp 69-82.

McGrath, H. (2010) *National evaluation of planning performance agreements*, London: HCA/Tribal.

McGregor, D. (1960) *The human side of enterprise*, New York, NY: McGraw Hill.

McGregor, A., Glass, A., Higgins, K., Macdougall, L. and Sutherland, V. (2003) *Developing people – regenerating place: Achieving greater integration for local area regeneration*, Bristol: Policy Press.

McKay, S., Berry, J. and McGreal, S. (2003) 'Planning enforcement: lessons for practice and procedure', *Planning Theory & Practice*, vol 4, no 3, pp 325-44.

McLoughlin, J.B. (1969) *Urban and regional planning*, London: Faber and Faber.

Megginson, D. and Whitaker, V. (2003) *Continuing professional development*, London: CIPD Publishing.

Memery, J., Megicks, P., Angell, R. and Williams, J. (2012) 'Understanding ethical grocery shoppers', *Journal of Business Research*, vol 65, no 9, pp 1283-9.

MHLG (Ministry of Housing and Local Government) (1970) *Development plans: A manual on their form and content*, London: HMSO.

Miliband, D. (2006) Speech to National Council of Voluntary Organizations (NCVO), London, 21 February, www.theguardian.com/society/2006/feb/21/localgovernment.politics1 (accessed 8 May 2014).

Minton, A. (2009) *Ground control: Fear and happiness in the twenty-first century city*, London: Penguin.

Mishan, E.J. and Quah, E. (2007) *Cost benefit analysis*, Abingdon: Routledge.

MoJ (2013) *Judicial Review Proposals for further reform*, Cm 8703 London: HMSO.

Mole, G. (2004) 'Can leadership be taught?', in D. Storey (ed) *Leadership and organizations: Current issues and key trends*, London: Routledge, pp 125-37.

Molyneux, P. (2007) *This is somewhere I want to stay: The voluntary sector's contribution to place-shaping*, London: Joseph Rowntree Foundation.

Monti, M. (2010) *A new strategy for the single market*, Brussels: CEC.

Morden, T. (2012) *Principles of strategic management*, Farnham: Ashgate Publishing.

Morgan, R. and Alden, J. (1974) *Regional planning: A comprehensive view*, Leighton Buzzard: Leonard Hill Books.

Morphet, J. (2007) *Delivering inspiring places: A report for the National Planning Forum*, London: NPF.

Morphet, J. (2008) *Modern local government*, London: Sage Publications.

Morphet, J. (2011a) 'Reflections on alterity in Irish and Scottish spatial planning: fragmentation or fugue?' *Journal of Irish and Scottish Studies*, vol 4, no 2, pp 173-94.

Morphet, J. (2011b) *Effective practice in spatial planning*, Abingdon: Routledge.

Morphet, J. (2013) *How Europe shapes British public policy*, Bristol: Policy Press.

Morphet J. and Clifford B. (2014) 'Policy convergence, divergence and communities: the case of spatial planning in post-devolution Britain and Ireland', *Planning Practice and Research*, vol 29, no 5, pp 508-24.

Morphet, J., Gallent, N., Tewdwr-Jones, M., Hall, B., Spry, M. and Howard, R. (2007) *Shaping and delivering tomorrow's places, effective practice in spatial planning (EPiSP)*, London: RTPI, CLG, GLA and JRF.

Morris, M. and Leung, K (2010) 'Creativity East and West: Perspectives and parallels', *Management and Organization Review*, vol 6, no 3, pp 313-27.

Muir, R. and Parker, I. (2014) *Many to many: How the relational state will transform public services*, London: IPPR.

Mulgan, G. (2010) *The art of public strategy*, Oxford: Oxford University Press.

Nadin, V. and Stead, D. (2008) 'European spatial planning systems, social models and learning', *disP-The Planning Review*, vol 44, no 172, pp 35-47.

Nairn, I. (1956) *Outrage*, London: Architectural Press.

NAO (National Audit Office) (2011) *Initiating successful projects*, London: NAO.

NAO (2013) *Over-optimism in government projects*, London: NAO.

NAO (2014) *Whole government accounts 2013-2014; guidance for preparers*, London: NAO.

NAO (2015) *Code of Audit Practice*, London: NAO.

Nesheim T., Fahle, B. and Tobiassen, A. (2014) 'When external consultants work on internal projects', in B.A. Koene, N. Galais and C. Garsten (eds) *Management and Organization of temporary agency work*, Abingdon: Routledge.

National Archive (2010) Archive of papers from the Prime Minster's Strategy Unit, http://webarchive.nationalarchives.gov.uk/20100125070726/http://cabinetoffice.gov.uk/strategy/publications/archive.aspx.

Neyroud, P. (2011) 'Leading policing in the 21st century: leadership, democracy, deficits and the new professionalism' *Public Money & Management*, vol 31, no 5, pp 347-54.

NHS (National Health Service) (2011) *The handbook of quality and service improvement tools*, London: NHS Institute for Innovation and Improvement.

Ni, N., Qian, C. and Crilly, D. (2014) 'The stakeholder enterprise: caring for the community by attending to employees', *Strategic Organization*, vol 12, no 1, pp 38-61.

Nijmeijer, K.J., Fabbricotti, I.N. And Huijsman, R. (2014) 'Making franchising work: a framework based on a systematic review', *International Journal of Management Reviews*, vol 16, no 1, pp 62-83.

Nolan, M. (1995) *Report of Committee on Standards in Public Life*, London: HMSO.

Noordegraaf, M. (2011) 'Risky business: how professionals and professional fields (must) deal with organizational issues' *Organization Studies*, vol 32, no 10, pp 1349-71.

Noordegraaf, M. (2013) 'Reconfiguring professional work: changing forms of professionalism in public services', *Administration & Society*, 6 November, DOI:10.1177/0095399713509242.

Noordegraaf, M. and Schinkel, W. (2011) 'Professional capital contested: a Bourdieusian analysis of conflicts between professionals and managers', *Comparative Sociology*, vol 10, no 1, pp 97-125.

Nye, J.S. (2004) *Soft Power: The means to success in world politics*, New York, NY: Public Affairs.

Nye, J.S. (2008) *The powers to lead*, New York, NY: Oxford University Press.

Nye, J.S. (2014) 'Transformational and transactional presidents', *Leadership*, vol 10, pp 118-24.

Oborn, E., Barrett, M. and Dawson, S. (2013) 'Distributed leadership in policy formulation: a sociomaterial perspective', *Organization Studies*, vol 34, no 2, pp 253-76.

ODPM (Office of the Deputy Prime Minister) (2004a) *The role of staff in delivering high quality public services*, London: ODPM.

ODPM (2004b) *The Egan review: Skills for sustainable communities*, London: ODPM.

ODPM (2004c) *Risk management: Technical notes*, London: ODPM.

ODPM (2004d) *Planning policy statement 12 local development frameworks*, London: ODPM.

ODPM (2004e) *Creating LDFs*, London: ODPM.

ODPM and LGA (2004) *Delivering delegation*, London: ODPM.

OECD (Organisation for Economic Co-operation and Development) (2001) *Local partnerships for better governance*, Paris: OECD.

OECD (2010) *Transfer pricing guidelines for multinational enterprises and tax administrations*, Paris: OECD.

OECD (2011) *Guidelines for multinational enterprises*, Paris: OECD.

OECD (2013) *How's life?*, Paris: OECD.

OECD (2014) 'Horizon scanning', www.oecd.org/site/schoolingfortomorrowknowledgebase/futuresthinking/overviewofmethodologies.htm (accessed 4 May 2014).

Ofcom (2014) *Adults' media use and attitudes report 2014*, London: Ofcom.

Oliver, C. (1997) 'Sustainable competitive advantage: combining institutional and resource-based views', *Strategic Management Journal*, vol 18, no 9, pp 697-713.

O'Reilly, D. and Reed, M. (2010) '"Leaderism": an evolution of managerialism in UK public service reform', *Public Administration*, vol 88, no 4, pp 960-78.

Orlitzky, M. (2007) 'Recruitment strategy', in P. Boxall, J. Purcell and P. M. Wright (eds), *The Oxford Handbook of Human Resource Management*, Oxford: Oxford University Press, pp 273-99.

Osborne, D. and Gaebler, T. (1992) *Reinventing government*, Reading: Addison-Wesley.

Osborne, G. (2014) *The Budget*, London: HM Treasury.

Osborne, S. and McLaughlin, K. (2004) 'The cross-cutting review of the voluntary sector: where next for local government voluntary sector relationships?', *Regional Studies*, vol 38, no 5, pp 573–82.

Owen, S., Moseley, M. and Courtney, P. (2007) 'Bridging the gap: an attempt to reconcile strategic planning and very local community-based planning in rural England', *Local Government Studies*, vol 33, no 1, pp 49-76.

Owens, S. and Cowell, R. (2013) *Land and limits: Interpreting sustainability in the planning process*, Abingdon: Routledge.

Palomino, M.A., Bardsley, S., Bown, K., De Lurio, J., Ellwood, P., Holland-Smith, D. and Owen, R. (2012) 'Web-based horizon scanning: concepts and practice', *Foresight*, vol 14, no 5, pp 355-73.

Park, A.J., Hwang, E., Spicer, V., Cheng, C., Brantingham, P.L. and Sixsmith, A. (2011) 'Testing elderly people's fear of crime using a virtual environment', Paper presented at Intelligence and Security Informatics Conference, EISIC 2011, Athens, Greece, 12-14 September.

Parker, D. (2012) *The official history of privatisation* (Vol. 2), London: Routledge.

PAS (Planning Advisory Service) (2008) *Finding the flow: Re-engineering business processes for planning*, London: IDeA.

PAS (2013a) *A competency framework for planners*, London: LGA.

PAS (2013b) *Local plan project management tool*, London: LGA.

PAS (2013c) *Guidance for local authorities: Approaching an investment (open for growth) peer challenge*, London: LGA.

PAS (2014a) *Report into the use, value for money and effectiveness of local development orders in implementing local authority objectives*, London: LGA.

PAS (2014b) *Neighbourhood plan project management tool*, London: LGA.

PAS (2014c) *Investing in our place*, London: LGA.

PAS (2014d) *Report into the use, value for money and effectiveness of local development orders in implementing local authority objectives*, Published as a Rough & Ready Report, Revision 3, London: PAS.

PAS and BPF (2014) *10 Commitments for effective pre-application engagement*, London: LGA.

Passmore, J. and Fillery-Travis, A. (2011) 'A critical review of executive coaching research: a decade of progress and what's to come', *Coaching: An International Journal of Theory, Research and Practice*, vol 4, no 2, pp 70-88.

Paun, A. and Harris, J. (2013) *Accountability at the top: Supporting effective leadership in Whitehall*, London: Institute for Government.

Peel D. and Lloyd, M. G. (2007), 'Neo-traditional planning: Towards a new ethos for land-use planning?' *Land Use Policy*, vol 24, pp 396-403.

Peltier, B. (2011) *The psychology of executive coaching: Theory and application.* Abingdon: Taylor and Francis.

Pemberton S. and Morphet J. (2014) 'The rescaling of economic governance: insights into the transitional territories of England', *Urban Studies*, vol 51, no 11, pp 2354-70.

Perdicoulis A. (2011), *Building Competences for spatial planners methods and Techniques for performing tasks with efficiency*, Abingdon: Routledge.

Peter Brett Associates (2014) *Local Development Orders: Impacts and good practice. Final report*, Cardiff: Welsh Government.

Peters, B.G. (2012) 'Machinery of government?', Explorations in Governance 10, www.executivepolitics.org/Executive_Politics/News_files/Explorations%20in%20Governance.pdf#page=7 (accessed 8 May).

Peters, B.G. (2014) 'Implementation structures as institutions', *International Journal of Public Administration*, vol 35, no 1, pp 46-57.

Pickvance, C. (1990) 'Introduction', in M. Harloe, C.G. Pickvance and J. Urry (eds) *Place, policy and politics: Do localities matter?*, Abingdon: Routledge.

Pierre J. and Peters, B.G. (2000) *Governance, politics and the state*, London: Palgrave Macmillan.

PINS (Planning Inspectorate National Service) (2007) *Local development frameworks: Lessons learnt examining development plan documents*, Bristol: PINS.

PINS (2014) *Major applications process: section 62A. Authorities in special measures. Frequently asked questions for local communities*, Bristol: PINS.

PMI (Project Management Institute) (2000) *A guide to the project management body of knowledge*, Philadelphia, PA: PMI.

Pollitt, C. (1994) 'The citizen's charter: a preliminary analysis', *Public Money & Management*, vol 14, no 2, pp 9-14.

Pollitt, C. (2013) 'Back in the OECD…an oblique comment on the World Bank's Better Results from Public Sector Institutions', *International Review of Administrative Sciences* vol. 79, no. 3, pp 406-412.

Pollitt, C. and Bouckaert, G. (2011) *Public management reform: A comparative analysis. New public management, governance, and the neo-Weberian state*, Oxford: Oxford University Press.

Popper, K. (1957) *The poverty of historicism*, London: Routledge

Porter, A.L., Cunningham, S.W., Banks, J., Roper, A.T., Mason, T.W. and Rossini, F.A. (2011) *Forecasting and management of technology*, Chichester: John Wiley & Sons.

Porter, M.E. (2011) *Competitive advantage of nations: Creating and sustaining superior performance*, London: Simon and Schuster.

Potter, J.R. and Hooper, A. (2005) *Developing strategic leadership skills,* London: Chartered Institute of Personnel and Development.

Powell, J. (2011) *The new Machiavelli: How to wield power in the modern world*, London:Vintage.

Powell, M., Greener, I., Szmigin, I. and Mills, N. (2010) 'Broadening the focus of public service consumerism', *Public Management Review*, vol 12, no 3, pp 323-39.

Priestley, R. (2011) *Managing change: Planning fact sheet*, Edinburgh: Improvement Service.

Prior, A. (2000) 'Problems in the theory and practice of planning enforcement', *Planning Theory and Practice*, vol 1, no 1, pp 53-69.

Pritchett, L. (2013) 'The World Bank and public sector management: what next?', *International Review of Administrative Sciences,* vol 79, no 3, pp 413-19.

PSU (Prime Minister's Strategy Unit) (2004) *Strategy survival guide: Overview*, London: Cabinet Office.

Pugh, D.S. and Hickson, D.J. (2007) *Writers on organizations* (6th edn), London: Penguin.

Putnam, R. (2000) *Bowling alone*, New York, NY: Simon and Schuster.

Pyper, R. and Burnham, J. (2011) 'The British civil service: perspectives on "decline" and "modernisation"', *British Journal of Politics & International Relations*, vol 13, no 2, pp 189-205.

Qaiser, K., Ahmad, S., Johnson, W. and Batista, J.R. (2013) 'Evaluating water conservation and reuse policies using a dynamic water balance model', *Environmental Management*, vol 51, no 2, pp 449-58.

Radnor, Z. and Johnston, R. (2013) 'Lean in UK government: internal efficiency or customer service?', *Production Planning & Control*, vol 24, nos 10-11, pp 903-15.

Radnor, Z. and Walley, P. (2008) 'Learning to walk before we try to run: adapting lean for the public sector', *Public Money and Management*, vol 28, no 1, pp 13-20.

Ratcliffe, J. (2000) 'Scenario building: a suitable method for strategic property planning?', *Property Management*, vol 18, no 2, pp 127-44.

Ray T., Clegg, S. and Gordon, R. (2004) 'A new look at dispersed leadership: power, knowledge and context', in J. Storey (ed) *Leadership in organizations: Current issues and key trends*, London: Routledge, pp 319-36.

Reade, E. (1987) *British town and country planning*, Milton Keyes: Open University Press.

Reid, R. and Botterill, L. (2013) 'The multiple meanings of "resilience": an overview of the literature', *Australian Journal of Public Administration*, vol 72, no 1, pp 31-40.

Renn, O. (2008) *Risk governance: Coping with uncertainty in a complex world*, London: Earthscan.

RIBA (Royal Institute of British Architects) (2007) *Designing for flood risk* (2nd edn), London: RIBA and CABE.

Riddell, P. (2013) *Ministers and mandarins: How civil servants and politicians can work better together*, London: Institute for Government.

Rigg, C. and O'Mahony, N. (2013) 'Frustrations in collaborative working', *Public Management Review*, vol 15, no 1, pp 83-108.

Robb, A.M. and Robinson, D.T. (2014) 'The capital structure decisions of new firms', *Review of Financial Studies*, vol 27, no 1, pp 153-79.

Roberge, M.É. and van Dick, R. (2010) 'Recognizing the benefits of diversity: when and how does diversity increase group performance?', *Human Resource Management Review*, vol 20, no 4, pp 295-308.

Rodgers, W. (1965) *House of Commons Debate 18 February 1965*, vol 706, cc 1342-4

Ross A. with M. Chang (2013) *Reuniting health with planning – healthier homes, healthier communities*, London: TCPA.

Rowlinson, M., Booth, C., Clark, P., Delahaye, A. and Procter, S. (2010) 'Social remembering and organizational memory', *Organization Studies*, vol 31, no 1, pp 69-87.

RTPI (Royal Town Planning Institute) (2012) *Royal charter*, London: RTPI.

RTPI (2014) 'RTPI survey', *The Planner*, March, pp 22-7.

Rumsfeld, D. (2011) *Known and unknown: A memoir*, Penguin: London.

Rydin, Y. (1999) 'Participation in the 1990s', in B. Cullingworth (ed) *British planning: 50 years of urban and regional policy*, London: Continuum Books, pp 184-97.

Rydin, Y. (2011) *The purpose of planning*, Bristol: Policy Press.

Sager, T. (2009) 'Planners' role: torn between dialogical ideals and neo-liberal realities', *European Planning Studies*, vol 17, no 1, pp 65-84.

Sainsbury, D. (2013) *Progressive capitalism: How to achieve economic growth, liberty and social justice*, London: Biteback Publishing.

Sampson, F. (2012) 'Hail to the chief? How far does the introduction of elected police commissioners herald a US-style politicization of policing for the UK?', *Policing*, vol 6, no 1, pp 4-15.

Sandford, J. (1966) Cathy Come Home, London: BBC.

Sandford, M. (2013) *Assets of community value*, Standard Note SN/PC/06366, London: House of Commons Library.

Schein, E. (1978) *Career dynamics: Matching individual and organizational needs*, London: Addison-Wesley.

Schilit, W.K. and Locke, E.A. (1982) 'A study of upward influence in organizations', *Administrative Science Quarterly*, vol 27, no 2, pp304-316.

Schon, D.A. (1983) *The reflective practitioner*, London: Temple Smith.

Scott, A.J., Carter, C., Reed, M.R., Larkham, P., Adams, D., Morton, N. and Coles, R. (2013) 'Disintegrated development at the rural–urban fringe: re-connecting spatial planning theory and practice', *Progress in Planning*, vol 83, pp 1-52.

Scottish Government (2008) *PAN 65 Planning and open space*, Edinburgh: Scottish Government.

Scottish Government (2011) *Customer Satisfaction Survey 2010-11*, Edinburgh: Directorate for Planning and Environmental Appeals, Scottish Government.

Scottish Government (2014) *National Planning Framework 3*, Edinburgh: Scottish Government.

Segers, J. and Inceoglu, I. (2012) 'Exploring supportive and developmental career management through business strategies and coaching', *Human Resource Management*, vol 51, no 1, pp 99-120.

Sell S. (2013) 'The "planning" consultancy survey', 15 November www.planningresource.co.uk/article/1220522/planning-consultancy-survey-2013 (accessed 23 May 2014).

Senior, B. (1997) 'Team roles and team performance: is there "really" a link?', *Journal of Occupational and Organizational Psychology*, vol 70, no 3, pp 241-58.

Sharma, S., Sharma, J. and Devi, A. (2011) 'Corporate social responsibility: the key role of human resource management', *Human Resource Management: Issues, Challenges and Opportunities*, vol 2, no 1, pp 205-213.

Shaw, D. (2006) *Spatial plans in practice: Supporting the reform of local planning. Literature review 2: Culture change and planning summary note for practitioners*, London: DCLG.

Shaw, D. and Lord, A. (2009) 'From land-use to spatial planning', *Town Planning Review*, vol 80, nos 4-5, pp 415-35.

Shaw, K. (2012) '"Reframing" Resilience: Challenges for Planning Theory and Practice', *Planning Theory and Practice*, vol 13, no 2, pp 308-312.

Shepherd, D.A., Patzelt, H. and Wolfe, M. (2011) 'Moving forward from project failure: negative emotions, affective commitment, and learning from the experience', *Academy of Management Journal*, vol 54, no 6, pp 1229-59.

Sheppard, A. and Smith, N. (2011) 'Delivering homes and infrastructure through incentivisation: the role of the growth points agenda and the New Homes Bonus', Paper presented at the 2011 UK/Ireland Planning Research Conference, Birmingham, 12-14 September.

Shiftan, Y., Kaplan, S. and Hakkert, S. (2003) 'Scenario building as a tool for planning a sustainable transportation system', *Transportation Research Part D: Transport and Environment*, vol 8, no 5, pp 323-42.

Shirky, C. (2010) *Cognitive surplus: Creativity and generosity in a connected age*, London: Penguin.

Shragai, N. (2014) 'Why we see bosses as parents', *Financial Times*, 6 March, p 14.

Singh, J.J., Iglesias, O. and Batista-Foguet, J.M. (2012) 'Does having an ethical brand matter? The influence of consumer perceived ethicality on trust, affect and loyalty', *Journal of Business Ethics*, vol 11, no 4, pp 541-9.

Simpson, J. (2008) *The politics of leadership*, London: The Leadership Centre.

Skeffington Committee (1969) *Public participation in plan making*, London: HMSO.

Slovic, P.E. (2000) *The perception of risk*, London: Earthscan Publications.

Smith, L. (2014) 'Neighbourhood planning', Standard Note SN/SC/5838, London: House of Commons Library.

Smith, M. (2011) 'The paradoxes of Britain's strong centre: delegating decisions and reclaiming control', in C. Dahlstrom, B.G. Peters and J. Pierre (eds) *Steering from the centre*, Toronto: University of Toronto Press, pp 166-90.

Smith, S.P. and Sheate, W.R. (2001) 'Sustainability appraisal of English regional plans: incorporating the requirements of the EU Strategic Environmental Assessment Directive', *Impact Assessment and Project Appraisal*, vol 19, no 4, pp 263-76.

Smith, T. and Young, A. (1996) *The fixers: Crisis management in British politics*, Aldershot: Dartmouth.

Smulian, M. (2009) 'Business methods cut cost', *Planning*, 30 January, pp 16-17.

Socitm (Society of Information Technology Management) (2013) *Better connected: Briefing for top management team*, London: Socitm.

Solace (Society of Local Authority Chief Executives and Senior Managers) (2013) *Asking the right questions: The need for transformational and new contextual leadership skills for local authority chief executives*, London: Solace.

Solace (2014a) *Middle managers: Dinosaurs or key innovation allies?*, London: Solace.

Solace (2014b) *Local roots to growth*, London: Solace.

Solesbury, W. (1974) *Policy in urban planning*, Oxford: Pergamon.

South, J., Hunter, D. and Gamsu, M. (2014) *What local government needs to know about public health: A Local Government Knowledge Navigator Evidence Review*, London: LGA.

Southgate, M. (2013) *Update on government policy*, NIPA National Conference, London, 9 May.

Spellman, C. (2009) Letter to Conservative local authorities on planning, August.

Spillane, J.P. (2012) *Distributed leadership* (vol 4), Chichester: John Wiley & Sons.

Spillane, J.P., Halverson, R. and Diamond, J.B. (2004) 'Towards a theory of leadership practice: a distributed perspective', *Journal of Curriculum Studies*, vol 36, no 1, pp 3-34.

Stead, D. and Meijers, E. (2010) 'Spatial planning and policy integration: concepts, facilitators and inhibitors', *Planning Theory and Practice*, vol 10, no 3, pp 317-32.

Stead, D. and Nadin, V. (2009) 'Planning cultures between models of society and planning systems', in J. Knieling and F. Othengrafen (eds) *Planning cultures in Europe. Decoding cultural phenomena in urban and regional planning*, Farnham: Ashgate, pp 283-300.

Steiner, G.A. (2010) *Strategic planning*, London: Simon and Schuster.

Stewart, J. and Walsh, K. (1992) 'Change in the management of public services', *Public Administration*, vol 70, no 4, pp 499-518.

Stewart, M. (1994) 'Between Whitehall and town hall: the realignment of urban regeneration policy in England', *Policy & Politics*, vol 22, no 2, pp 133-46.

Stiglitz, J. (2012) 'Resources: from curse to blessing', www.project-syndicate.org/commentary/from-resource-curse-to-blessing-by-joseph-e--stiglitz (accessed 8 May 2014).

Stocker, N. and Thompson-Fawcett, M. (2014) '"It's not like never-the-twain-shall-meet": politician–staff relationship structures in local government', *Local Government Studies*, DOI:10.1080/03003930.2014.887563.

Stoker, G., Gains, F., Greasley, S., John, P. and Rao, N. (2007) *The new council constitutions: The outcomes and impact of the Local Government Act 2000*, London: DCLG.

Storey, J. (2004a) 'Signs of change', in J. Storey (ed) *Leadership in organizations: Current issues and key trends*, London: Routledge, pp 3-10.

Storey, J. (2004b) 'Changing theories of leadership and leadership development', in J. Storey (ed) *Leadership in organizations: Current issues and key trends*, London: Routledge, pp 11-37.

Storper, M. (2011) 'Why do regions develop and change? The challenge for geography and economics', *Journal of Economic Geography*, vol 11, no 2, pp 333-46.

Sturdy, A. and Wright, C. (2011) 'The active client: the boundary-spanning roles of internal consultants as gatekeepers, brokers and partners of their external counterparts', *Management Learning*, vol 42, no 5, pp 485-503.

Sturges, J. (2004) 'The individualization of the career and its implications for leadership and management development', in J. Storey (ed) *Leadership in organizations: Current issues and key trends*, London: Routledge, pp 249-68.

Sullivan, H. and Gillanders, G. (2005) 'Stretched to the limit? The impact of local public service agreements on service improvement and central–local relations', *Local Government Studies*, vol 31, no 5, pp 555-74.

Sullivan, H., Williams, P. and Jeffares, S. (2012) 'Situated agency in practice', *Public Management Review*, vol 14, no 1, pp 41-66.

Sunstein, C.R. and Thaler, R. (2008) *Nudge: Improving decisions about health, wealth, and happiness*, London: Penguin.

Sutherland, W.J. and Woodroof, H.J. (2009) 'The need for environmental horizon scanning', *Trends in Ecology and Evolution*, vol 24, no 10, pp 523-7.

Sweeting, D. (2003) 'How strong is the Mayor of London?', *Policy & Politics*, vol 31, no 4, pp 465-78.

Sykes, R. (2003) *Planning reform: A survey of local authorities*, Research Briefing 1.03, London: LGA.

Taleb, N.N. (2010) *The black swan: The impact of the highly improbable fragility*, London: Random House.

Tallon, A. (2013) *Urban regeneration in the UK*, Abingdon: Routledge.

Taylor, M. and Warburton, D. (2003) 'Legitimacy and the role of UK third sector organizations in the policy process', *Voluntas: International Journal of Voluntary and Nonprofit Organizations*, vol 14, no 3, pp 321-38.

Terk, E. (2013) 'Opportunities for combining quantitative and qualitative approaches in scenario building: the experience of the 'Estonia 2010' project', in M. Giaoutzi and B. Sapio, *Recent developments in foresight methodologies*, New York, NY: Springer, pp 297-307.

Tewdwr-Jones, M. (2005) '"Oh, the planners did their best": the planning films of John Betjeman', *Planning Perspectives*, vol 20, vol 4, pp 389-411.

Thake, S. (2001) *Building communities, changing lives: The contribution of large, independent neighbourhood regeneration organisations*, York: Joseph Rowntree Foundation.

Therivel, R. (2012) *Strategic environmental assessment in action*, Abingdon: Routledge.

Thomas, H. (2012) 'Values and the planning school', *Planning Theory*, vol 11, no 4, pp 400-417.

Thomas, K. (2013) *Development control*, Abingdon: Routledge.

Thomas, K. and Littlewood, S. (2010) 'A European programme for skills to deliver sustainable communities: recent steps towards developing discourse', *European Planning Studies*, vol 18, no 3, pp 467-84.

Thomas, P. and Panchamia, N. (2014) *Civil service reform in the real world patterns of success in UK civil service reform*, London: IfG.

Thornley, A. (1991) *Urban planning under Thatcherism: The challenge of the market*, London: Routledge.

Toplis, J., Dulewicz, V. and Fletcher, C. (2005) *Psychological testing: A manager's guide* (4th edn), London: Chartered Institute of Personnel and Development.

Toth, A.G. (1992) 'The principle of subsidiarity in the Maastricht Treaty', *Common Market Law Review*, vol 29, 1079-1105.

Travers, T. (2002) 'Decentralization London-style: the GLA and London governance' *Regional Studies*, vol *36, no* 7, pp 779-788.

Turok, I. and Taylor, P. (2006) 'A skills framework for regeneration and planning', *Planning Practice and Research*, vol 21, no 4, pp 497-509.

United Nations (2011) *Global compact*, New York, NY: UN.

Varney, D. (2006) *Service transformation: A better service for citizens and businesses, a better deal for the taxpayer*, London: HM Treasury.

Vespermann, J. and Wald, A. (2011) 'Intermodal integration in air transportation: status quo, motives and future developments', *Journal of Transport Geography*, vol 19, no 6, pp 1187-97.

Vigar, G. (2012) 'Planning and professionalism: knowledge, judgement and expertise in English planning', *Planning Theory*, vol 11, no 4, pp 361-78.

Vigar, G. (2013) *The politics of mobility: Transport planning, the environment and public policy*, Abingdon: Routledge.

Vigar, G.I., Healey, P., Hull, A. and Davoudi, S. (2000) *Planning, Governance and Spatial Strategy in Britain: an institutionalist analysis*, Basingstoke: Macmillan.

Waldrop, M.M. (1992) *Complexity: The emerging science and the edge of order and chaos*, London: Simon & Schuster.

Walker, J.W. and LaRocco, J.M. (2002) 'Perspectives: talent pools: the best and the rest', *Human Resource Planning*, vol 25, no 3, pp 12-15.

Warburton, D. (ed) (2013) *Community and sustainable development: Participation in the future*, Abingdon: Routledge.

Ward, M. (2014) *Enterprise zones*, Standard Note SN/EP/5942, London: House of Commons Library.

Wates, N. and Knevitt, C. (2013) *Community architecture (Routledge Revivals): How people are creating their own environment*, Abingdon: Routledge.

Watkins, M.D. (2012) 'How managers become leaders', *Harvard Business Review*, vol 90, no 6, pp 65-72.

Weerakkody, V., Janssen, M. and Dwivedi, Y.K. (2011) 'Transformational change and business process reengineering (BPR): Lessons from the British and Dutch public sector', *Government Information Quarterly*, vol 28, no 3, pp 320-8.

Welford, R. (2013) 'From green to golden: hijacking environmentalism', in R. Welford (ed) *Hijacking environmentalism: Corporate responses to sustainable development*, Abingdon: Routledge, pp 16-39.

Welsh Government (2004) *People, places, futures Wales spatial plan*, Cardiff: Welsh Government.

Welsh Government (2008) *People, places, futures Wales spatial plan update*, Cardiff: Welsh Government.

Wenger, E. (2000) 'Communities of Practice and Social Learning Systems', *Organization, vol 7*, no 2, pp 225-246.

White, A. and Dunleavy, P. (2010) *Making and breaking Whitehall departments: A guide to machinery of government changes*, London: Institute for Government.

White, I. and Howe, J. (2002) 'Flooding and the role of planning in England and Wales: a critical review', *Journal of Environmental Planning and Management*, vol 45, no 5, pp 735-45.

Whitehead, C. (2010) *How can the planning system deliver more housing?*, York: Joseph Rowntree Foundation.

Wideman, R.M. (2002) 'Comparing PRINCE2® with PMBoK®', http://www.logro.sk/na_stiahnutie/project_management_-_comparing_prince2_with_pmbok.pdf (accessed 26 May 2014).

Wilkinson, M. and Craig, G. (2002) *New roles for old: Local authority members and partnership working*, York: Joseph Rowntree Foundation.

Williams, P. (2002) 'The competent boundary spanner', *Public Administration*, vol 80, no 1, pp 103-24.

Williams, P. (2012) *Collaboration in public policy and practice: Perspectives on boundary spanners*, Bristol: Policy Press.

Wilson, W. (2014) *The New Homes Bonus scheme*, Commons Library Standard Note SN05724, London: House of Commons Library.

Wokingham Borough Council (2014) *Adopted managing development delivery local plan*, Wokingham: Wokingham Borough Council.

Wollmann, H. and Thurmaier, K. (2012) 'Reforming local government institutions and the New Public Management', in K. Mossberger, S. Clarke and P. John, *The Oxford handbook of urban politics*, Oxford: Oxford University Press, p 179-209.

Womack, J.P. and Jones, D.T. (2010) *Lean thinking: Banish waste and create wealth in your corporation*, London: Simon and Schuster.

Wong, C. (2013) *Indicators for urban and regional planning: The interplay of policy and methods*, Abingdon: Routledge.

Wong, C., Baker, M., Hincks, S., Schulze Bäing, A. and Webb, B. (2012) *A map for England: Spatial expressions of government policies and programmes. Final report to the Royal Town Planning Institute*, Manchester: Centre for Urban Policy Studies, University of Manchester.

Woodruffe, C. (2007) *Development and assessment centres: Identifying and developing competence* (4th edn), London: Human Assets.

Woolcock, S. (2010) 'Trade Policy', in H. Wallace, M. A. Pollack and A. R. Young (eds), *Policy Making in the European Union*, (Sixth Edition) Oxford: Oxford University Press, pp 381-99.

Wray, I. (2014) 'Bring back regional planning strategies', *The Planner*, 3 January www.theplanner.co.uk/news/bring-back-regional-planning-strategies (accessed 4 May 2014).

Wright, J.S., Dempster, P.G., Keen, J., Allen, P. and Hutchings, A. (2012) 'The new governance arrangements for NHS foundation trust hospitals: reframing governors as meta-regulators', *Public Administration*, vol 90, no 2, pp 351-69.

Yaghootkar, K. and Gil, N. (2012) 'The effects of schedule-driven project management in multi-project environments', *International Journal of Project Management*, vol 30, no 1, pp 127-40.

Yarnall, J. (2011) 'Maximising the effectiveness of talent pools: a review of case study literature', *Leadership & Organization Development Journal*, vol 32, no 5, pp 510-26.

Young, K. (ed) (1988) *New directions in county council government*, London: ACC/INLOGOV.

Young, K. and Garside, P. (1982) *Metropolitan London: Politics and urban change, 1837-1981*, London: Hodder and Stoughton.

Zachary, L.J. (2011) *Creating a mentoring culture: The organization's guide*, Chichester: John Wiley & Sons.

Zattoni, A. and Cuomo, F. (2010) 'How independent, competent and incentivized should non-executive directors be? An empirical investigation of good governance codes', *British Journal of Management*, vol 21, no 1, pp 63-79.

Zebrowski, C. (2013) 'The nature of resilience', *Resilience: International Policies, Practices and Discourses*, vol 1, no 3, pp 159-73.

Zeeman, E.C. (1977) *Catastrophe theory. Selected papers, 1972–1977*, London: Addison.

Zibarras, L.D. and Woods, S.A. (2010) 'A survey of UK selection practices across different organization sizes and industry sectors', *Journal of Occupational and Organizational Psychology*, vol 83, no 2, pp 499-511.

Index

A

Absenteeism 91, 177
Accountability 3, 5, 22-5, 29, 30-1, 121, 162, 174, 180
Action centred leadership 44
Adair, John, 41, 44, 46, 93
Adams D. 2, 4, 14, 118, 121, 159
Amenities 4, 95, 172
Allmendinger P. 9, 22
Assets 14, 32, 81, 101-4, 112-4
Audit 10, 26-7, 31, 37, 106-110, 122-6, 134, 146, 152, 165-7, 174-5

B

Barker K. 1, 16, 17, 134, 182
Belbin's team roles 88, 89
Benchmarking 165
Blame 12, 41, 124
BPR (business process re-engineering) 135-9
Business case 67, 77, 138, 144, 146, 154, 161, 165

C

Capital finance 6, 28, 31, 39, 55, 80, 101-5, 118-9, 147, 157
Carmona m. 4, 14, 16, 37, 63, 118, 125, 126
Case officers 131
Central government 6, 9-12, 14-17, 21, 23-7, 35, 38, 45, 48-9, 61-4, 75, 98, 105, 119, 122-5, 134-8, 141, 146, 151, 154, 183-4
Client 2-7, 13, 27-8, 31-8, 47, 54-6, 66, 79-80, 85, 92-98, 104, 108-111, 121-5, 143, 146-7, 158-9, 177-8, 180-1, 186-190.
Change management 42, 49, 60, 157-8
Charging 107, 109-11, 115
CIL (community infrastructure levy) 110, 115-7
CIPD 22, 38, 70, 84, 85
Civil servants 17, 24, 38, 61-2, 65, 83, 90, 160, 177
Clifford B. xii, 4, 6, 16, 18, 38, 160, 168
Coaching 39, 89-90, 131, 190
Collaborative planning 29, 38, 45, 48, 51, 167, 174, 181
Communication 43, 45, 55-6, 60, 73, 79, 85, 93-6, 122, 145, 149, 153, 156, 171-2
Community 1-5, 7-8, 11, 14-15, 18, 21, 26, 28-9, 33-4, 46, 50-2, 56, 63, 69, 77-9, 82, 93-6, 110-14, 116-9, 125-128, 130, 134, 145-8, 167, 173, 179-81, 187-9
Competency framework 48-9, 183
Contingent leadership 43-44

Contributions *see developers' contributions*
Councillors 1-2, 9, 16-18, 22, 25-6, 47, 63, 79, 86, 95-7, 110, 116, 121-6, 135, 180-1
Co-production 35
Corporate responsibility 161, 164-6
CPD (Continuous professional development), 90, 93, 177, 180
Crisis leadership 14, 26, 27, 40-1, 124
Cullingworth B. 2, 9, 10, 13, 14, 61, 159
Culture 3, 15-7, 24-9, 34, 39-41, 49, 51, 55-6, 61-3, 66, 69, 81-4, 89, 91-4, 110, 119m 148, 157-60, 161, 168-72, 184-8
Customers 12, 17, 26-7, 31, 38, 55-6, 85, 93, 95-7, 104, 107, 125-7, 136-139, 149-52, 162-6

D

Delivery 4-11, 15-6, 23-6, 34-5, 37, 42, 45, 50-2, 59, 61-7, 70, 73-6, 80, 95, 106-110, 116-8, 121-2, 134-5, 140-1, 143-9
Deregulation 10
Design 4-5, 12-16, 46, 61, 69, 84, 90, 110, 114-19, 126-8, 134-6, 140-5, 149-51, 162-7, 172-7, 182-3
Developer 2, 4, 8, 28, 47, 51-3, 59. 111.115-9, 130-3, 160, 168, 183, 187, 190
Developers' contributions 2, 5,-6, 26-7, 44, 53, 79-80, 101, 110-1, 115-7, 119, 148, 160
Development control 124, 134 *see also development management*
Development management 4, 9-13, 15-6, 48, 52, 88, 115, 123-127, 131-141, 159-160, 184, 188 *see also development control*
Distributed leadership 44, 45, 75
Diversity 82, 83.
Drucker P. 53, 59, 60, 62

E

Egan review 16, 48, 183, 185
Employment law 80
Enforcement 4, 133, 173
England 1, 7-12, 16, 22-6, 29, 40, 47-8, 50-2, 63-4, 75, 95-6, 112-115, 119, 122-3, 159-60, 180, 184
e-planning 164
Equality 38, 82-3, 86
Ethics 178
Evidence 3, 6, 10, 13, 37, 48, 50, 62-5, 72, 89, 93-7, 123, 133, 139, 146, 154, 160-4, 178, 182-190
EZ (Enterprize zones) 10

F

Financial appraisal 72
Forecasting 68-9, 72, 183

G

Gap analysis 72

H

Handy, Charles, 44, 53
Healey P. 3, 45, 64, 178, 181
Health 5, 18, 22-3, 28-9, 38, 52, 76, 103, 111, 116-19, 138, 146, 149, 151, 161-9, 173-6
Hendler S, 3, 178, 179, 182
HMT Five case business model 154-5
Horizon scanning 67
Housing 3-8, 10, 12, 14, 17, 21, 26-9, 32, 50, 60-1, 76, 105-6, 112-119, 131, 134, 143, 147, 178, 189-90
Human capital 80
Human resources 28, 80-2, 91, 153
Hybrid organisations 8, 21, 27,-8, 34-5, 47, 105, 113, 119

I

IFRS (International finance reporting standard) 101, 105
Implementation 7, 14-5, 40, 44, 51, 62, 65, 73-6, 101, 130-1, 137-8, 143-7, 153-4, 160, 179, 182, 185, 187
Income 11, 26, 30-4, 79-80, 91, 97, 102-6, 109-119, 167
Infrastructure 4-8, 12-15, 21, 25-9, 50, 66-8, 72-6, 80. 88. 96, 101-5, 110, 115-119, 131, 140, 143, 147, 158-60, 170, 174, 183-5
Innovation 27, 31, 38, 53-4, 69, 80, 97, 145

J

Job description 84-9
Job specification 85

L

Leadership skills 42, 47-9, 124
Lean thinking 138-9
Local authority 1, 7-13, 18, 22, 25-7, 33, 48, 50-2, 62-6, 79, 86, 95-8, 101, 106, 110-19, 121-5, 127-31, 132, 136, 139-40, 144-7, 164, 169, 173-7, 186-7 *see also local government*
Local government 1-5, 12, 17-8, 22-29, 47-50, 62-66, 76, 90, 98, 101-3, 112, 122-3, 136-7, 146, 180, 183, *see also local authority*
Local plans 5, 7-8, 15, 25, 29, 40, 61, 73, 76, 117-9, 135-7, 147, 160

M

Management team 123, 132, 136
Marketing 94-8, 103, 107, 163
Mentoring 39, 89-90, 131, 190
Modelling 11, 14, 23, 68-9, 72, 77, 112, 126, 139, 154-5, 166, 183

Monitoring 65, 73-7, 129, 143, 147, 159, 166, 175-7
Motivation 33, 42, 84, 91-2, 182
Muddling through 60, 65
Mulgan G. 40, 60, 65
Multidisciplinary teams 29

N

Nadin V. 2, 9, 10, 13, 14, 61, 159, 185, 186
Negotiation 4, 87, 98, 116, 117, 125, 182, 188
Neighbourhood 3, 8, 21, 23, 33, 52, 117, 147, 189
New towns 3, 14, 15
Northern Ireland 1, 7, 10, 12, 22-3, 75
NPM (new public management) 122-3

O

OECD 7, 8, 50, 64, 67, 105, 122, 134, 161, 163, 165, 168
One stop shops 17, 113, 123
Options appraisal 72-3, 154

P

Parish 8, 21-2, 95, 147
Participation 37, 67, 95-6, 152
Participative 6, 43, 51, 95, 126
Partnership 13-4, 23, 30, 42, 47-8, 50-1, 61-66, 74-7, 83, 135, 148, 181
PAS (Planning Advisory Service) 10-11, 15, 48-9, 79, 101, 117, 127-8, 132-6, 146, 183
PDG (Planning delivery grant) 134
Peer review 49-50, 123, 132
Performance 8-11, 27-30, 37-9, 41-8, 50, 55, 60, 62-3, 73, 82, 87-9, 90-3, 98-9, 102, 115, 121-6, 131-6, 147, 160, 165-6, 170, 172
Performance management 37, 60, 63, 82, 91-2, 98, 122-6
PINS (Planning Inspectorate National Service) 25, 40, 124
Places 3, 6, 10, 14, 18, 26, 35-7, 50, 74, 118-20, 159, 163, 173-5, 182-3, 187
Plan making 4, 6-9, 13, 15, 17, 55, 65, 72-3, 88, 93, 95, 118, 143-6, 157. 159-60, 164, 178, 184
Planning applications 1, 5, 8-13, 15-6, 21, 25, 35-37, 53, 55, 87-88, 91, 95-8, 101, 108, 114-147, 164, 181-2, 185, 190
Planning consent 2, 4, 10-12, 15, 32, 92, 124, 130, 133,
Planning consultants 2,4, 6, 8, 13-14, 28, 32, 47, 55, 67, 82, 85, 88-9, 109, 116, 124, 146-9, 153, 160, 186
PMBOK 150-15
PPA (Planning performance agreement) 11-12, 115, 140
Pre-panning application advice 128
Presenteeism 92
Pricing 8, 105, 107-9, 111, 113, 155
PRINCE2 150, 153-4, 156

Private sector 1-8, 13-17, 21-37, 47, 51-54,
    66-9, 79-85, 90-98, 104-9, 113-114, 124,
    134-9, 157, 160-165, 177-187, 190
Process improvement 122, 126, 135-7
Professional 79-90, 102, 126, 129, 160, 167-8,
    174-190
Programme management 143, 155, 158-9
Project board 145, 148, 150, 156-7, 170
Project initiation document (PID) 156
Project management 2, 9, 14, 40, 53, 124, 132,
    138, 143-160
Project manager 133, 138, 144, 146, 148-9,
    156-9, 170
Public sector 4, 7-8, 92-8, 101-119, 121-3,
    139, 146, 150, 153-4, 164—6, 169-187,
    190

Q

Quality 2, 4-5, 16, 27-8, 38, 46, 53, 63, 72, 82,
    91, 96, 118, 120-8, 132-4, 139-40, 144-5,
    149-52, 159, 162, 165-8, 186
Quality assurance 28, 126, 132, 144, 149, 152,
    167
Quality management 126, 132, 150, 152

R

Recruitment 38-9, 82-9, 92-3
Recycling 4, 111
Regeneration 13-15, 22, 57, 88. 97, 111
Regulation 3-4, 9-13, 19, 21, 25, 81, 98, 105,
    111, 121, 131-2, 136, 161, 164-9, 171-4,
    187
Reputation management 56, 93, 98
Resilience 41, 68, 167, 172-3
Revenue funding 32, 101-6, 110, 111, 113
Risk 2, 27-31, 41, 55, 64, 79-80, 107, 110,
    124-126, 138, 144-148, 150-157, 161-177
RTPI 1, 21, 79, 101, 177
Rule based judgement 132, 188
Rydin Y. 37, 178, 183

S

Scenario 68-70, 88, 152, 170, 173
Scoping 133, 144, 150, 152, 160
Scotland 1, 7-8, 10, 12, 22-4, 29, 50-2, 63-4,
    73-6, 94, 115, 119, 123, 149, 184
Scrutiny 22, 37, 49, 54, 86, 95, 139, 146, 158,
    161
Self-management 6, 177
Shared services 139
Sheppard A. 10
Skills 16, 34, 38-9, 41-52, 56, 72-3, 80-5, 88-9,
    91, 93, 105, 124, 132, 145, 153, 157, 177,
    182-190,
SMART 145
Smith N. 10
Soft power 45, 94
Sounding board 148, 149-50
Spatial planning 50, 118, 185

SRO (senior responsible owner) 144, 147-8,
    150, 159
Stakeholders 5, 36, 46, 49, 56, 127, 135-7, 144-
    50, 150, 152-3, 156-161, 184
Strategic choice 62-3, 73
Strategic planning 25, 40, 48, 59-62, 65, 69,
    74-7, 183
Strategy 7-8, 16, 27, 32, 35, 46-7, 59- 80, 93,
    102, 112 154-5, 165, 172
Sub-regional 3, 75, 160
Sustainability 37, 48, 74, 111, 119, 161-177,
    182, 183, 187
SWOT 71-2

T

Talent pools 91
Targets 10, 61, 77, 98, 122-3, 166, 172, 185
Teams 13, 16, 25, 28-32, 39-49, 53-6, 67, 69,
    85-94, 123, 126, 131-3
Therivel R. 72
Third sector 7, 14, 21, 26, 33-37, 47, 52, 64-
    66, 106-111, 139, 146, 157, 161-4, 180-187
    see also voluntary sector
TQM (total quality management) 126, 152
Training 18, 27, 39, 46, 50, 56, 79, 81-3, 89-90,
    102-3, 116, 131-4, 141, 145-6, 151, 153,
    160, 168, 172, 176, 183, 190
Transport 8, 22-3, 26, 68, 76, 80, 89, 102, 109-
    114, 119, 144, 163, 168-9, 171, 173-4

U

Unintended consequences 40, 170
Utilities 8, 21-2, 28, 105, 113, 119

V

Viability 117, 168
Vigar G. 8. 9, 180. 182, 184
Voluntary sector 21, 27, 54, 98, 121, 162, 177,
    181-3 *see also third sector*
Volunteers 8, 33-5, 46-7, 52, 149, 173, 183

W

Wales 1, 7, 10-12, 22-3, 29, 75-6, 119
Waste 4, 12, 106, 110, 132, 168-9
Wong C. 37, 45